Up the Lake
with a Paddle

VOLUME FOUR

Canoe and Kayak Guidebook

HIGH COUNTRY

CENTRAL SIERRA NEVADA:

The Lakes and Reservoirs off

California Scenic Highways 88 and 4

WILLIAM VAN DER VEN

FINE EDGE
Nautical & Recreational Publishing

Important Legal Notice and Disclaimer

Outdoor activities are an assumed risk sport. This book cannot take the place of appropriate instruction for paddling, swimming, or lifesaving techniques. Bodies of water by nature contain hazards and they change with time and conditions. Every effort has been made to make this guide as accurate as possible, but it is the ultimate responsibility of the paddler to judge his or her ability and act accordingly.

The editors, author, publishers, and distributors accept no liability for any errors or omissions in this book or for any injuries or losses incurred from using this book.

Credits

Cover Photo: William Van der Ven
Author Photo: Jason Bates
Photographs within text: William Van der Ven
Book design: Melanie Haage
Maps: Farinaz Wadia
Editor: Leslie Bunzel
Copyeditor: Pat Hillis

LIBRARY OF CONGRESS CATALOGING-ON-PUBLICATION DATA

Van der Ven, William, 1949—
    Up the lake with a paddle : canoe and kayak guide / by William Van der Ven.
— 1st ed.
        p.   cm.
      Contents: v.   1.   Sierra Foothills and Sacramento Region
      ISBN 0-938665-54-5 (v. 1)
      1.   Canoes and canoeing—California, Northern—Guidebooks.
2. Kayaking—California, Northern—Guidebooks.   3.   California, Northern—Guidebooks.   I. Title.
GV776.C2V36 1998   98-16844
917.94—dc21   CIP

Address requests for permission to:
Fine Edge , 14004 Biz Point Lane, Anacortes, WA 98221
www.fineedge.com
Printed in the United States of America
First Edition

Dedication

To the memory of my mother:
Mrs. Lydia (Broet) Van Der Ven, June 22, 1925–June 06, 2004.

Alone, she brought two small boys to America,
where they blossomed into men.

Robert William (Bill) Cherry, November 9, 1925–March 2, 2004:
Sailor, Soldier, Husband, Father and Father-In-Law.

Bill, wherever you are, thank you for all your support and generosity.
May you always sail with a fair wind.

I dedicate this book to Sergeants Eric and Devine (Grant) Butler,
and the rest of the soldiers of Taskforce Ironhorse, 4th Infantry Division,
Operation Iraqi Freedom: *Deeds not Words*.

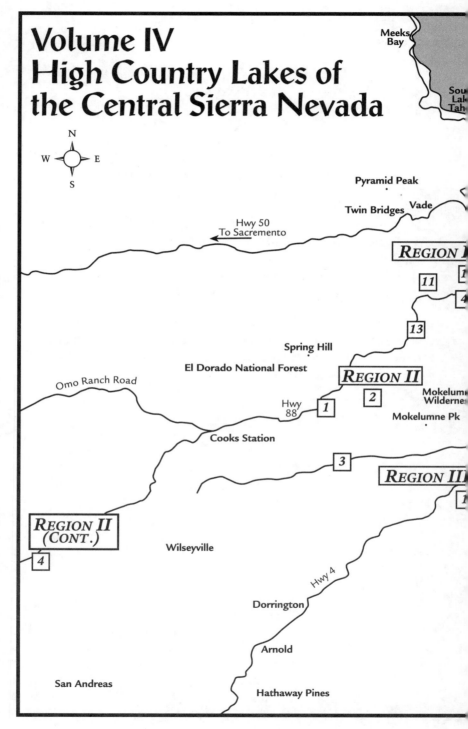

Volume IV
High Country Lakes of the Central Sierra Nevada

Meeks Bay

South Lake Tahoe

N
W — E
S

Pyramid Peak

Twin Bridges Vade

Hwy 50
To Sacramento

REGION I

11

13

Spring Hill

El Dorado National Forest

REGION II

2

Mokelumne Wilderness

Hwy 88   1

Mokelumne Pk

Cooks Station

3

REGION III

*REGION II
(CONT.)*

4

Wilseyville

Omo Ranch Road

Hwy 4

Dorrington

Arnold

San Andreas

Hathaway Pines

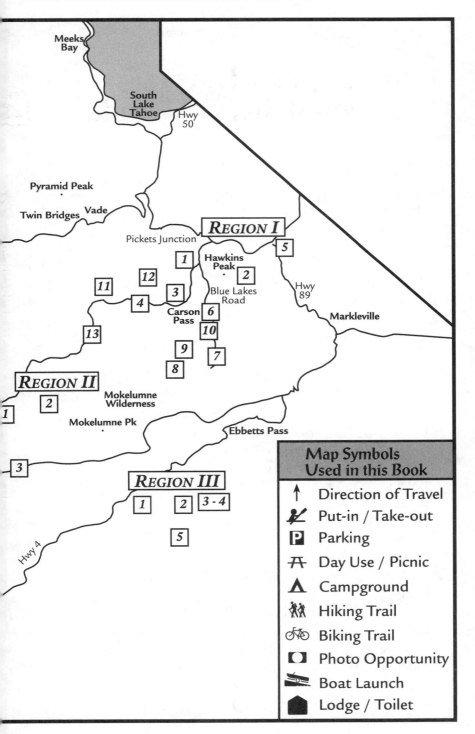

Table of Contents

Acknowledgments

Along the winding way in preparation of this book, I met some wonderful people; some even stayed around to become friends. If I forget to mention your names, please forgive me, but know that your memory has a warm spot in my heart, and I do cherish those memories.

This volume would never have been published without the generous support of my publisher, Mark Bunzel. When a busy publisher takes the time to answer his e-mail promptly, even to soothe a writer's ego—you never treat that relationship lightly.

Leslie Bunzel and Pat Hillis, my editing team, their kindness and good humor made the touchy process of editing a valuable learning experience rather than a nasty chore.

A special *Motshakeram* to Farinaz! Her diagrams were always completed on time and easy to comprehend.

Melanie Haage, designer and coordinator. Your professionalism and easy manners allowed me to feel comfortable negotiating the complexities of electronic files and other computerized widgets. You take a pile of pages and slides and turn it all into a book that I am proud of . . . my humble thanks.

Elizabeth *Liz* Mihslov, your last minute editing allowed me time to meet deadlines on other projects.

As always, the tip of the paddle to the Love of my life, Louise, for her unyielding support and understanding of this writing thing.

To my Father, Mr. Peter Theodore Van Der Ven, you not only gave me your name, but, more importantly, your unconditional love and support: may I be as gracious and loving in return.

Warren and Trina Harding, Muffet McCleneghan and Heather Carlson for taking the time out from your very busy lives to read and write generous comments on the rough manuscript. I raise the paddle high!

In the field:

The always-gracious Ms. Kim Parrino. I don't know how you do it Kim; even after a full day of paddling and hiking, your demeanor never frays.

Dan Crandall, you took a chance, just on hearsay, gave me the key to your warehouse and let me play! Seriously, Dan, you are not just a good employer, but a fine friend as well. Muchas gracias, compadre!

To my new paddling companion Spencer Parker, your contribution, both on the water and with those e-mails, allowed me to complete this book on time; no small thing amigo.

Mr. John Brissenden, that cup of coffee and morning conversation will always contribute to my growing love affair with Hope Valley and the surrounding Region.

To all of you, my fine friends, a heart-felt thank-you; however, any faults or mistakes that may creep out from the text: those are mine and mine alone.

The canoe / Courage! / You have the power to succeed in reaching the other side, so that you may get where you want to go . . .

— Chumash Indian Canoe Song,
recorded by John P. Harrington

Using This Guide

Use of the Terms: Lake and Reservoir

The majority of California lakes, and Sierran lakes in particular, are man-made and designed to hold water for a specific use; therefore, these bodies of water are technically reservoirs. Many of the reservoirs originated as natural lakes whose original shorelines have been altered to increase water storage.

In the book, I use the terms interchangeably for continuity and clarity.

Book four is divided into *three Regions* and their accompanying *Paddling Areas.*

The paddling areas are numbered to reflect the total number described within that region only. Subsequently, there are three sets of paddling areas of varied amounts.

The first section of each paddling area contains the highlighted main facts that pertain specifically to the lake or reservoir to be described.

I include the appropriate, and when necessary, the adjoining *7.5-Minute Quadrangle Topographical Map* to each paddling area. For road maps, I include maps made by Compass Maps, Inc. and those of the California State Automobile Association (AAA). From many years of using both companies' maps, I have noticed that the maps appear interchangeable.

If any lake resides within the jurisdiction of a national forest, wilderness area, national, state, or regional park, I include the maps (if any), from that governing body.

Portages exist, but only for two paddling areas: in Region One, a short portage between the first and second Lost Lake, and in Region Two, a true bear (pun intended) of a carry between Lower and Upper Bear River Lakes.

The Heads Up section includes brief bullets of pertinent information about each paddling area.

The *Sources and References* section includes materials I used for reference in describing that paddling area.

Readers wishing to view updates, additional information and my recommended good books to read, can access more details on this book's web page at the Fine Edge website (www.FineEdge.com). The websites listed will provide the reader with more specific information on any aspect of the paddling area, be it on the history, geology or interesting background that I could not cover in the book.

The Regions

Region One describes the lakes, reservoirs and countryside within the North Fork of the Carson River Drainage, between Carson Pass and Markleeville. These bodies of water are reached primarily by way of California State Highways 88 and 89.

Region Two covers the lakes and reservoirs that make up a part of the Mokelumne River Drainage. These lakes are reached off of California State Highway 88.

Region Three includes the high country lakes that are part of the Stanislaus River Drainage. These lakes are approached from California State Highway 4.

In The Eddy and Paddle Note

The side bar, *In the Eddy*, provides the reader with additional information that pertains to the paddling area but does not fit within the context of the data that specifically describes a paddling area. For example, when you paddle Burnside Lake, you cannot help but view the dominant mass of nearby Hawkins Peak. Those readers wishing to know more about this peak may do so by reading a description of a hike to the top of Hawkins Peak contained in, In the Eddy.

Paddle Notes are just that, bits of information I have discovered that may enhance your paddle at a specific paddling area.

For additional information on retailers, clubs, and specific source material pertaining to canoeing and kayaking, places to stay or dine located within the regions described in this book, please see the appendices section at the back of the book.

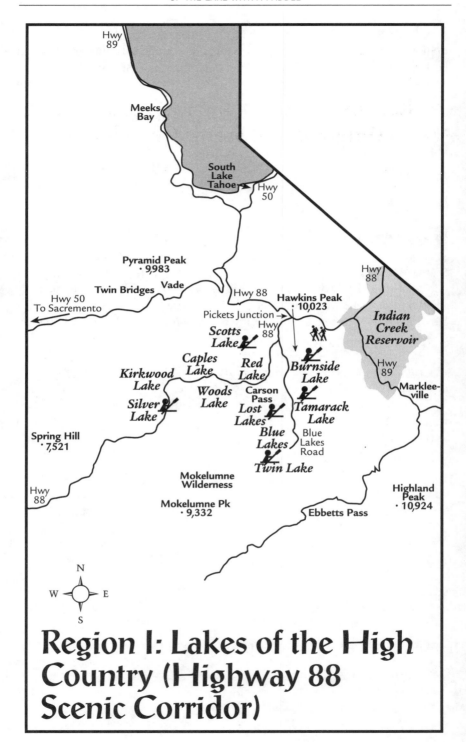

Region I: Lakes of the High Country (Highway 88 Scenic Corridor)

Region I: Lakes of the High Country (Highway 88 Scenic Corridor)

A s you drop down onto the floor of Hope Valley you are surrounded by majestic snow-capped Sierra on one side and the rain-starved Carson Range on the other side, your heart beats fast with excitement. The West Fork of the Carson River stretches out in braids of sun-speckled shimmers, and meanders through the valley. Looking down on your map, the names of the lakes start to collect on your tongue: Scotts, Burnside, Upper Blue and Lower Blue, Red, Silver, Twin Lake and the Lost Lakes, Caples, Kirkwood, and finally, the alpine gem of Woods Lake. So many lakes, so little time!

Long before the arrival of modern man and the quest for a wilderness experience, be it on a hike, or in a canoe or kayak, the land was home to various tribes of Paiute (Pah-Ute), Shoshone(Sho-sho-nee), and the Washoe (Washo) Indians, whose territories extended from the eastern Sierra throughout present day Nevada, Utah and portions of California's High Country. On the western slopes that extend out to the foothills, various tribes of Miwok and Maidu were sometimes trading partners with tribes living on the eastern side. Carson Pass existed as a primary trading route long before the first emigrant train crested its summit. As a matter of fact, it was a Washoe, given the name Mélo (meaning friend) by the whites, who guided Fremont, the first white man to guide and record his expedition through the Sierra, at the present location of the Pass.

Not long after Fremont passed through this region, gold was discovered in California and life as the Native Americans knew it was destined for a tragic end. The abundance of the land that sustained the Washoe and other tribes now fed and watered the pioneers and their stock as they followed the same valleys where the rivers flowed. Fremont's Carson Pass became a major thoroughfare for the hardy pioneers and their prairie-schooner wagons, as they negotiated the infamous Devil's Ladder before cresting the pass and descending into California's goldfields.

This is the former haunt of the notable John A. "Snowshoe" Thompson (1827-1876), a Norwegian immigrant turned mail carrier. His exploits on skis (between 1856-1876), carrying an 80 pound mail pack over the Sierra

Snow capped Carson Range with Hope Valley below.

through Carson Pass into Placerville and then retracing his track back to Genoa, still stands as a record of pioneer will and endurance. Snowshoe's grave marker is still on view in Genoa, Nevada.

Burnside Lake is one of the first accessible lakes, approximately five miles off Highway 88 near Pickett Junction, and it is an ideal family vacation spot. The lake was named after Ambrose Everett Burnside, a Union General during the Civil War. The general is also credited with popularizing the men's beard style, a full mustache and beard with a clean chin, called *burnsides*. This style was later altered to the current sideburns. Today the only burn will come from the sun if you stay too long as you glide lazily on the sedge-covered waters of the lake.

A hike to the top of Hawkins Peak or the rocky knobs that border the peak, leaves you breathless not just from the hike, but also for the eagle's-eye view of all three valleys: Faith, Hope, and Charity, as well as the snow-capped peaks of the distant Carson Range.

Traverse the ridge-hidden valley, cross Highway 88, then climb the flanks of the southern portion of the Carson Range to see Scotts Lake. A small earthen cowboy dam contains the waters of this man-altered lake. Although it's a bone-crunching drive to reach it, once you arrive, the surrounding granite walls, carpeted with conifers and aspens, provide a majestic backdrop to the deep blue lake. From this height you have a clear view of Hope Valley, the meandering Carson River, and the lofty peaks that encompass the valley.

The pine odors mixed with sage, scent the air with their natural fragrances and stimulate the senses as well as the appetite. With luck and skill, rainbow or brown trout may soon sizzle in a pan.

Following Highway 88 south as it parallels the West Fork of the Carson, you'll find a side road taking you into Faith and Charity Valleys, named in 1855 by O.B. Powers and the government surveyors, as an analogy to the earlier named Hope Valley. Henry W. Bigler, a member of the disbanded Mormon Battalion en-route back to Salt Lake City on July 28, 1848, named Hope Valley. Set within the borders of the Mokelumne Wilderness and Toiyabe National Forest, these valleys act as the gateway to the Blue Lakes, and the (not so lost) Lost Lakes.

Before arriving at the sight of Lower Blue Lake, enjoy the scenic splendor of the three biblically inspired valleys from a newly asphalted road. A shoreline of pine frames the lovely oval-shaped lake and provides a peaceful setting for the family seeking a weekend away from the hustle and bustle of modern life. The fact that the lake is stocked each year with 14,000 10-12-inch rainbow trout and 15,000 fingerling brookies, just adds to the fun.

A short drive over the lake's dam and down the road apiece is Twin Lake, named as a twin to Lower Blue Lake. As a day-use area, you can't beat the quiet and serenity of this lake. Paddling on the wind-rippled waters, it is not uncommon to see a bald eagle or view the osprey's fishing prowess.

If you drive farther down the Twin Lake road, you dead-end at the parking area with its breathtaking view of Meadow Lake, which lies in a glacially-shaped gorge. Unfortunately, the portage down to the lake, although doable, is extremely rugged and steep.

Back on the main road, a short drive from lower Blue Lake, is Upper Blue Lake. Except for Meadow Lake, no other member of the Blue Lake family of lakes sits in such

Monument to Snowshoe Thompson erected by Nevada Members of E. Clampus Vitus, Carson Pass Management Area Visitor's Center.

Visitor's Center, Crest of Carson Pass, Highway 88. The center is also the source for information on the nearby Carson Pass Management Area.

an imposing setting. Rising to a height of 9,342 feet, the desiccated mass of a former volcanic eruption, known as The Nipple, dominates the northern shoreline of the lake. Glacially shaped granite ridges rising 500 feet above the surface of the lake, help define the lake's southwestern boundary. Splendid stands of pine, fir, junipers and aspens add color and softness to the harsh contrast of ice-scarred rock.

Exit the Blue Lakes valley and begin your climb toward Forestdale Divide and Highway 88 near Red Lake. Be sure to take the side road to the Lost Lakes. These two lakes may be small in size, but they're long on scenery. Paddle the first lake and portage to the second, and more southerly, Lost Lake. Once on the second lake, paddle your boat to its northeasterly cove; then hike to the top of the rocky, windswept knob that separates the two lakes. I won't give away the view, you will have to earn it yourself . . . but yes, it is worth every stroke and boot step! As an added bonus, look for the sandy beach tucked in a small cove on the southernmost end of the lake beneath the base of The Nipple. If you seek a campsite with lots of privacy and character, then this cove will surpass your needs.

As you reach Highway 88 at Red Lake, you have two options. Either paddle on the waters of this historically important lake, fishing for trout, hiking the adjacent trails that were once part of the Emigrant Trail, or follow the highway via Carson Pass to the high mountain lakes: Woods, Caples, Kirkwood, and Silver Lakes.

Drive into little Woods Lake in the spring when the wildflowers are in bloom and are especially delightful. Once at the lake, slide your boat into the wind-rippled water, fish for trout or just build up an appetite for a picnic lunch at one of the tables that dot the shore of this miniature lake. A hike up to the Lost Cabin Mine, or nearby Emigrant Lake, will round out your stay.

At Caples Lake, you have not only splendid scenic vistas to enjoy, but also the opportunity to paddle and camp the back country that was once part of the former Carson River Route of the California Emigrant Trail. Enjoy your time at Caples Lake, either at one of the nearby campsites or in rustic comfort with a room or cabin at the historic Caples Lake Resort.

For those of you with small children, or those just starting to camp with your canoe or kayak, a weekend at secluded and friendly Kirkwood Lake may build your confidence and skills for more adventuresome locations later. Conifers and granite ledges surround and protect tiny Kirkwood Lake from the strong winds that blow in a small valley on nearby Caples and Silver Lakes. A small campground adjacent to the lake provides easy access for those wishing to boat, fish or swim.

Silver Lake has a long history of admirers. William Brewer, the famous early California geologist, describes the lake's many splendors:

> *"Here we descended into the Valley of Silver Lake, a lovely little sheet of water very deep and blue, resting in a basin of granite, high picturesque peaks of volcanic rock visible on the east."*

> *—William H. Brewer's journal entry of August 23, 1863*

Main and only dining room of Sorensen's Resort; note the table at far left, made from a round from an old growth pine tree.

This large lake with its magnificent Sierran scenery, coves and islands, stimulates any paddler fortunate enough to spend time on its surface.

It comes as no surprise, therefore, that Alpine County is the new destination for outdoor enthusiasts. With many year-round activities, ranging from paddling, biking, fishing, hiking and rock climbing in the spring and summer, to skiing and snowshoeing in the winter, time spent in this high country will always be memorable.

Sources and References:

Acker, Roy M., *Historical Summit City: An 1860s Mining Center In Alpine County California*. Los Angeles: Self Published, 1999, 2nd Ed.

The only booklet out on the history of the mining town that existed off Blue Lakes Road between Lost Lakes and Red Lake at Carson Pass.

www.ghosttowns.com/states/ca/summitcity.html

Grossi, Mark, The *Longstreet Highroad Guide to the California Sierra Nevada*, Marietta: Longstreet Press, Inc, 2000, 336 pp.
An excellent guidebook on all things relating to the Sierra Nevada. (http://sherpaguides.com/california/mountains/)

Sorensen's Resort, renowned for its hospitality, good food and more importantly, as a center for conservation issues pertaining to Alpine County and Hope Valley, in particular.

REGION I: LAKES OF THE HIGH COUNTRY
PADDLING AREA 1: SCOTTS LAKE

Position: 38°45.50'N, 119°57.55'W

Difficulty: Fierce afternoon winds blow through the saddle from the southwest.

Trip Length: This small oval lake may be paddled comfortably in one hour.

Portage: None.

Paddle Distance: The lake's size is too small for any measurable paddling distances.

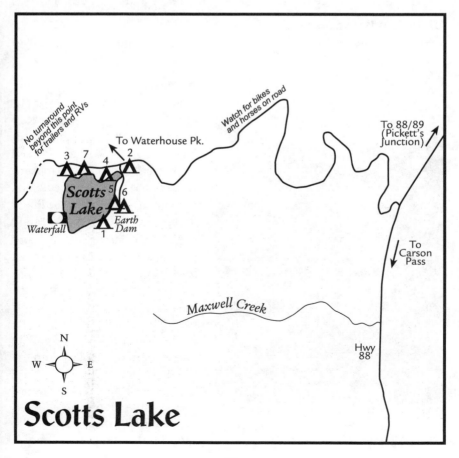

Scotts Lake

Season: From late spring (if the snow melt is sufficient to dry the road) through fall.

Lake Size: 1,750 feet long.

Elevation: 8,012 feet.

County: Alpine County.

National Forest: Toiyabe National Forest (Carson Ranger District).

Maps:

USGS 7.5-Minute Quadrangle Topographical Map Series: Freel Peak, CA.

National Forest Service/Wilderness Area: Toiyabe National Forest (Carson Ranger District) and Eldorado National Forest.

Road Maps:

Compass Maps, Inc.: Alpine Amador and Sacramento Counties.

California State Automobile Association (AAA) Map: Central California—California Bay Area to Lake Tahoe, Lake Tahoe and Northern Sierra.

Historical Background:

Scotts Lake was named for J. B. Scotts, a local dairyman in Hope Valley (*Place-Names of the Sierra Nevada*, p. 194).

Campsite # 2, with a view of the lake and the south trending peaks of Toiyabe National Forest and the Mokelumne Wilderness.

Access:

Hwy. 50 E to Meyers, turn right onto Hwy. 89 (Luther Pass Rd.) to Markleeville. At junction of Hwys. 88 and 89, locally known as Pickett Junction, turn right (west), onto Hwy. 88 Carson Pass National Scenic Byway. Continue for approximately 1.25 miles.

Note: It is important to watch your odometer, because there are no signs posted for the lake or the turnoff.

Look for a yellow gate with a cattle guard. Turn onto the dirt road. This is forest route 079, the main road to Scotts lake. The lake is located 2.6 miles from the gate entrance.

Follow Route 079 as it takes you past the pine-covered meadow and begins to ascend the ridge.

You will come to a fork just before you begin the ascent. Stay to the left, passing through an open gate. From here to the lake, the road is rough and contains numerous cobbles, and ruts making it difficult for a passenger car to negotiate.

Note: You will come to several side routes leading off the main route. Be sure you stay on 079 to reach the lake.

Upon reaching the lake, note that the road forks to the left, heading toward the dam. Another side road begins to ascend the flank of Waterhouse Peak.

The route you are on continues around the east side of the lake.

The road leads to two camp spots and continues farther into the gorge before ending.

Unless you have a high-clearance vehicle, 4 x 4 do not attempt to drive past the turnoff leading to the lakeside campsites.

The road making a left fork at the lake's entrance leads to the dam and the stream that empties out of the lake. You will cross a stream before you reach the dam.

An excellent alternative for those not wishing to drive farther is to take the left fork as if heading for the dam, and immediately park in the flat, grassy meadow adjacent to the lake and stream.

Heads Up:

- Campfire permit is necessary for any overnight camping at lake.
- Winds blowing through the pass are fierce; bring proper clothing.
- Mosquitoes are prevalent.

On Scotts Lake, looking east past the cowboy dam towards Pickett Peak in foreground, and Hawkins Peak in background.

Overview of Scotts Lake from the trail to Waterhouse Peak.

- 7 prior campsites (there are no formal agency-maintained campsites at Scotts lake); in order of preference *(See map for site locations):*

  Site 1: Opposite side of dam (south end).

  You may either pack in your gear by carrying it across the dam or by packing the boat and paddling to the shoreline below the site.

  The site is located among a small grove of junipers and pine immediately past the south end of the dam.

  Site 2: Meadow adjacent to the road fork between route 079 and cutoff to the dam.

  Site 3: West end of the lake. This site is located at the turn-around for the road that leads off Route 079 just before you start ascending the ridge leading away from the lake.

  Site 4: Finger extending outward on east end of lake.

  Look for a small road to your left just past the fork leading to the dam.

  At the end of the road is a small site containing a built-up fire circle and small turnaround.

  Site 5: The aspen grove at the east end of the dam.

  It is necessary to cross a stream at a deep pool to reach this site by vehicle.

  Site 6: A cleared site below the dam. Provides an excellent windbreak, but allows mosquitoes to swarm, and there is no view of the lake.

  Site 7: Northeast side adjacent to site 3. The first small site off the cutoff from 079. A very exposed site, muddy and damp.

- Exceptional views of Hope Valley, Pickett Peak, Hawkins Peak and the range paralleling Hwy. 88.

- Limited access heightens the possibility of privacy and having the lake to yourself.
- Great mountain biking.
- Easy-to-strenuous hiking trails nearby.
- The road up to the lake has become a popular mountain biking trek; watch for cyclists negotiating the ruts and cobbles of the road.

Description:

For those willing to make the extra effort and drive on an unmaintained forest road, Scotts Lake is a high-alpine delight offering exceptional views of the Carson Range and adjacent mountain vistas.

For an added bonus, make the drive in the fall to see the color changes in the aspen groves. Before you reach the lake, look for the mature Western Junipers *(Juniperus occidentalis)* that are growing nearby. Their longevity (they live 800-1,000 years), incredible girth, and handsome profile earn them the sobriquet, *grandfather trees.*

Bunches of wildflowers add spots of color to the green drab of the forest. The large yellow woolly mule's ears or Mountain mule ears *(Wyethia mollis)* is the predominant species, whose large fleshy leaves look like, well . . . a mule's ear. The bright yellow mule's ears blossoms complement the red-to-orange stems of the Paintbrush *(Family: Castillja)*. This partially parasitic plant requires the use of other plant species' roots in order to thrive. The third predominant flower is the blue-blossomed Lupine *(Family: Lupinus)*. If you are from Texas, you will recognize this plant, affectionately known as the blue bonnet, as your state flower.

Occasionally, a large furry animal will stick its head out from the rocky outcrops on the side of the road, look to see if it is safe to dart across and disappear among the boulders on the other side. At first you may think it's a rather large ground squirrel; however, its distinctive yellow underside and loud whistle, given to warn of an intruder's approach (hence, it's nickname, The Whistler) identifies this rodent as the Yellow-Bellied Marmot *(Marmota flaviventris)*. The marmot prefers to dwell in the talus that accumulates near mountainous terrain. It sometimes will dig a burrow in a nearby meadow.

The marmot is the preferred food choice of many carnivores. Eagles, larger raptors, coyotes, foxes, bobcats, mountain lions and bears all prey on this sun-loving member of the squirrel family.

When you finally reach the lake, you'll spot the shimmer of its waters as you crest the ridge and look through the wall of junipers and aspen that grow near a meadow (south side). Continue on until you break free of the trees and are in the open where the road forks left and right. *(See the Heads Up Section at the beginning of the chapter to decide to park or explore the campsites listed.)*

If you arrive in the afternoon, you will likely encounter the strong wind that funnels through the saddle visible to the southwest across the lake. Explore for your new temporary home as you wait for the winds to die down. If no other visitors are camping nearby, check out all the campsites and pick the one you feel is right for you.

If bikes are among your toys, this is the perfect opportunity to explore the road ahead or attempt to ride up the steep cutoff leading to the top of Waterhouse Peak (9,497 feet).

If you fly fish, the stream that empties out of the lake only a short walk from the road and meadow, contains trout. The lake itself is known for its rainbow and brown trout.

A meadow with snow covered Cascade Range in background at Scotts Lake.

If those activities leave you cold, you can soak up the spectacular scenery, watch and listen for birds or attempt to identify the variety of trees and flowers.

Sometime in the late afternoon when the wind dies down to a steady breeze, and as the afternoon progresses, this, too, will die. It's paddling time! Slip the canoe or kayak into the cold water, adjust the fit of your PFD (Personal Flotation Device), smear on some more bug juice, set the water bottle in its place and shove off.

The first feature that you notice is the lone ghost tree standing near the center of the northwest end of the lake. As you draw near the snag, you see the burn scars that reshaped the features of this forlorn former conifer.

Cruise past the standing deadwood and pass one of the campsites listed in the Heads Up Section, and you will hear the sound of rushing water. On the west end of the lake, two western junipers frame a picturesque waterfall that slides and tumbles over slick granite before it enters the lake. Tiny clusters of broken ferns survive harsh climate changes tucked in various niches and fractures within the wet zone. The majestic grandfather junipers growing along the banks of the stream, tower over the many varieties of wild flowers showing off their blooms.

If time permits, wait until morning to photograph this Kodak moment as, early light reveals the subtle details of the falls and surrounding vegetation.

Follow the shoreline to the southern bend of the lake and enter a small inlet where stands of deadwood are cast in the golden glow of late afternoon. The color of the aspen groves provides a contrast against the deeper greens of the conifers. As a breeze stirs, their leaves tremble to the movement and cast a silvery shimmer as sunlight penetrates the leafy cover.

The late Donald Peattie, in his delightful book, *A Natural History of Western Trees*, succinctly describes the reason for the leafy shimmer:

" . . . *[The] leaves of the Aspen are hinged upon leafstalks longer than the blade and flattened contrary to the plane of the blade, with the result that the leafstalk acts as a pivot and the foliage cannot but go into a panic whispering every time the slightest breeze flows down the canyon."—p. 318.*

If the water level is high enough, paddle up close and personal to the trees growing in and around the elevated shoreline. In the background, lichen-covered and chemically stained boulders lie in jumbled masses.

Make your way around the forested south end of the lake, and approach the earthen dam. If you haven't already explored the area, this is a good time to get out, stretch and walk up the embankment for a grand view of Hope Valley (7,100 feet), and the peaks that reach south and make up the borders of Toiyabe National Forest and Mokelumne Wilderness Area. The two peaks, from north to south, are Pickett Peak (9,118 feet) and Hawkins Peak (10,023 feet). (*See Paddling Area 2, In the Eddy: The Hike to Hawkins Peak.*) Pickett Peak was named after Edward M. Pickett who operated the Pickett Place stage station at the junction of present day Highways 88 and 89, now called Pickett Junction. The sun glistens over the water as the West Fork of the Carson River snakes along the valley floor.

Step over the rocky ground and notice small, slender upright clusters of yellow flowers; these handsome members of the mustard family are called Western Wallflowers (*Erysimum capitatum*). They are recognizable by their four rounded yellow, or sometimes orange, petals that form a symmetrical cross. The former scientific name for this species was *Cruciferae* (Latin for cross). Their narrow, and sometimes saw-toothed, leaves grow irregularly on a one-to-three foot stem. The name *wallflower* comes from their preference for growing in old walls or against rocks. If you bend low, you will catch their fragrant scent. This fragrance also captivates many insects that feed on the nectar, thus helping to propagate the species through pollination.

As you complete your paddle, be sure to work your way among the snags near the small finger that juts out from the eastern bank of the lake. Blackbirds sometimes nest in the exposed weathered roots and branches of the snags. If you spot a nest, look, but do not touch any of the nesting area, as your scent may stress the birds to abandon the nest.

Paddle Note:

Use the wind to your advantage when fishing or using a camera from a canoe or kayak. At Scotts Lake, paddle to the far west shore, cast out and let the wind push you quietly across the lake. You will maintain a steady drift without having to disturb the surface of the lake with paddle strokes.

To photograph the shoreline, again let your boat drift slowly across your intended view, line up your view finder and slowly depress the shutter release. Your rate of drift is usually slow enough to provide a sharp and clear print, as long as you do not jerk the camera. To photograph a bird or animal, paddle past the wildlife and let your boat drift back toward them, rather than approach head on. This allows the bird or animal to become used to your growing presence; in addition, no noise accompanies your approach.

Sources and References:

Blackwell, Laird R., *Wildflowers of the Tahoe Sierra.* Redmond: Lone Pine Publishing, 1997.

Browning, Peter, *Place-Names of the Sierra Nevada.* Berkeley: Wilderness Press, 1992.

Durham, David L., *Place-Names of California's Eastern Sierra.* Clovis: Word Dancer Press, 2001.

Orr, Robert T. and Margaret C. Orr, *Wildflowers of Western America.* New York: A Chanticleer Press Edition, Alfred A. Knopf, Inc., 1974.

Peattie, Donald, Culross, *A Natural History of Western Trees.* Boston: Houghton Mifflin Company, 1981.

Sprout, Jerry and Janine, *Alpine Trailblazer.* Markleeville: Diamond Valley Company Publisher, 1999.

REGION I: LAKES OF THE HIGH COUNTRY
PADDLING AREA 2: BURNSIDE LAKE

Position: 38°42.45'N, 119°53.20'W

Difficulty: The gusty afternoon winds are the only drawback to paddling this small natural lake.

Paddling Distance: The Lake is too small for any measurable distances.

Lake Size: 1,250 feet long.

Elevation: 8,100 feet.

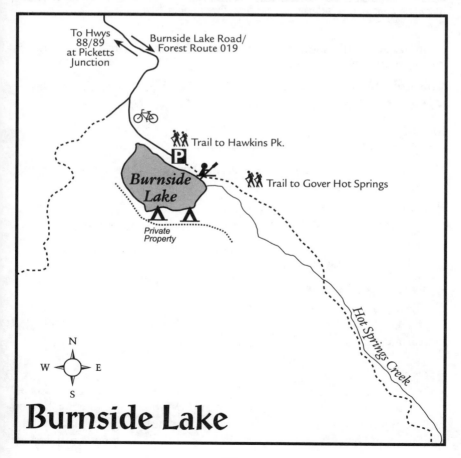

Morning calm; a view of Burnside Lake from the primitive boat ramp.

Season: When the snow melts and the road opens in late spring, through summer and early fall.

County: Alpine County.

National Forest: Toiyabe National Forest (Carson Ranger District).

Maps:

USGS 7.5-Minute Quadrangle Topographical Map Series: Carson Pass, CA.

National Forest Service: Toiyabe National Forest (Carson Ranger District) and Eldorado National Forest.

Road Maps:

Compass Maps, Inc: Alpine, Amador and Sacramento Counties Map.

California State Automobile Association (AAA) Maps: Central California – Bay Area to Lake Tahoe.

Historical Background:

The Lake was named after Gen. Ambrose E. Burnside, a Union General during the Civil War and the originator of the *burnsides* beard style, later called sideburns.

Access:

From South Tahoe, exit from Hwy. 50 onto Hwy. 89 South (Luther Pass Road). Continue on this highway until you reach the Hwy. 89 and 88 junction, known as Pickett Junction. Cross over Hwy. 88 and enter the open gate that marks the beginning of Forest Road 019, Burnside Lake Road. Look for a Forest Service display board describing the Hope Valley Wildlife Refuge, plants and wild-life living in the area. Continue on Burnside Lake Road for approximately 5.7 miles until it ends at the lake, which will appear on your right.

Note: 2.7 miles from the road entrance, the road forks to the left. Stay to the right to reach the lake.

Heads Up:

- The road deadends at the lake. The short, rugged turnaround is not suitable for a trailer or recreational vehicle (RV). Leave the trailer or RV at the wider junction that leads off to the Cal-Pine Mine and Hawkins Peak, approximately 0.75 miles from the lake.
- A campfire permit is mandatory prior to camping in the area.
- Bear country—pack and camp smart!
- There are no developed campsites at the lake; dispersed primitive camping only.
- No toilet facilities.
- Observe the posted Private Property signs when hiking the borders of the lake.
- Be prepared for mosquitoes.
- Excellent hiking and mountain biking nearby.
- On your return from the lake, stop by Sorensen's Resort and Restaurant.

Description:

California is blessed with many fine recreational lakes; however, only a small percentage are natural, and of those, the majority are located in hard-to-reach wilderness areas.

Reach the small but picturesque Burnside Lake with almost any standard vehicle.

Bring your fishing pole, favorite book, and make a day or weekend of it to appreciate the natural beauty of this high alpine lake.

When I camp here, I paddle out to the center of the lake, set up my pole and let the line out with a bobber, stretch out in the canoe (no easy task), and let the breeze push me as it may.

As a result of this lazy mode of locomotion, I enjoy a 360-degree view of the surrounding peaks. To the west (stretching in a south to north direction), is an 8,600-foot tree-covered ridge; the West Fork of the Carson River flows on the opposite side.

The breeze blows the boat around, and a majestic lone spire of rock comes into view. Hawkins Peak is a 30-million-year-old remnant of a former volcanic vent rising to the grand height of 10,023 feet. The peak was named after John Hawkins, who squatted on a ranch east of the peak in either 1854 or 1858. He eventually sold part of the property to Alvin Grover, for whom

Grover Hot Springs is named. As part of the local lore, a rock with Harry's name scripted on it is somewhere near the top of the peak *(See In the Eddy: Trail to Hawkins Peak and Vicinity)*.

Note: For additional local lore and information on activities in Alpine County, obtain Jerry and Janine Sprout's delightful guidebook, Alpine Trailblazer *(See Sources and References on p. 32)*.

When the boat slowly turns, you're facing the south end of the lake. Hot Springs Creek is the stream flowing out of Burnside Lake and the same that flows into Grover Hot Springs State Park approximately four miles down stream.

Burnside Lake with surrounding cover of Lodgepole Pines; the view is to the northeast.

Watch the shoreline as the boat moves with the rhythm of the breeze on the water. The rocky, rubble ridges bordering the lake infer the origins of the lake may be moraine fields created by a former glacier as it scraped the surface during its progression. When the glaciation period ended, depressions and debris-bordered localities such as this one, acted as natural catch basins for future lakes.

Explore the lake from the shore and notice the carpet of green that marks the shallow areas of the lake. The grass-covered shallow zones consist of sedges with triangular-shape stems *(Family: Cyperaceae)*. The sedges are a favorite food source for ducks that dabble, such as mallards, as well as the Canada geese that visit the lake in the spring and summer.

The Pine Siskin *(Spinus pinus)*, with its streak of yellow on the flight feathers and along the base of its tail, flit from conifer to conifer. The Clark's nutcracker *(Nucifraga columbiana)* displaces the Steller's jay *(Cyanocitta stelleri)* at this higher elevation, and its ability to locate and abscond with any tasty morsel of food left by careless campers earns it its name, the "camp robber." Gray, with black and white wings, and smaller than a crow, this noisy, gregarious and bold bird plays a dominant role in the distribution of the Whitebark Pine *(Pinus albicaulis)*. As the Clark's nutcracker strips the pine's seeds from cones and caches those it does not eat, it enlarges the growing area of the tree. Another significant attribute of this remarkable bird is its ability to store extra seeds in a pouch located in the bottom of its mouth.

" . . . Roughly 150 Whitebark Pine seeds can fit onto the pouch. Only two nutcracker species in the world own such pouches: Clark's in North America and the Eurasian nutcracker (Nucifraga caryocatactes) *in Europe and Asia."*

—*Verna Johnson, California Forests and Woodlands, p. 146.*

The Lodgepole Pine *(Pinus contorta)* is the predominant conifer around Burnside Lake and is a pioneer tree that springs up in flat, wet meadows and eventually closes an open space with dense stands of pine.

Take the time and effort to load your boat and paddle across the lake to the southwest end where a small stream feeds into the lake, as it is a good location for an overnight stay. The stream inlet, whose current does not allow the sedges to form thick mats, is a good spot to take-out. In the early summer, beach your boat and look for the pale green stalks whose buds resemble green cigars that sprout from the ground. The plants that emerge are Corn Lilies *(Veratrum californicum)*, whose flower will appear later in the season. This plant is extremely poisonous.

" . . . [It] paralyzes the respiratory system, reputedly after turning everything green!"

—*Laird R. Blackwell, Wildflowers of the Sierra, p. 54.*

Carpets of small, yellow flowers belonging to the buttercup family *(Family: Ranunculus)* intermingle with the corn lilies. Step into the coolness

Upper end of Burnside Lake, amongst the sedges.

On the lake with clear view of Hawkins Peak.

of the trees and look for the beautiful Crimson Columbine or Red Columbine (*Aquilegia formosa*). The red and yellow flowers hang upside down on long thin stalks. These flowers act as a humming bird magnet, as their bright coloration attracts the birds to their nectar. An interesting note on the coloration of the columbine is that red is visible to birds but not insects, but yellow attracts both birds and insects. The red and yellow coloration of the columbine, therefore, insures the plants' chances for survival.

Behind a shoreline screen of pine is a spacious clearing, complete with a rock fire ring. Adjacent to the fire ring is a large, flat slab of granite that is just the right angle to allow you to sit and catch the warmth of the morning sun.

The property beyond the clearing is private and posted. Respect the wishes of the owners and do not trespass on their land.

Eventually, the day will draw to a close. The knobby capstone of Hawkins Peak bathes in a reddish glow as the sun sets, and an aromatic fragrance of pine and sage scent the air, leaving an indelible memory of the high country.

Sources and References:

Blackwell, Laird R., *Wildflowers of the Tahoe Sierra*. Redmond: Lone Pine Publishing, 1997.

Browning, Peter, *Place-Names of the Sierra Nevada*. Berkeley: Wilderness Press, 1992.

Sprout, Jerry and Janine, *Alpine Trailblazer*. Markleeville: Diamond Valley Company Publisher, 1999.

In the Eddy:
The Trail to Hawkins Peak and Vicinity

A hike to Hawkins Peak is in order if the fish don't bite and the wind is too strong to boat, or you just want to stretch. Start at the turnoff to the Cal-Pine Mine, 0.90 mile back on Burnside Lake Road (see map).

Park your vehicle under the canopy of the juniper that straddles the turnoff. Follow the road as it climbs up to Hawkins Peak. Approximately one mile from your starting point you come to a gate. View the mine by following the left junction to where it dead ends at the mine site.

Note: Heed the written caution regarding no entry due to poisonous mine gases. Carbon monoxide gas is odorless and tasteless; you will lose consciousness before you realize anything is wrong.

The wooden portal at the entrance to the adit (a horizontal shaft where the mine's entrance and exit are the same) protects it from falling rock and snow accumulation. Notice the narrow-gauge track that runs into the mine. At one time, ore carts carried the ore out the entrance and into an ore chute that stood at the edge of the entrance near the dead pine. The ore was then either crushed into smaller more manageable pieces by a now missing stamp mill, or transported directly to a mill for milling *(See Vol. 3, In the Eddy: A Paddle to Yellow Metal Mine, for a picture of a still-standing stamp mill and assorted mining hardware)*.

First view of Hawkins Peak after leaving the forest that surrounds Burnside Lake.

Throughout the late spring and early summer, wildflowers bloom along the stream below the mine and on the opposite hillside; in the late fall, the aspen growing the length of the gorge that harbors the stream undergo a gorgeous color change. To regain the road that leads to Hawkins Peak, backtrack by way of the road that leads to the mine, and to the former main jeep road and continue upwards. Pass the tree line and come out onto the brushy slope of the hill that leads to the base of Hawkins Peak. A splendid view of Burnside Lake and the adjacent ridge that borders the lake awaits you where the slope levels before your final push to the base of the peak.

Reach the top of this ridge for your first, full close-up view of Hawkins Peak. If your energy level is on empty, or the prospect of another uphill hike in the thin mountain air leaves you gasping, an alternative is to hike down to the twin knobs facing southwest from the

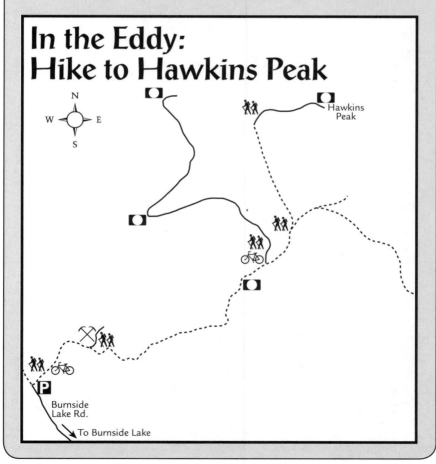

In the Eddy:
Hike to Hawkins Peak

Fin of igneous rock that was once part of a lava flow located at the western base of Hawkins Peak.

base of Hawkins Peak on the opposite side of the stream valley below, visible from where you stand. This valley is the head of the same stream that flows downward passing the Cal-Pine Mine site before joining Hawkins Creek.

Your reward for shifting gears and destination is to hike through a delightful alpine forest of mixed conifers and junipers before exiting onto a rocky knob (elevation 9,010 feet) with a grand view of Carson Pass, Red Lake, Hope Valley and the peaks that make up the Carson Range. Views of Markleeville Peak (9,415 feet) and Jeff Davis Peak (8,754 feet) are unobstructed to the south. Hike back into the trees and sit quietly to watch a variety of birds and animals go about their lives. The antics of the Clark's nutcracker will be a real treat. Identify the bird's presence by listening for the harsh *kraaa* call. A pair of binoculars comes in handy to view the bird tearing apart a cone from one of the nearby conifers. Although the bird eats a few of the seeds, it can slip as many as 70 into a special pouch called a *sublingual pouch*, located under its tongue. The bird will then fly off and cache the seeds (usually in groups of three), with an uncanny ability to locate each cache and retrieve the seeds months later.

Stay on the main road and follow it to the fork to reach the top of Hawkins Peak. The right fork follows the southeasterly base of the peak before turning south following the ridgeline adjacent to Millberry

Canyon. The main fork, on your left, rounds the southern base of the peak as it climbs toward the exposed flank of a columnar jointed igneous rock thrusting outward from the western base of the main peak. Look to your left at the exposed desiccated rock that forms a small overhang leading to the start of the valley below before you reach the small grove of juniper and the last upward section of the road. Pass over the remains of an old ash flow whose fiery descent has left behind this eroding exposure consisting of rocks and cinders in a matrix of hardened cement-like ash. The bright yellow and orange stains on the rock are various lichens that grow on the rock's surface.

The best approach to the summit is to hike to the base of the jointed rock, using the last of the trees as shade before the final push to the top. Where the trees end, leave your pack on a prominent boulder, and continue to scramble your way upward, following the base of the old flow. Come to a break in the sidewall and follow the rubble into a small level area where krummholtz-shaped (German for crooked wood) conifers grow. The path continues through the pine grove to the base of the last portion of rock, to the visible shiny structures of the relay station. Your last pitch is a hand scramble onto the rock pile that holds an antenna array. Once there, stay away from the dish and work your way to the southeastern end of the knob. You may now throw your hands upward and wheeze out a yell, for you are on top of the peak . . . all 10,024 feet of it!

Sources and References:

Lanner, Ronald, M., *Made for Each Other: A Symbiosis of Birds and Pines.* New York: Oxford University Press Inc., 1996.

http://www.frontiertrails.com/oldwest/typesmining.html
   Great site on history of mining, with links to other history-related topics.

REGION I: LAKES OF THE HIGH COUNTRY
PADDLING AREAS: 3 and 4:
WOODS LAKE and RED LAKE

Difficulty: The small size of both lakes, and their protected settings, make for a paddle that may be enjoyed by paddlers of all levels of experience.

Length: The lakes are too small for measuring any paddling distances.

Portage: None.

Paddling Distance: Both lakes are small ponds with Red Lake the larger of the two. Perfect for day excursions.

Season: Spring, after the snow melts, through fall.

Red Lake: 0.75 mile long by 0.25 mile wide.

Woods Lake: Approximately 0.25 mile long.

Elevation: Red Lake is 7,880 feet and Woods Lake is 8,240 feet.

County: Alpine County.

Maps:

Red Lake is on the USGS 7.5-Minute Quadrangle Topographical Map Series: Carson Pass, CA and Woods Lake is on the adjoining USGS 7.5-Minute Quadrangle Topographical Map Series: Caples Lake, CA.

Note: Purchase both quadrangle sheets if plan to hike within the Carson Pass area.

Forest Service: Both lakes appear on Toiyabe National Forest (Carson Ranger District) Map, Eldorado National Forest Service, and Mokelumne Wilderness Maps.

Road Maps:

Compass Maps, Inc: Alpine, Amador and Sacramento Counties Map.

California State Automobile Association (AAA) Maps: Central California – Bay Area to Lake Tahoe.

Historical Background:

Red Lake is situated on the east side of the historical Carson Pass, named after Kit Carson, the scout and guide for the expedition led by John C. Fremont. They were the first non-Native Americans to record their traverse through the area. Red Lake was described as, "... *a small marshy lake all drying up,*" by Fremont. Red Lake and the nearby Lost Lakes are the headwaters of the Carson River.

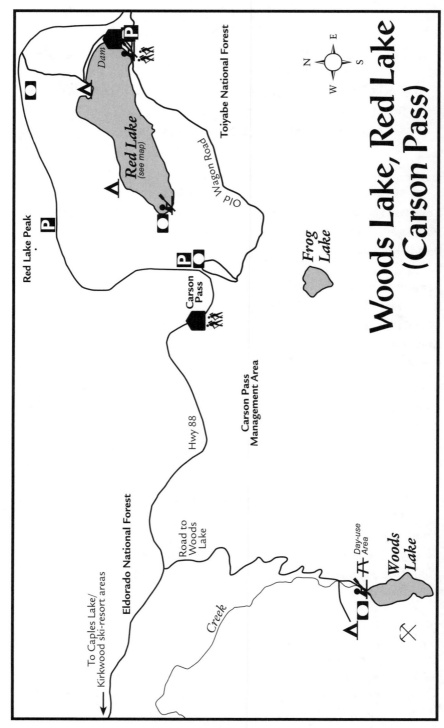

Woods Lake, Red Lake (Carson Pass)

Woods Lake, early morning calm.

Woods Lake was named by Joseph N. LeConte after Robert Martin Woods, a sheepman who spent summers between 1871 and 1900 in the Sierra.

Access:

Both lakes are located just off California State Hwy. 88. To reach Woods Lake from the west, take Hwy. 88 east from Jackson. The signed turnoff for the lake is approximately 70 miles east of Jackson and a few miles after you pass Caples Lake. Exit is on your right (south) and the lake is 2 miles from the turnoff.

Note: The road leading into Woods Lake is very narrow, with little to no turning room for RVs and trailers. The few day-use parking spots fill fast, so arrive early.

Red Lake sits at the eastern base of Carson Pass, approximately 6.5 miles beyond the Woods Lake exit and 2.5 miles below the crest of Carson Pass. Take the first right exit just before the highway starts to bank to the left. This exit was not marked the last time I was there. A rough cut into the bank at the end of the paved road paralleling the lake serves as a primitive boat launch. If you plan on camping, the best sites are located across the dam on the opposite shore. Follow the dirt road across the dam to the sites.

Note: If approaching Red Lake from the west, be sure to turn off at the two vista points descending Carson Pass. The view of the lake and surrounding terrain is a grand one!

Heads Up:

- Woods Lake does have an established campground; contact the Eldorado National Forest Information Center 530.644.6048 or fax 530.295.5624.

- Woods Lake is also a popular day-use area with picnic tables and a cinder block vault toilet.
- The lake is stocked with rainbow trout.
- The entire Carson Pass area is well known for its spring-through-summer wildflower displays.
- Be sure to stop at the Carson Pass Visitor's Center, located in the main parking lot at the top of the pass. The center has a small but informative display of the natural history/history of the pass and surrounding area. A bookstore has well-chosen books, cards and souvenirs.
- From this same lot, you can also view the stone obelisk monument to Snowshoe Thompson, a hero of the 1800s. The lot serves as the trailhead to Frog Lake, Round Top and Winnemucca Lake.

One of the cabins located near Woods Lake.

- Dispersed primitive camping is found at Red Lake. The best sites are on the north side of the lake. A free campfire permit will be necessary.
- Red Lake contains rainbows, brookies, cutthroats and brown trout.

Description:

Individually, Woods Lake and Red lake are two small lakes whose size precludes them from being a destination choice for paddling; however, collectively, their closeness to each other, and their setting within the picturesque Carson Pass Management Area (C.P.M.A.), allow you to enjoy not only the lakes, but also their surrounding ecosystems, through a myriad of other activities.

The Carson Pass Management Area

Note: This entry is a fee area in summer and a snow park in winter.

Start west from the Carson Pass Interpretive Center, as the Carson Pass Area boundary angles southwest, and generally follows the unmaintained road leading to forest road 10N01 into Woods Lake. The boundary horseshoes around the Woods Lake access road and the outlying area. On the west side of Woods Lake, the boundary parallels Woods Creek, which flows south of Highway 88, before turning south 0.25 mile before the southeastern shoreline of Caples Lake. *(See map.)*

The C.P.M.A.'s western border covers everything east of the Emigrant Lake Trail as it runs south from Caples Lake for the first mile. The boundary wraps around Melissa Coray Peak, continues south before looping around Fourth of July Lake and follows Summit City Creek for approximately one mile before turning north toward the Sisters. From this peak the boundary follows the ridgeline eastward past Round Top Peak to the Amador Ranger District Boundary at the base of the Pacific Crest National Scenic Trail (P.C.T.). The C.P.M.A. border follows the boundary northward to close the loop at the Carson Pass Interpretive Center parking lot. Frog Lake is within the management area. Located within the management area's borders are trailheads that lead to some of the premier scenic landscapes within the Central Sierra.

As a bonus, both Woods Lake and Red Lake sit just outside the Carson Pass Management Area boundary, but well within hiking distance of destinations that are protected within the C.P.M.A. Before you enter the heart of the management area via the Lost Cabin Mine Trailhead, reserve a campsite at Woods Lake to paddle, fish and swim. At Red Lake, on the opposite (eastern) side of he area, you do not need a reservation. There too, you can enjoy the beauty of the lake before you drive the short distance to the Carson Pass Interpretive Center. Spend time visiting the small museum and the monuments to Snowshoe Thompson and Kit Carson before hiking into the area by way of Frog Lake. Options include a hike to the summit of Red Lake Peak (10,063 feet), Stevens Peak (10,059 feet) or to Meiss Meadow and Meiss Lake. The trailhead and parking area are located across the highway on the north side, just west of the monument.

REGION I: LAKES OF THE HIGH COUNTRY
PADDLING AREA 3: WOODS LAKE

Position: 38°41.00'N, 120°00.30'W

It takes longer to drive the entrance road into Woods Lake than to paddle the breadth of the lake itself. Once you arrive at the lake site, its charm and scenic beauty reinforce your decision to launch your boat. After so many sierran lakes with steep access routes and boat crunching put-ins, it is a joy to walk the short distance on a paved road to the firm sandy beach and casually load your boat before you paddle out. Once on the lake, paddle out to the granite outcrop on the north side and find a slab for sun bathing, or just drift with the breeze. Either choice slows down the day and brings you closer to the natural rhythms that the warm sun and blowing breeze provide.

A few paddle strokes and you reach the dramatic cascading of Woods Creek as it tumbles down from a steep rocky ledge into the waters of the lake. Cast a line, either with a fly or just a spinner, as this lake is known for its rainbow trout. For a photographer's delight, take the trail that leads from the campground, and hike to Round Top Lake by way of the Lost Cabin Mine *(See: Alpine Trailblazer, Chapter References)* or hike the roadside that follows Woods Creek for great wildflower displays. Whatever your choice, Woods Lake is a great place to unwind for either a day or a weekend on river time.

Late afternoon trout fishing; the twin peaks, known as the Sisters, are in the background.

REGION I: LAKES OF THE HIGH COUNTRY
PADDLING AREA 4: RED LAKE

Position: 38°41.55'N, 119°58.25'W

The payback for easy and free access into Red Lake is the sight and sound of traffic that negotiates the Carson Pass grade, as Red Lake, unfortunately, sits at the bottom of the pass immediately off Highway 88. From the center of the lake, watch the vehicles climb and descend the pass. At the far western end, you can even wave to the onlookers who stop at either of the two vista points and busily photograph your antics.

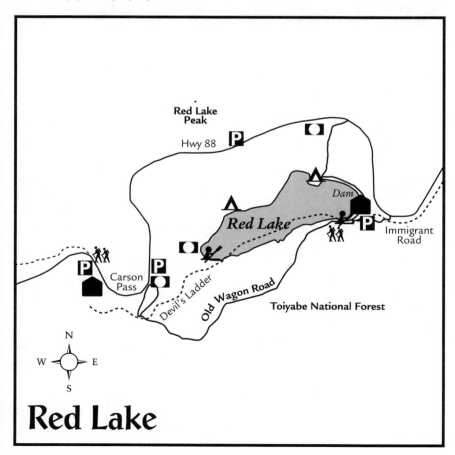

43

View of Red Lake with blooming flowers of mule's ears in foreground.

This bit of news should not, however, keep you from spending a day or longer at the lake. The lake's setting, at the base of a north-south trending granite ridge, surrounded by a forest of conifers, surpasses any of the drawbacks heard from the highway. Once you're on the lake, the sound of the breeze through the pines easily mutes the noise of traffic. Choose one of the sites bordering the northern shore where the base of Red Lake Peak (10,063 feet) meets the lake if you plan to camp. If any of the sites there are taken or if you seek privacy, load up your boat and paddle to the conifer stand along the northwestern shoreline. There are two small, level sites within the stand of Jeffrey pine and juniper, just beyond the bleached deadwood standing in the lake. A second site, is a short distance down lake. Your take-out is just where the sedges and willows begin. The site is on top of the first bluff above the lake. Pull your boat onto the sedges where the willows grow. Follow the animal trail that borders the bluff. Walk between the pine tree and the juniper, following the trail through the sage and mule's ears. At approximately 100 yards, you will round the bluff and see a small trail that goes up the moderate end of the bluff. Follow it up to the top. The level site is at the base of a large Jeffrey pine with a scattering of granite boulders as your eastern border.

Camp here in the fall, as well as in late spring. Spring offers high water and colorful wildflowers and fall offers changing colors and maturing pinecones—and (don't forget) the antics of the Clark's nutcracker (*See Burnside Lake Paddle for a description of this remarkable bird*).

44

What really makes Red Lake a surprisingly busy place is the fishing. According to Tom Stienstra, who writes in his book, *California Fishing*, Red Lake is:

" . . . *stocked with 6,000 "catchable" rainbow trout, 5,000 brook dinkers and 300 to 500 fingerling cutthroats and browns."*

For activities other than fishing, paddle to where the second of two streams enters the lake at its southern end. Hopefully, you are at the lake during spring or summer when the wildflowers bloom. Paddle through the lush green grass and sedges that grow from the shallow silt-filled bottom that extends outward from the mouths of the two streams that enter the lake, and parallel the entire southern end of the lake.

Beach your boat on the small patch of recent sand deposits and gravel at the mouth of the stream. An old beaver lodge is visible under some brush at the mouth of the stream on the left bank. Make your way to shore, partially visible beyond the willows, to the pines and granite boulders that make up the shoreline. Look for a narrow fishermen's trail that follows the lake alongside the base of the ridge. Hike toward the stream's brush-covered canyon. All along the trail and the nearby brush, you spot the telltale color of blooming wildflowers. Many of them use the shade of the brush to keep the sun from drying out their blossoms. Others grow in patches along the streambed or in a cleared area moist from snowmelt. Just before you reach the rocky bank of the stream, look for the exposed trunks of large pine where beavers have gnawed through the outer bark. Eventually, you come to the impassably dense streambed, overgrown with a lush cover of brush and wildflowers. Tall stalks of the Alpine Lily (*Lilium parvum*), whose Latin species name describes the flower as small, contain multiple flowers and hide in the shade, as if too shy to be seen. Other flowers that you will see are the Crimson Columbine (*Aquilegia Formosa*), a source of nectar for hummingbirds, the delicate purple of Lupine (*Family: Lupinus*) and the orange-red blooms of the Paintbrush (*Family: Figwort*). One plant you will smell before you see it is the aromatic Nettlemint Horsemint (*Agastache urticifolia*). If your last meal disagrees with you, according to sources, *"some Native Americans used the leaves from this plant to make a tea to induce sweating and expel gas."*(K. Wiese, *Sierra Nevada Wildflowers, p. 57*).

Once you view the wildflowers, retrace your steps to your boat and make your way past the grassy shore onto the main body of the lake. Follow the south shoreline, paralleling the former wagon road, visible as a diagonal slash above the trees midway up the southeast ridge that borders the lake (*See In the Eddy: Hiking the Pioneer Road to Devil's Ladder*).

As soon as you pass the thick, brush-covered cove midway down the southern shoreline, you will round a small point of aspen and pine and arrive at the primitive boat launch from which you started.

Paddling through the sedges, with a full view of Carson Pass and Red Lake Peak.

In the Eddy:
Hiking the Pioneer Road to Devil's Ladder

The air smells of pine and wetness, flashes of lightning with the distant sounds of thunder are heard, as my hiking partner, Kim Perrino and I begin our hike. We are at Red Lake to follow an infamous trace of the former Carson River Route of the longer Oregon-California Emigrant Trail, known as the *Devil's Ladder*.

Our first task is to hike to the dam at the north end of the lake and orient the terrain features near the trail with those on the map. As I take photographs, Kim matches the route of the former Emigrant Trail to the sketch in our guidebook. On the Emigrant's guidebook map, the trail follows the shoreline of the original Red Lake—a much smaller and nondescript meadow lake. Today, this portion of the trail is underwater because the earthen dam that Kim and I stand on, enlarged the lake. The dam provides a clear vantage point from which to view the former trail as it emerges from the lake and begins to ascend the forest-covered granite we plan to explore. To reach that part of the trail that ascends Carson Pass, we hike on another historical route, a section of the Amador-Carson Valley Wagon Road that was later improved and served as the main road until it was abandoned after the construction of the modern day State Highway 88. This first section of road is clearly visible from the two viewpoints where Highway 88 ascends Carson Pass. Look for a diagonal road slashing across the upper mid-section of

Dispersed camping along the shore of Red Lake.

the ridge, trending north/south along the southern flank of Red Lake. People mistakenly confuse this portion of the Old Highway with the Emigrant Trail. This mistake is easy to make because both sections are near each other and do, briefly, intersect at the crest of the pass.

Kim and I shoulder our packs and proceed to the trailhead of the first leg of the hike. The section that remains of the old highway starts where the paved portion of the exit road to Red Lake ends. Look for a string of boulders that delineate the exit road from the trail. On our right, a belt of Aspen (*Populus tremuloides*), and a copse of mixed conifers hide the waters of Red Lake. To our left, an unstable slope of a former volcanic ash-flow provides a constant source of rocks, cobbles and cinders that slowly bury the pavement of the old highway. We proceed upward, passing the small point of conifers bordering the lake, and begin our ascent to the crest of Carson Pass and location of Devil's Ladder.

Keeping a wary eye out for any change in weather, we note that a Sierran storm seems to be rotating around us. The brief moments of sun that we enjoy will surely be followed by rain. Our hope is that we can complete the hike before the next go-round of rain, with the accompanying deadly lightening. Even with the threat of unstable weather, the view of the lake and the surrounding peaks is breathtaking. We hike upward. The breadth of the lake and the vista of Hope Valley, lying beyond the lake to the East, slowly begin to emerge. Massive white and gray-tinted cumulonimbus clouds roll majestically overhead. To the east, flashes of distant lightening occasionally pierce the inky black skyline. Rolls of thunder gravitate across the valley and bounce off the nearby granite. Here, for the moment, on the ridge bordering Carson Pass, silvery streaks of sunlight flash in and out through the passing clouds. The flank of the ridge protects us on the trail, as only wisps of a breeze remind us of the storm's movement. Although we hike steadily, the beauty of the terrain attracts us and causes us to stop occasionally. Late blooming wildflowers grow out from shady areas. Stray blossoms of purple-colored lupine still bloom in various spots along the trail. Hiding among the lupine, is a lone Orange Agoseris (*Agoseris aurantiaca*), whose rare orange-colored flower head stands out among the green background. Small bands of purple Alpine Aster (*Aster alpigenus*) dot the trail as we pass in and out of wet areas where a small stream flows.

As we look downward toward the lake from the roadbed, Kim attempts to locate the area where the wagons started their ascent away from the former shoreline. It is not easy to discern anything (let alone a hundred-year-old wagon trail) as we look down onto a tree- and brush-covered slope, although the sketch map and its guidebook description are

Standing at the top of Devil's Ladder, looking down on Red Lake. Hawkins Peak in center background, with Pickett Peak on the left.

helpful. We use a bit of *terrain-windage* to decide that the slope here is too steep, and out-wash from a nearby stream-flow makes the ground too soft for the weight of wagons.

This break feels good to my lungs as they burn from the exertion of the climb. I forget that we arrived from almost sea level to the present height of 8,000 feet. I pay for that now, as the shortness of breath and droplets of sweat that drip onto my notebook remind me that we began our hike without allowing our bodies to adjust. As we sit on a nearby rhyolite boulder that came down from the volcanic slope above us, I notice that Kim has barely broken a sweat. Her recent training for the Ironwoman portion of Eppies Race pays her dividends. I'm glad that she never even so much as hints at my huffing and puffing.

After a few moments, I am ready to go, and we soon round the bend where (according to the guidebook) the Wagon Trail intersects the section of the Old Highway. I verify the map and we both spot the tin Emigrant Trail markers attached to pines that grow above the former highway. We now straddle two historical sections of road. At our feet runs the original Amador-Carson Valley Wagon Road, which later became the improved road bed of the Old Highway; above and below us run the remnants of the Carson River Route of the California Emigrant trail. Both the guidebook and the trail markers give us a good visual image of the trail direction. We look for clues as we first try to locate the easy section of the old highway above us and to the south. As I follow the markers, Kim hikes higher to look for additional signs and markings.

One of the large pines that has a trail marker tin attached to it bears a visible notch similar to a *rope scar* (markings from ropes that attached to pull the wagons up the steep trail). The tree is also in direct line with this section of the trail. Farther along on the trail bed is an iron T-Marker. This consists of two sections of T-iron, similar to a piece of railroad track, with the top section affixed to form a T and bolted to an inscribed plaque. A few yards past this marker is a boulder outcrop with names painted on several of the boulders. A large brass plaque, honoring a group of Odd Fellows Fraternal Organization who made the crossing, is set into one of the prominent granite boulders.

This section of trail officially ends at the gravesite of the Unknown Pioneer. It picks up again on the opposite side of Carson Pass near the Visitor's Center.

We head back to where the trail intersects the former wagon road and Old Highway and peer down onto the granite slabs that make up the Devil's Ladder. In addition to the more thought-provoking name, this section of the Trail is also known as "Three Quarter Mountain, First Summit, Dividing Ridge, and others." (See: *From Gold Rush Trail*, p. 37).

We descend following the trail markers, and spot several sections where piles of rock and cobbles have been pitched and form a crude border. The early emigrants cleared the trail to make a more passable route. Even after 150 years, the trail is still discernible through the trees and brush. It is not wide—the width of one wagon at a time. It snakes up from the lake that follows the least grade and avoids the large granite outcrops. Going down is a snap, and we soon reach a fairly level clearing. The clearing sits as the first and only large, level area above the lake where a number of wagons could be grouped. According to Mr. Tortorich, this clearing could have been used as a staging area for the wagons prior to their last struggle to the crest. Just below the clearing, where the trail ascends past the creek, I notice orange-colored stains on the granite. Beneath the stain, the rock has a slight polish, approximately 2-3 inches in width and the same in length. The coloration stains my fingers and pants and appears to be rust, which matches the description I read about iron wheels that stained and polished the rock as they passed.

Kim and I start our ascent after a late summer rain passes; we're now in the heat of the late afternoon and now understand the reason for the name given to this section of inhospitable terrain. As one of the pioneers so aptly states:

> " . . . *we pushed up the step. The most astonishing thing respecting the road, is, that any man of common sense should have first thought of taking a wagon over it. There is about a half mile of road that is nearly perpendicular as a horse can well travel up alone, and the road is filled with large blocks of granite as it is in the can [y] on below. Nearly half way up is a sudden bend in the road and an increase, if possible, of steepness. Below this mountain falls off almost in a precipice. At the foot may be seen three wagons which have run backwards and gone over, . . . "*
>
> —William Tell Parker, 1850, Gold Rush Trail, pp. 38-39.

Sources and References:

Eppies Race, Officially known as Eppie's Great Race, is billed as the World's Oldest Triathlon. The race was originated by Eppie (Eppaminonda) Johnson, a well-known Sacramento restaurant chain owner with a flair for dramatic advertising. The race is held in Sacramento, CA, along a portion of the American River Parkway and the adjacent Jedediah Smith Bike Trail. The Triathlon features a 5.82-mile run, a 12.5-mile cycling race and a 6.35-mile paddle. The first race was held in 1974 with 51 teams and 153 entrants.

Tortorich, Frank, Jr., *Gold Rush Trail: A Guide to the Carson River Route of the Emigrant Trail.* Pine Grove: Wagon Wheel Tours, 2002.

http://www.emigranttrailswest.org/caltrail.htm
Sponsored by Emigrant Trails West, a historical society concerned with the preservation of Emigrant Trails. This portion of the site provides information on the segment of the California Trail through Carson Pass.

REGION I: LAKES OF THE HIGH COUNTRY
PADDLING AREA 5: INDIAN CREEK RESERVOIR

Position: 38°45.05'N, 119°46.35'W

Difficulty: May be paddled by paddlers of all skill levels. Paddlers should be aware of strong afternoon winds blowing through the valley.

Lake Size: Covers 160 acres and is 4,200 feet long.

Trip Length: This small reservoir may be paddled and explored in one full day.

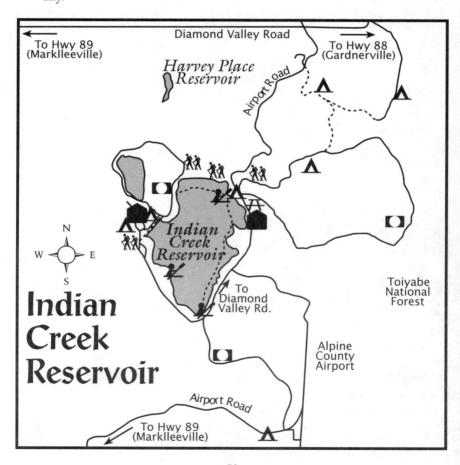

First view of Indian Creek Reservoir from Airport Road. Note the typical High Desert vegetation, sagebrush and juniper. Carson Range looms in the background.

Portage: None.

Paddling Distances: The lake is too small for any measurable paddling distances.

Elevation: 5,600 feet.

Season: Spring through fall.

County: Alpine County.

National Forest/Wilderness Area: Indian Creek Reservoir Recreation Site/Bureau of Land Management and adjacent Toiyabe National Forest, Carson Ranger District.

Maps:

USGS 7.5-Minute Quadrangle Topographical Map Series: Markleeville, CA and Woodfords, CA.

National Forest Service/Wilderness Area: Indian Creek Reservoir Recreation Site/Bureau of Land Management and adjacent to Toiyabe National Forest (Carson Ranger District).

Road Maps:

Compass Maps Inc.: Alpine Amador and Sacramento Counties.

California State and Northern Sierra Map and Guide.

California State Automobile Association (AAA) Maps: Alpine Amador and Sacramento Counties, Lake Tahoe.

Historical Background:

Constructed in 1967 by the South Tahoe Public Utility District; recreation facilities and adjacent lands are managed by the Bureau of Land Management, Carson City District.

Heads Up:

- 19 campsites able to handle RVs up to 19 feet and tents. Secondary location contains 10 tent campsites.
- The campsites that border the access to Stevens Lake at northern end of campground are the best choice.
- Campground contains running water, hot showers and flush toilets. A sanitary dump station is provided.
- Campground usually is opened the first weekend in May, closes the last weekend in September.
- Best sites are those bordering Stevens Lake (See map).
- Camping fees are charged. Phone 775.885.6000 for current fee information.
  Sites are filled early; be prepared to camp at adjacent areas outside the official campground (See map).
- Campfire permit necessary if camping in non-designated camping areas.
- Bear country—pack and camp smart!

Looking across the upper end of the reservoir toward the primitive camping area and boat launch.

- Excellent location for birding and fishing.
- Pets OK, but must be on leash.
- 24-hour ATM gas purchase off Hwy. 89 south on the west side at Sierra Pines Country Store Restaurant and Trailer Park. Incidentally, the restaurant is famous for its "Giant Burger" served for over 25 years —and yes, it is good!

Note: For any vehicle emergencies such as a breakdown or flat tires, the only local towing and garage service in the area is located in Woodfords, CA: Woodfords Auto Service and Towing (530.694.2916). The garage services several major motor clubs and insurance companies.

Access:

Hwy. 89 to Airport Road (midway between the community of Woodfords and the town of Markleeville, and across from the entrance to Turtle Rock County Park). The entrance to the reservoir and the main campground is approximately 3 miles from the turnoff. *(See map for access to the primitive camping locations.)*

Note: You may also access Indian Springs by way of Diamond Valley Road; take the exit out of Woodfords off Hwy. 89 South or Paynesville, located off Hwy. 88.

Description:

Unlike the lakes you find on the western side of the Sierran crest, Indian Creek Reservoir sits within the rain shadow of the mountains and has a dryer environment. As a result, your first view of the lake is of a blue-green body of water surrounded by a forest of ponderosa, Jeffrey and piñon pine trees. Huge expanses of open ground, covered by juniper and sagebrush *(Artemisia)*, which are two definitive plants of the high desert, stretch away from the reservoir and its conifer forest.

Continue down the winding road to reach the turnoff for the main campground. The scent of sage and juniper fills the air. At the turnoff, choose either a traditional campground near the lake or the main campground with its excellent campsites within a pine-shaded grove. If the campground is full, or you wish to camp at your own chosen site, continue on Airport Road, which is now unpaved. Look for side roads that lead off the main road and head into the open country (Several possible campsites and locations are noted on the map).

A third alternative is to camp free at the northeastern end of the reservoir near the dam. Although it is free, there are no amenities other than one Porta-potty and slight shade from the late afternoon sun. This location is best for RVs and vehicles with camper shells. A primitive boat ramp provides access to the water. If you camp outside the reservoir's boundaries, then the boat ramp serves as your closest put-in.

A small boat ramp is located in the main campground. Access the ramp from of the day-use parking lot.

It is best to put-in as early as possible, before the heat of the day creates the strong afternoon winds that blow almost every day. The wind peaks in the late afternoon and begins to die by 5 p.m. By midday, the heat is intense, and combined with the wind, it feels like a blowtorch. So why mention this place? As a high desert lake, Indian Creek has a unique beauty of its own. Its setting, surrounded by a forest of pine, juniper and sage, and capped by the stark mass of the Carson Range, makes for a dramatic backdrop as you paddle along the shore. This impressive wall of the Carson Massif is composed of several peaks and drainages pertinent to the local history of the area. The peak to the far left (the western end of the range) is known as Cary Peak (8,727 feet). It is named after John Cary, who operated a lumber mill nearby in 1864. On the opposite side of the peak is Horse Thief Canyon, a steep drainage that was used by horse thieves in the 1850s. The thieves stole livestock on the western side of the range, then drove the horses up the canyon before turning eastward into Carson Valley, where they resold their stolen animals. It is not out of the realm of possibility that many of these stolen animals made more than one journey through Horse Thief Canyon. Washoe Falls is adjacent to Cary Peak and is a sacred site to the Washoe Tribe. The falls are located in one of the steep canyons that drains into the West Fork of the Carson River. The remaining peaks are Wade (9,367 feet) located to the right of Cary, and Freel Peak (10,900 feet), the highest point in the Lake Tahoe region which the US Coast Survey used for its triangulations in 1870s. The two adjacent peaks are: Jobs Sister (10,820 feet) on the left and Jobs Peak (10,580 feet) on the right. Originally, these two peaks, along with Freel, were

Rocky shoreline with juniper and pine; an excellent spot for a picnic and a morning of fishing.

known as the *Job's Group of Mountains*. The peaks are named after Moses Job, who ran a store in the Carson Valley in 1854.

On another scale, Indian Creek is the home of several interesting species of birds. The majestic Bald Eagle *(Haliaeetus leucocephalus)* has a nesting site nearby, Ospreys *(Pandion haliaetus)* and terns cruise the surface to hunt for fish, Canada geese breed their young, Pied-billed Grebes *(Podilymbus podiceps)* and Common Mergansers *(Mergus merganser)* cruise the lake to search and dive for fish, and the Double-crested Cormorant *(Phalacrocorax auritus)* and the American White Pelican *(Pelecanus erythrorhynchos)* spend spring and summer at the reservoir *(See: In the Eddy)*.

On the Water:

The two best sections of the reservoir to launch from are at the northwestern end, or following the southwestern shoreline. The best approach for the northwestern end is to put-in at the undeveloped boat ramp at the no-fee entry access on the extreme northeastern end of the reservoir. The put-in at the southern end of the reservoir is at the boat launch ramp in the day-use area of the official campground.

The Upper Reservoir

Once you put-in, the first area of interest may be a bald eagle as it roosts atop a lone dead pine across the lake. Follow the lake past the dam and make your approach from the dam. With a pair of binoculars, you can obtain an excellent view of the birds. Sometimes, the entire family perches on the adjacent limbs. As more and more people come to use the reservoir, the nests are abandoned, but the eagles still breed nearby—just not at the reservoir's edge.

Beach your boat, and hike the nearby area by following the shore to a trail that intersects it at the end of the dam. The trail follows the shoreline around the entire lake below the dam. Cross the dam or drop down to the bed of Indian Creek. Use the creek bed to follow the trail back to the restricted-use area of Harvey Place Reservoir. The area that surrounds this reservoir is teeming with birds and animals. Very few people make their way back there because no fishing, camping or boating is allowed; therefore, the birding and wildlife viewing is excellent.

Back on the water, paddle southward and follow the shoreline around the rocky juniper-studded outcrop which makes up the small rounded point bordering the northern end of the second smaller dam on the lake. This outcrop is the highest point surrounding the lakeshore and makes a great picnic spot. The junipers or piñons provide some shade, and the height of the outcrop catches the breeze. From this vantage point, you have a clear view of the lake and the forested ridges beyond. The high peaks, visible to the south, are, from left to right: Highland (10,955 feet), Silver (10,774 feet) and Raymond (10,075 feet).

Caution: These same outcrops of rock provide shelter for rattlesnakes! Pay attention to where you step, sit, or place your hands.

Lower Reservoir

Note: As the waters recede in this section of the reservoir, which is higher in elevation, it becomes shallower and difficult to paddle. If possible, do a vehicle shuttle leaving one vehicle at the main camp area and the second at the primitive boat launch across the lake. This eliminates the need to paddle back to your starting point.

Launch out onto the reservoir from the sheltered boat ramp which provides you with a panoramic view of the sloping, sage-covered shore and the tops of individual tents that peek out from the cover of piñon and juniper. If you seek trout, try your skill in the deep water of the nearby cove. If you want to explore by paddle, point your bow southward and follow the shoreline as it leaves behind the piñon and juniper forest that opens up onto an open expanse of sedges and sage. Bring plenty of water, and wear a hat, for no shade is found on this paddle. Include a pair of binoculars and a guidebook to the local birds and plants as this section of shoreline brings you in contact with a variety of bird life and wildflowers that grow along the shore when the reservoir is full. On my paddles around this section of the reservoir, I am pleasantly surprised that the presence of the Airport Road (a mile up from the lake) does not reduce the variety and numbers of birds I spot. The barren appearance and variable depth (an unwary motor-boater can lose a prop to the rocky bottom) of this lake may cause few people to frequent the area, which is a paddler's delight.

Round the southern point of the cove that borders the day-use area. You will spot a green mat of sedges that grows out from the water's edge. Use your binoculars to look for small bands of Canada Geese *(Branta canadensis)* feeding on the plants. Down-covered goslings hide among the parent birds in the spring. Wherever there are helpless young, there are predators ready to pick off the unwary. For a good chance to view one or more types of hawks as they perch on a limb, point your binoculars up from the shoreline towards the distant pines that grow by the road. Although a hawk's primary interest is field mice or ground squirrels that live nearby, a lone gosling, separated from its parents, is too tempting to pass up. Even in the daylight near the campground, don't be surprised to spot a coyote *(Canis latrans)* or two checking out the odds against running the gauntlet of aggravated adult geese to snatch a gosling. Look high overhead to seek the telltale circular soaring flight of a Golden Eagle *(Aquila chrysaetos)*.

Paddle past the sedge-covered cove and round the lower end of the lake to start your trip's up-leg segment. Just past the sedges is a small barren beach that leads upward toward the tree line. Land your boat far enough away from the grazing geese to prevent any undue stress on the flock. As

A quiet morning for fishing.

you step out, note the white, crusty coating that covers the rocks and surface of the shoreline. This coating is a sodium-carbonate mixture with other heavy metals, such as sodium sulfate (a telltale indicator of poorly-drained arid soils). The mixture of these chemicals produces alkali soils, which are poisonous to most plants and useless for agriculture.

Walk farther away from the shoreline and look down among the grasses to spot the delicate white bloom of a Prickly Poppy (*Argemone platyceras*), one of the few plants that tolerates these soils. The short but sharp prickles resemble thistles, but in actuality, the plant is very different.

"Like most poppies, it contains isoquinolins (opium-type) alkaloids which are known to be toxic to man and other animals."

Look for the bright, yellow blossoms of the buckwheat family sometimes called sulphur flowers or Desert Buckwheat (*Eriogonum umbellatum*). These flowers, when young are bright yellow but turn yellow-orange as they age.

The bright blue and reddish blossoms of lupines and paintbrush provide a contrast to the drab tones of the desert. Sagebrush (*Artemisia species*) tickles your nostrils with its pungent scent as you brush against its gray-green stalks. Tall sagebrush or Great Basin Sagebrush (*Artemisia tridentate*) is the state flower of Nevada. For a plant of such humble origins, it's name comes from a royal pedigree:

"The genus was named in honor of Artemisia, wife of Mausolus, ancient ruler of Caria (Southwest Asia Minor). Mausolus died in 353 BC and his bereaved wife perpetuated his memory by the erection of a magnificent monument-

mausoleum- which became one of the Seven Wonders of the World. Artemisia herself was named in honor of the Greek goddess Artemis, the virgin huntress of wild nature."

—*Wildflowers 2: Sagebrush Country, p. 19.*

Green ephedra, commonly known as Mormon Tea *(Ephedra viridis)*, is an interesting shrub that grows in the open area that surrounds the lake. The plant lacks flowers and appears as a series of pale-green jointed stems that remind me of the Tinker Toys I played with as a child. The anti-depressant and anti-congestion drug known as *ephedrine* is a natural alkaloid derivative from the *Ephedra* plant species.

Walk away from the lake toward the belt of piñon and juniper to spot the gray California Ground Squirrels *(Spermophilus beecheyi)* and small colorful Chipmunks *(Family: Eutamias)* as they scurry rapidly toward the safety of their burrows.

Be wary where you place your feet as you explore the open ground. Rattlesnakes are common here, especially in the spring, due to the variety of prey. The most common rattlesnake is the well camouflaged Western Rattlesnake *(Crotalus viridis)* and possibly the Great Basin subspecies *(lutosus)*.

Stand and take a break under the piñon and juniper that grow parallel to the road, as it is your only shade source. The Single Leaf Piñon *(Pinus monophylla)* is named *piñon* in Spanish and refers to the tree's large edible seeds. The seeds, or pine nuts, provide nourishment to a host of birds and animals, from the corvids such as the Clark's nutcracker, scrub, Steller's and piñon jays, to the mammals of various sizes, from the tiny Piñon Mouse *(Peromyscus truei)*, chipmunks, squirrels, deer, coyotes, black bears and even Bighorn Sheep *(Ovis canadensis* subspecies calforniana) all thrive on a diet of piñon nuts.

Before the arrival of the Europeans into the region, Native Americans living in the Great Basin and the Eastern Sierra considered the pine nut a staple of their diet. As a matter of fact, in January 1844, when Major John Charles Fremont's expedition was on its last legs from cold and hunger, their survival was assured by the timely purchase of pine nuts from a passing Indian. Later, Fremont along with a well-known botanist by the name of John Torrey, described and named this species of pine.

The tree companion to the piñon is the Utah Juniper *(Juniperus osteosperma)*. Ronald Lanner writes in his classic book, *Trees of the Great Basin*:

"A powerful argument could be made that Utah juniper is the most important tree in the Great Basin. . . . there are more acres covered with Utah junipers than with any other of the Basin's trees. It grows in virtually every mountain range in Utah and Nevada, and is dominant in the desert ranges of California." p. 112.

Continue to follow the shoreline to the primitive boat launch at the no-fee camping area located at the eastern end of the dam, or paddle across the main body of the lake back to your original launch spot.

Sources and References:

Lanner, Ronald M, *Trees of the Great Basin: A Natural History*. Reno: University of Nevada Press, 1984.

Taylor, Ronald J. and Rolf W. Valum, *Wildflowers 2: Sagebrush Country*. Beaverton: The Touchstone Press, 1974.

Thomas, John Hunter and Dennis R. Parnell, *Native Shrubs of the Sierra Nevada*. Berkeley: University of California Press, 1974.

Nearby American Bald Eagle's nest with parent bird on the nest.

In the Eddy:
The American White Pelican: A Bird of High Desert Lakes

Oh, a wondrous bird is the pelican!
His beak holds more than his belican.
He takes in his beak food enough for
A week.
But I'll be darned if I know how the
Helican.
  —Dixon Merritt, US Writer
    Nashville Banner *April 22, 1913*

The writer of this ditty does not take poetic license when he states that the bird's beak can hold more than its belly. The American White Pelican (*Pelecanus erythrorhynchos*) holds more than twice the capacity of its stomach in its beak, as it catches fish by scooping close to three gallons of water. Unlike it's cousin the Brown Pelican (*Pelecanus occidentalis*), the American White ranges beyond the coast and even breeds on several islands that make up the remnants of ancient Pleistocene lakes, such as Pyramid Lake, 30 miles northeast of Reno, Nevada. The pelican nests at the large lakes in the Klamath basin of Northern California, es-

White Pelican in flight over main body of the reservoir.

Lift off!

pecially at the Clear Lake National Wildlife Refuge and at various sites along the Salton Sea in southern California. Flocks of white pelicans make their way to feeding grounds throughout the west in the summer months. It is not uncommon for pelicans to fly 50-60 miles one-way to an abundant feeding ground. Indian Creek is an active feeding stop for the pelicans that breed at Pyramid Lake.

The two most splendid characteristics to observe are the flock in flight and their unique cooperative fishing technique.

The white pelican is known for its ability to soar. In fact, their arrival at the lake is rather sudden. One minute the sky overhead is clear and empty, and the next minute a silent flock of white pelican's descends majestically upon the lake in a strung-out V-formation. The flock banks to the left or right before landing silently in a bay away from nearby campers and boaters. Like ravens, white pelicans delight in aerial aerobatics. It is not uncommon for the bird to soar motionless on afternoon thermals, climb high and suddenly drop rapidly onto the surface of the lake. At the last minute, the pelican will check its descent and glide across the lake before ascending again for another run.

Unlike the brown pelican, the American White pelicans' quest for dinner is a communal affair, so they do not as a rule, dive for their food. To observe this organized, group mayhem, paddle to a spot where the flock has grouped itself on the water. Don't forget the binoculars, camera, or video cam, but keep a reasonable distance!

The best place to view the pelicans is on the shallow eastern side of the lake's southernmost bay or along the shoreline parallel to Airport Road.

When pelicans on the water spot a school of young fry, they form either a straight or oblique line. The leader gives a silent signal which starts a commotion of feathered wings beating rapidly on the water, causing sparkling droplets to fly over their heads. Each pelican plunges its head in and out of the water in a rapid staccato. At the same time all this movement is taking place, the line of birds advances toward a shallow section of the lake. Pelicans wait patiently with hangers on such as the Common Merganser and the Double-Breasted Cormorant, either on shore or bobbing in the water, who glide out to join the thrashing group. The pelicans fill a pouch full of fish with each dip of their beak; this continues until the school is depleted or the survivors escape into deeper water.

When satisfied, or the fish are gone, the flock breaks up into individuals or small groups until the next feeding.

Sources and References:

http://www.brrc.unr.edu./data/animal/
Animals of the Great Basin, with some nice photos of American White Pelicans at Pyramid Lake, Nevada.

Beating the surface to scare the fish toward a specific direction.

REGION I: LAKES OF THE HIGH COUNTRY
PADDLING AREA 6: TAMARACK LAKE

Position: 38°36.45'N, 119°54.00'W

Note: Tamarack is a common name for several lakes within Northern California. This particular lake is located off the Blue Lakes Road within the Humboldt-Toiyabe National Forest.

Difficulty: Boaters of all skill levels may paddle this lake.

Trip Length: May be enjoyed as a day trip or as an overnight stay.

Portage: None.

Lake Size: 0.5 mile long.

Paddling Distances: This lake is too small for any measurable distances.

Elevation: 7,890 feet.

Season: Accessible when the snow melts, either in late spring or early summer.

County: Alpine County.

Ranger District: Carson Ranger District.
1536 S. Carson Street, Carson City, Nevada 89701 (tel. 702.884.8123)

Wilderness Area: Tamarack Lake's northern shoreline abuts the boundary of the Mokelumne Wilderness.

Maps:

USGS 7.5-Minute Quadrangle Topographical Map Series: Pacific Valley, CA and Carson Pass, CA.

National Forest Service/Wilderness Area: Humboldt-Toiyabe National Forest (Carson Ranger District) and Mokelumne Wilderness Maps.

Road Maps:

Compass Maps, Inc: Alpine, Amador and Sacramento Counties Map.

California State Automobile Association (AAA) Maps: Central California – Bay Area to Lake Tahoe.

Historical Background:

One of the many smaller reservoirs maintained by PG&E within the Blue Lakes Region.

Access:

From State Hwy. 88, exit onto Blue Lakes Road, located approximately 6 miles west from Pickett Junction (Hwys. 88 and 89). Stay on the recently paved Blue Lakes Road for an additional 10 miles. (There is no sign for the lake; use your odometer to track the mileage.)

Just before the Tamarack Lake and OHV Information board visible ahead and to your right, turn left onto Tamarack Lake Road. Follow the road; it becomes dirt shortly after you pass through the Forest Service gate, to the lake approximately one mile ahead.

Heads Up:

- A campfire permit (obtained free of charge) is necessary when camping in dispersed campgrounds.
- The campgrounds are primitive with NO water or sanitation facilities. For health and common sense reasons, please bring your own portable toilet.

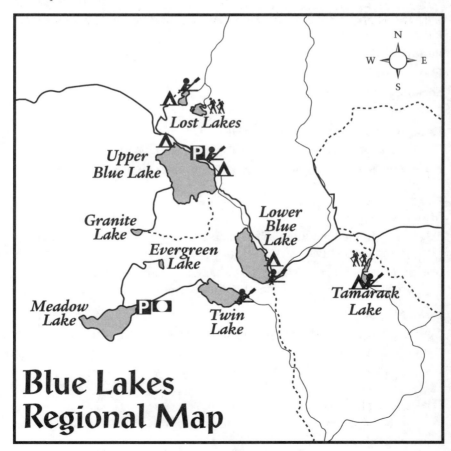

Blue Lakes
Regional Map

The remains of an old cabin visible from Blue Lakes Road. Markleeville Peak in background.

- Bear country—pack and camp smart!
- Excellent hiking throughout the area surrounding the lake.
- Vehicles with high clearance may continue on to the Sunrise Lakes, located several miles to the southeast of Tamarack Lake.
- Mosquitoes are prevalent, especially in the spring.
- By late summer, the lake has receded and is unsuitable for boating.

Description:

'Tis a lovely sheet of water indeed!

You can't help but smile as the lake makes its first shy appearance through a screen of its namesake, the tamarack, also known by its other common name, lodgepole pine.

Pull your vehicle into one of the spaces open to the view of the lake and wait a moment for the dust to settle before stepping out into the pine-scented air.

Wow, what a view!

Tamarack Lake stretches out as a perfect oval and is bordered on all sides by pines, while crystals in the barren patches of granite sparkle in the morning sun. Look north to make out the looming presence of the former volcanic plug known as Jeff Davis Peak (9,065 feet).

After that first impression, you just know that your time here will be well spent.

Lakeside

To approach Tamarack Lake, leave on the newly paved Blue Lakes Road, noting that the last mile is on a dusty corrugated road.

If you arrive at the lake in a standard vehicle, your best choice for a campsite is along the southern shoreline; choose either the single site at the west end of the main dam or the first two sites along the southeastern end of the dam.

Vehicles with high clearance should continue on to the sites bordering the eastern shoreline and closer to the secondary dam. Another possibility, especially if you seek quiet and privacy, is to park the vehicle, load your boat, and paddle across the lake to set up camp on the opposite shore.

On the Lake

Now that camp is set up and chores are done . . . its paddling time!

The beauty of this small lake is that it is long enough to explore, but small enough to keep it from being work.

When the lake is full in the spring through early summer, throw in a lunch, a fishing pole (many people fish, but few seem to catch any) and your hiking boots and don't forget the day pack with binoculars, a camera, and a guidebook or two on the flowers and birds of the area to make a day of it on the lake.

To start your day right, paddle toward the center of the lake, sit back and let the water and air take hold of your boat while you reacquaint yourself

First full view of Tamarack Lake from the top of the lower lake dam. Jeff Davis Peak visible in the background.

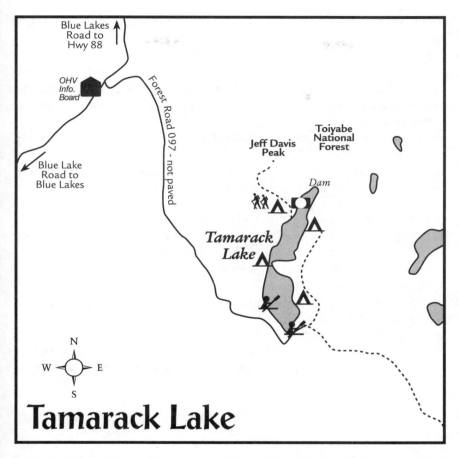

Tamarack Lake

with your five senses. Feast your eyes on the splendor of the immediate surroundings, especially the view toward Jeff Davis Peak. Look at the blue of the sky and enjoy the antics of the raven as it bullies a bald eagle away from its territory. Close your eyes and listen to the breeze rustling the pines, the many languages of the birds, and the water slapping against the hull of your boat. Breathe in the turpentine-scented air from the pines, the tang of wood smoke and the freshness of the rising breeze. You are now ready to start your day!

Begin your paddle by crossing toward the southerly edge of the lake where the pines cast deep shadows over the water. With your binoculars, scan the upper tops of the pines for birds. The first bird you will spot, as well as hear, will be the brassy Steller's jay *(Cyanocitta stelleri)*. The jay is named after George W. Steller, who discovered the bird in 1741 on the coast of Alaska. Steller's jays are so common to the forest and campsites that we often ignore them. With binoculars, observe the rich coloration of the bird; the deep blue and black of its plumage is effervescent in the sunlight. Observe how it bobs its pointed crest up and down, an interesting behavioral trait. Keep your binoculars on the jay as it moves about the tree. Jays are members of the family *Corvidae* (the same group as ravens, crows and magpies), which is noted for its intelligence and aggressive behavior. They are opportunists and, therefore, quick to turn a situation into a meal. Observe the jays long enough and you will see such an encounter. Leave out nuts at your campsite and the jays that come to snatch them are likely to be both young and old, as they tend to congregate in small family flocks.

In addition to the jays, you may also spot (as well as hear) the vociferous chatter of the Douglas Squirrel or Chickaree *(Tamiasciurus douglasii)*. These small, compact rodents are full of energy, as they run from limb to limb, gathering pinecones to husk in preparation for winter. It is probable that the first encounter involving a Steller's jay will also include the curious chickaree. Steller's jays know that after husking the pinecone, the squirrel may either eat or store the nuts. The squirrel takes its nuts to its cache, but the knowing jays will fly-in and attempt to rob the site. Sometimes the squirrel spots the jays and all hell breaks loose—the squirrel runs after the jays chattering loudly, and the jays answer back in their harsh cries and make off with the chickarees' hard-earned nuts.

Spend enough time observing, and you will see similar confrontations between the jays and the woodpeckers and among the jays themselves. Steller's jays are aggressive opportunists and are very adept at exploiting a situation for their benefit.

Lower Lake

Move away from the shaded section of the lake and paddle across the rock-filled dam, passing the shoreline adjacent to the lakeside road. This side of the lake contains a string of vehicles that access primitive campsites as well as trails that intersect the Pacific Crest Trail. Paddle leisurely along the campsites and note the round, protruding point that squeezes the center of the lake. A natural cove with an adjoining campsite on the northern end of the lake is a nice location to camp.

Upper Lake and Lily Pond

Beach your boat and take a short stroll to the adjacent lily pond at the end of the lake where the dam blocks the flow of Pleasant Valley Creek. The pond is approximately 100 yards southeast from the dam, through a grove of immature pine and an outcrop of glacially scattered erratics. Lather on mosquito repellent prior to visiting the pond, because you are visiting their home ground.

The pond's stillness allows you to see the surrounding pines along with the blue sky in the mirror-like reflection of the pond. The distinctive, large,

Looking back from Blue Lakes Road onto Hope Valley, Hwy. 88, and Carson Range with Hawkins Peak in far background.

heart-shaped leathery leaves of the Yellow Pond-Lilies *(Nuphar lutea* subspecies *polysepala)* are found across the surface of the pond. The water lily was a food source of the Native Americans. They harvested the seeds, which were dried and roasted and ground into flour, or popped as popcorn.

A short walk beyond the pond brings you to the Pacific Crest Trail. Hike in either direction to obtain a wonderful view of Pleasant Valley Creek Gorge and the surrounding terrain.

Back at the lake, walk along the top of the small dam to the center to get a photo of the entire lake.

Rather than continue across the dam, paddle over to the opposite shore. The small, shady beach location, a few yards south of the dam, but before the miniature island topped with pine, is perfect for a take-out. Hike to the top of the first ridge overlooking the lake. The view of Tamarack below, and the adjacent view of the Sunset Lakes Region with Pleasant Valley in the distance, is worth every uphill step. On your way down, take the time to admire the mature Sierra Junipers also known as the Western Juniper *(Juniperus australis).*

The best description of these handsome trees comes from R. Lanner's, *Conifers Of California*:

> "In high-elevation habitats, Sierra juniper grows near lodgepole, Jeffrey, and whitebark pines, mountain hemlock, and California red fir.
>
> It does not form intimate associations with these other species . . . It survives in places these pine-family trees cannot invade, where only its search-

ing roots can thread themselves into rocky fissures in quest for water. . . . the Sierra junipers are scattered in ones or twos, or in small groves— never, in the Sierra Nevada, in extensive woodlands." (p. 221.)

A shady cove, with a small but delightful beach, allows you to cool off and (if brave enough) swim in the bracing water of the lake as you return to your boat.

From here on down to your original put-in at the main dam are several small pine- enclosed coves that beg for exploration. Paddle your way down, being wary of the area around the small island just below the beach where you put-in. Extending out from this island is a shallow that contains rocks you cannot spot until on top of them.

Mileage markers, some more colorful than helpful.

Skirt around the island, either out toward the main body of the lake or inside, parallel to the shore.

By the time you paddle back to camp and beach the boat, the late afternoon sun will highlight Jeff Davis Peak and cast soft shadows to accentuate its shape. With camp chair in place, and something cool and refreshing in hand, your time on Tamarack Lake is now a series of stories around the campfire.

Sources and References:

Grater, Russell K, *Discovering Sierra Mammals*. Yosemite Association and Sequoia Natural History Association, 1978.

Lanner, Ronald M, *Conifers of California*. Los Olivos: Cachuma Press, 1999.

Wiese, Karen, *Sierra Nevada Wildflowers: A Falcon Guide*. Helena: Falcon Publishing, Inc., 2000.

REGION I: LAKES OF THE HIGH COUNTRY
PADDLING AREA 7: LOWER BLUE LAKE

Position: 38°36.30'N, 119°55.35'W

Difficulty: Sheltered by a tall conifer forest and a nearby ridge, this small mountain lake is well protected from strong winds, suitable for paddlers of all levels.

Trip Length: A great day-use lake.

Portage: None.

Paddling Distance: 0.25 mile long.

Season: Primarily in late spring when the snows melt, through summer and into early fall.

Lake Size: Approximately 1 mile long.

Elevation: 8,055 feet.

County: Alpine County.

National Forest / Wilderness Area: The entire Blue Lakes straddles the boundaries of El Dorado, Humboldt-Toiyabe (Carson Ranger District) National Forests and the Mokelumne Wilderness.

Maps:

USGS 7.5-Minute Quadrangle Topographical Map Series: Pacific Valley, CA and Carson Pass, CA.

National Forest Service/Wilderness Area: Humboldt-Toiyabe National Forest (Carson Ranger District) and Mokelumne Wilderness Maps.

Road Maps:

Compass Maps, Inc.: Alpine, Amador and Sacramento Counties.

California State Automobile Association (AAA) Map: Central California—Bay Area to Lake Tahoe.

Historical Background:

As early as the 1870s, the Amador Canal Company was using these natural lakes for water storage. Later when Pacific Gas and Electric Company (PG&E) acquired the rights to the area, the company raised the level of the lakes by constructing the present dams in the 1940s.

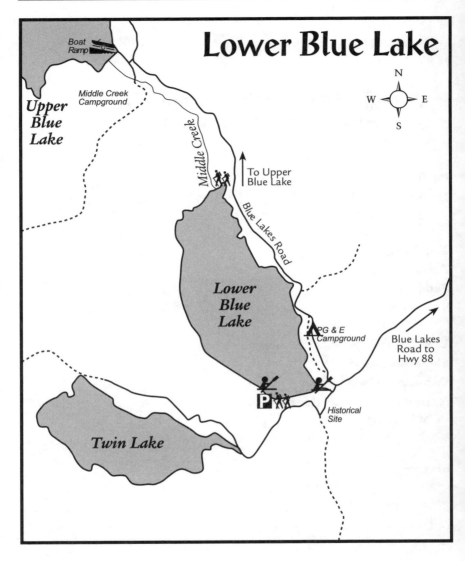

Access:

From State Hwy. 88, exit onto Blue Lakes Road, located approximately 6 miles west from Pickett Junction (Hwys. 88 and 89). Stay on the recently paved Blue Lakes Road for an additional 12 miles.

Heads Up:

- A new two-lane paved road provides access into the lakes for all vehicles.
- Contains 16, fee campsites bordering the eastern shoreline and adjacent to Blue Lakes Road. The sites contain running water, vault toilets and fire pits.

- As of this writing, the campsites are on a first-come basis.
- Maintained by PG&E (http://www.pge.com/about_us/environment/recreational_areas/carson_pass/).
- Primitive camping not allowed except at official campgrounds.
- Bear country—pack and camp smart!
- Well stocked for fishing, both on shore and with boat.
- Excellent lake for family camping.
- Close access to other lakes that make up the Blue Lakes Region.

Description:

The oval-shaped lake precludes any coves or hidden inlets into which to take the canoe or kayak. The lack of varied features does make for a safe lake to allow the older kids a chance to master their paddling skills while you keep an eye on them. The best area for exploration is at the upper north end of the lake where Middle Creek enters. At high water, there are several islands worthy for take-out. The Middle Creek area is also a great place to take the kids on a nature hike. Wild flowers grow in abundance along the banks of the stream in spring. Signs of raccoons, skunk, coyote and even Mr. Black Bear *(Ursus americanus)* are evident by their tracks, as they hunt along streams. In the willows and adjacent vegetation, blackbirds, both the Red-winged *(Agelaius phoeniceus)* and the Brewer *(Euphagus cyanocephalus)*, build their nests. Don't be surprised if these fiercely territorial birds make you the target of their wrath as they attempt to drive you away from their nesting territory.

View of Lower Blue Lake, from the west end of the dam.

75

The still standing pioneer cabin located below the Lower Blue Lake dam, on road to Twin Lake.

Paddle along the conifer-covered west shoreline and note the large barren slope that makes up the southern flank of a former volcanic feature known as The Nipple (9,342 feet), which dominates the immediate skyline. At the base of the slope, a portion of Sierran rock is weathered into the classic rounded shapes characteristic of exfoliating granite. Approach the southern bend of the lake near the dam to spot a cleared area that extends parallel with the shore; this is a service road, allowing access to the west end of the lake. (*See the Access section of Twin Lake for directions to this road*). Take-out at the roadside and hike to the dam, before you round the bend that takes you past the dam, as it is worth the time. Examine the granite blocks that make up the face of the dam. Those grooves are from drill bits used to carve and square each block. Smaller stones, called chinking, fill up the irregular spacing and fissures between the larger blocks. A cement mortar holds the entire assemblage in place.

From the top of the dam, walk to the discharge site below, where the stream pours out. Hike the dirt road where your boat is beached to reach this site and look for the wooden pump house built at the base of the dam. Watch for the presence of an American Dipper, formerly called a Water Ouzel (*Cinclus mexicanus*), on the nearby rocks, as this stout robin-sized slate-gray bird lives along swift-rushing streams. This special bird hunts for aquatic larvae as it dips its head under water (hence the name) or flies into the water and walks along the bottom in the course of its hunt.

Continue past the discharged stream and pump house to the other end of the dam. Look to your right for a lone structure in partial disrepair standing in a clearing surrounded by pines. The building, with a second-story loft and adjacent support beams, appears to be a barn. No matter what its function, there is no doubt as to its early history. Walk around to the sunlit eastern side before noon and examine closely the weathered roof shingles, and note all the square-headed nails. The square-head style of nail denotes a nineteenth or early twentieth century construction.

Sources and References:

Usinger, Robert L. and Tracy I. Storer, *Sierra Nevada Natural History* Berkeley: University of California Press, 1963.

REGION 1: LAKES OF THE HIGH COUNTRY
PADDLING AREA 8: TWIN LAKE

Position: 38°36.25'N, 119°56.15'W

Note: The road to Twin Lake terminates at the parking area that overlooks Meadow Lake. Although there is a portage route to Meadow Lake, it is extremely steep and rugged. Therefore, it is not included in this book.

Difficulty: Although a cover of pines screens this small lake, afternoon breezes still whip across it; however, the shoreline is easily accessible around the entire lake.

Trip Length: The lake may be paddled in its entirety in one afternoon.

Portage: None.

Paddling Distances: Due to the small size of the lake there are no measurable distances to consider when paddling.

Season: From spring through fall.

Lake Size: 4,000 feet long.

Elevation: 8,145 feet.

County: Alpine County.

National Forest / Wilderness Area: Eldorado National Forest, Humboldt-Toiyabe National Forest, Carson Ranger District; also, adjacent to the Mokelumne Wilderness Area.

Maps:

USGS 7.5-Minute Quadrangle Topographical Map Series: Pacific Valley, CA and Carson Pass, CA.

National Forest Service/Wilderness Area: Humboldt-Toiyabe National Forest (Carson Ranger District) and Mokelumne Wilderness Maps.

Road Maps:

Compass Maps, Inc.: Alpine, Amador and Sacramento Counties.

California State Automobile Association (AAA) Map: Central California-Bay Area to Lake Tahoe.

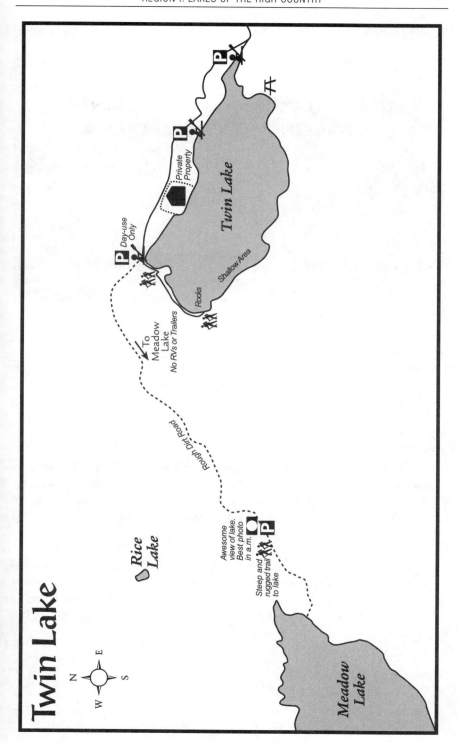

Twin Lake

N
W · E
S

Twin Lake

Rice Lake

Private Property

Day-use Only

P

Shallow Area

Rocks

To Meadow Lake
No RVs or Trailers

Rough Dirt Road

Awesome view of lake. Best photo in a.m.

Steep and rugged trail to lake

P

Meadow Lake

Put-in for upper Twin Lake. View is to the west, with dam located at far end of lake.

Historical Background:

Listed as Twin Lakes on the Markleeville 1889 30-Minute Quadrangle Topographical Map. The two lakes were joined when the present dam was constructed and the water level rose.

Access:

From State Hwy. 88, exit onto Blue Lakes Road, located approximately 6 miles west from Pickett Junction (Hwys. 88 and 89). Stay on the recently paved Blue Lakes Road for an additional 12 miles. The turnoff for Twin Lake is on your left, at the dam site of Lower Blue Lake. The road to Twin and Meadow Lake is not paved and not recommended for standard passenger vehicles or vehicles towing trailers.

Twin Lake contains no parking area except alongside the access road. One small area that may be utilized for parking is by way of a turnoff on your left, just as you crest the ridge and make the bend that allows you to first see the lake. You will have to walk your boat through the sedges to the water's edge.

Heads Up:

- Day-use area only.
- Excellent lake for birding and wildlife viewing, especially early morning and late afternoons.

- Do not attempt to drive to this lake with a large RV or trailer—No turnaround available.
- Bear country—pack and camp smart!
- For wildflowers, the meadow located at the southern end of the lake is superb. This meadow area also allows access to the ridge and trails above the lake.
- Do not leave without visiting the overlook for Meadow Lake, a short driving distance from Twin Lake dam.

Description:

Twin Lake maintains a quiet charm separate from the visible and more visited Lower and Upper Blue Lakes. Tall conifers and forested granite ridges surround the lake, and time appears to slow to the rhythm of the breeze that blows at set times. Arrive early, just as the sun lights the top of the pines that surround the lake. Walk quietly to the shore and look for any bald eagles resting in the branches of nearby pines before you take the boat off your vehicle.

Launch, and keep an ear ready for the loud, distinct *kyew, kyew, kyew* of an osprey. Twin Lake is a favorite fishing lake for ospreys in the early morning and late afternoon, especially when its surface is calm and glassy. Sometimes bald eagles sit and wait for an osprey to catch a fish before the eagles launch and hairy the osprey to drop its catch. The eagles then drop down and enjoy their ill-gotten meal.

Your best bet for fishing is either by the dam or along the northern shoreline. Both areas are in the deepest part of the lake. Almost the entire southern section is shallow and covered by layers of silt. To spot the shallower areas of the lake, notice the growth of green sedges that grow outward from small coves along the shore. For birders, these beds of sedges are prime areas to view with binoculars. Young, down-covered mergansers pass through the stalks learning the rudiments of fishing as they hunt the fry that hide among the grasses. Larger goslings of the ever-present Canada geese feed on the young shoots of

Having a high clearance makes the drive easier into Twin Lake.

the emerging sedges. Working your boat closer to the coves of the opposite end of the lake, keep a vigilant eye out as you pass the shadows. A great blue heron, standing still with its beak aimed at its prey, waits patiently for a frog, crustacean or small fish to come within striking range. These birds are solitary and extremely wary, but they are not shy, letting you know their disgust at your approach or presence. With a loud primeval *squawk,* the heron flaps huge wings and, as it slowly departs its hunting area, voids a copious stream of whitish liquid feces onto the rippled surface where it once stood. Nothing subtle in that message!

To erase that last scene, paddle to the wide meadow located near the inlet of a small stream at the southern end of the lake to view some wildflowers. Your eyes deceive you, and you believe that the ground is moving as you beach your boat and step out. Upon closer examination, you quickly realize why the heron was so upset about your intrusion onto its hunting area—masses of hopping young frogs cover the entire shoreline. The heron had the entire beach to itself as it feasted on the emerging mass. Gather your gear and cover the cockpit so as not to find any unwanted surprises, and beat a hasty retreat inland, away from the rituals of spring.

Beyond the shoreline, and past the screen of willows, pines and brush, lies a vast expanse of a lush meadow. In the late afternoon the breeze has the scent of pine, sage and wildflowers. The variety of spring blooms is astounding against a background of various shades of green. A carpet of mixed yellow, white and purple blossoms leads away from the beach. Toward the crest of the ridge, a vast cover of purple lupine contrasts against the dark green

The boardwalk is for launching in spring when the water level is high.

A nice overall view of the lake from the dam.

of the conifers and the surrounding gray of the granite. Game trails criss-cross the mats of vegetation and are the best bet to gain the ridge top and overlook the lake. Hike through the thick cover of plants to spot evidence of animals that have passed through. The deer prints are everywhere, but so are the crisp paw prints of a Black Bear *(Ursus americanus)*. A downed trunk, torn apart by the bear seeking to locate insects such as the termites that infest the rotting wood, is more evidence of a bear's passing. Near an open area where the soil is rich and soft, the bear has attempted to dig out a mound that marks the presence of either a Pocket Gopher *(Thomomys)* or a California Mole *(Scapanus latimanus)*.

Work the game trails upward to reach the trail that follows the contour below the ridge crest. The trail follows the high ground back to the dam, and the adjacent road leads to Meadow Lake. From this height, view the spectacular lake with its surrounding forest and a clear panorama of the distant Jeff Davis Peak (9,065 feet).

Back on the water, paddle near the southwest end of the lake to approach the dam, and watch for partially submerged rocks. The large knobby finger extending away from the dam harbors many granite boulders whose tips will scrape your boat. If you explore this granite protrusion, you will come upon a surprise feature: a metal, heraldic, pommee-styled cross, erected no doubt, as a memorial. The cross style is unusual because of the knobs at the end of each arm, which are described in French as pommes or apples, and represent the fruits of Christian life.

If you explore this area in the spring, keep your eyes on the shoreline where the sedges grow. Along with the large numbers of yellow-legged frogs, probably the mountain species *(Rana muscosa)*, young Common Garter Snakes *(Thamnophis sirtalis)* are also abundant as they hunt the frogs. Pale blue Damselflies *(Zygoptera)* flit about and skittishly sit for short periods of time on a blade of sedge; they most likely are Pond Damsels *(Family: Coenagrionidae)*. Walk past the large granite boulder that hides the pommee cross and look for a wide, whitish band that streaks the length of the boulder, as this is a good example of a dike. An intrusion of magma that forces its way into a weak zone of the surrounding granitic rock where it cools and hardens is a dike. This particular one comprises a very light-colored and fine-grained mineral called aplite. Similar dikes, consisting of a course-grained mineral, are called pegmatite dikes. Both types are common geological features in the Sierra mountain range; they may run for a few feet to several miles in length, and inches or yards in width.

From the granite boulder, hike to the top of the rock dam to a service road that terminates on the other side and continue along. The stream below the dam is the continuation of Blue Creek whose waters help fill Twin and Meadow Lakes. Walk to the dam's northern edge and reach the berm that marks the continuation of Forest Road 9N01 and terminates at Meadow Lake.

Back in your boat, paddle along the northern shoreline, paralleling the road and passing the only private structure built near the lake. Many passing visitors probably wish they, too, could have a cabin in such an ideal setting. Immediately past the cabin, notice several protruding points of rock, which

Common Garter Snake shows off its stripes.

emerge from the lake. Be wary as you approach, because these mark a rocky reef that may scrape the bottom of your boat. On the opposite side of the reef is a lovely cove with a nice sandy beach. When camping was allowed here, this entire side of the lake was a popular area. Now, only the campfire rings remain. This cove is the last location from which to easily take-out, enjoy a swim or just lie in the sun protected from the wind. This cove is only a short paddle to the sedge-covered meadow where your day began.

The elegant Bishops Cross *memorial located adjacent to a granite outcrop near the dam.*

Sources and References:

Biggs, Kathy, *Common Dragonflies of California*. Sebastopol: Azalea Creek Publishing, 2000.

Moore, James G., *Exploring the Highest Sierra*. Stanford:Stanford University Press, 2000.

Storer, Tracy I. and Robert L. Usinger, *Sierra Nevada Natural History*. Berkeley: University of California Press, 1963.

REGION I: LAKES OF THE HIGH COUNTRY
PADDLING AREA 9: UPPER BLUE LAKE

Position: 38°37.40'N, 119°56.20'W

Difficulty: Exposed to winds, this lake is best paddled in morning or late afternoon before the gusty afternoon winds arrive.

Trip Length: A great day-use lake.

Portage: None, unless you use the beach located off the road between Upper Blue Lake and the Dam Site Campgrounds. A short walk down the berm road is required to reach the beach (See map).

Lake Size: 1 mile long.

Paddling Distances:

From the boat launch facility to the shoreline of Upper Blue Lake Campground: 0.99 miles.

From the beach at mid-lake to The Point: 0.66 miles.

From the boat launch facility to the mouth of Granite Lake Creek: 0.66 miles.

From the shoreline at Upper Blue Lake Campground to The Point: 0.86 miles.

Elevation: 8,136 feet.

Season: Primarily in the late spring when the snow melts through summer and into fall.

County: Alpine County.

National Forest: The entire Blue Lakes straddles the boundaries of El Dorado, Humboldt-Toiyabe, Carson Ranger District, National Forests and the Mokelumne Wilderness.

Maps:

USGS 7.5-Minute Quadrangle Topographical Map Series: Pacific Valley, CA and Carson Pass, CA.

National Forest Service/Wilderness Area: Humboldt-Toiyabe National Forest (Carson Ranger District) and Mokelumne Wilderness Maps.

Road Maps:

Compass Maps, Inc.: Alpine, Amador and Sacramento Counties.

California State Automobile Association (AAA) Map: Central California – Bay Area to Lake Tahoe.

Historical Background:

Originally, both upper and lower lakes were called the Blue Lakes when penned on the 1889 Markleeville 30-Minute Quadrangle Topographical Map. Present-day Deadwood Peak, located to the west of Upper Blue Lake, was originally named Blue Lake Peak on Wheeler's 1876-77 map. Somewhere on present day Blue Lakes Road, between lower and upper Blue Lakes, stood a way station, or stopping place, called Harmonial City.

Access:

From Hwy. 88, exit onto Blue Lakes Road, located approximately 6 miles west from Pickett Junction (Hwys. 88 and 89). Stay on the recently paved Blue Lakes Road for an additional 12 miles. You will pass Lower Blue Lake and the adjacent campground. Continue on for an additional mile to the unimproved launch ramp located on your left, immediately past the spillway of the dam.

The beach access that requires a portage is located approximately one mile past the boat launch and campground. Look for a turnout on your right,

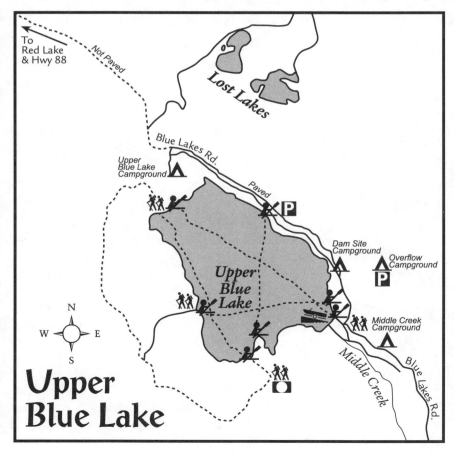

next to a mature pine tree. The trail to the beach is visible when you cross the road. You may also launch from the beach access adjacent to the campsites of Upper Blue Lake Campground, on the northwest end of the lake.

Heads Up:

- A free campfire permit is mandatory when camping outside designated campgrounds. You must obtain the permit in person.
- A new, paved, two-lane road allows easy access into the Blue Lakes.
- There are three PG&E first-come, first-served fee campgrounds at Upper Blue Lake. Upper Blue Lake Campground has 32 units, Blue Lake Dam Campground has 25, and Middle Creek Campground has 5 units. An overflow area has 34 units and is open on Friday nights to contain overflow campers. All units have vault toilets, piped water, picnic tables, grill and fire rings. For additional information, contact PG&E 800.743.5000 or 916.923.7142 or call Humboldt-Toiyabe National Forest (Carson Ranger District) 702.882.2766.
- Bear country—pack and camp smart!
- Due to the improved road conditions, the already popular area will be even more crowded. For a best bet on camping without too big a crowd, use the area mid-week or arrive zero-dark early to obtain a site.
- In addition to the boating, bring hiking gear as the area surrounding the lakes has some incredible views that may be appreciated only by hiking to them.
- These destination points have no set trails so you reach the site the old fashioned way, by trail blazing; consequently, bring a topographical map.

Description:

Upper Blue Lake's setting is grand in comparison to all the other lakes located within this area. Approach this lake from Lower Blue to view its magnificent background, which is not readily apparent until you turn off the main road and see the lake from the parking area of the boat launch. The raw beauty of rock, forest, and sky hits you all at once, like an ice cube sliding down your back on a hot summer day.

If the water level is below the ramp, drive closer to the shoreline to launch your boat. Do not leave your vehicle parked at the launch site; instead, drive back up the road and park nearby.

Several destinations await you once you paddle out. Whichever you choose, be sure to bring your boat about and view the panorama as it unfolds on the northeast side of the lake. The spectacle that spreads before you is the second half of the one-two punch that you experienced from the earlier goose-bump view to the west, and as you scan eastward you get a simi-

The main boat launch and put-in/take-out for Upper Blue Lake. Deadwood Peak rises in the background.

lar skin-tingling sensation. The blue sheen that comes off the lake's surface ends abruptly at the base of multi-colored bands of rock that rise skyward from the shoreline of Upper Blue Lake. The bareness of the ridges contrasts sharply against the thin line of conifers and brush that mark where the lake ends and the rock strata begin. If your first view of these rock layers is in the late afternoon, tints of purple, orange to red, and black against white, leave impressions of a painter's giant palette streaked across the horizon.

Oh, joy! With views like these, you know that the rest of the day will be memorable.

For ease of description, the lake is divided into two sections: the Upper/North End and the Lower/South End.

South End

The southern end is the first section of the lake you will see, and it contains a variety of coves, beaches and inlets that await exploration. In addition, this end of the lake provides a windbreak against the strong afternoon breezes that arise as the air warms. Use the easily accessible boat launch area, located adjacent to the spillway and above the dam, to start your paddle. Head for the conifer-covered point near the dam. A dense belt of conifers near the tip of the point provides a nice windbreak and coats the water's surface with sheen of yellow-green pollen, primarily from Lodgepole pines (*Pinus contorta*). The strip of green along the strandline below the pines appears at first

Early morning launch. A portion of the campground bordering the lake is visible behind the canoeists.

to be a lush patch of grass, but in actuality, it is another member of the grass family, namely, the Sedges *(ssp. Carex)*. Sedges, as a species, are difficult to identify, but as a group:

> " . . . they can be distinguished from grasses and rushes (another type of grass- like plant) by rolling the stems between your fingers. Since grasses and rushes have round stems, they feel smooth. But 'sedges have edges,' to quote a familiar botanical refrain; the three angles of the triangular stem can be felt easily."

This particular variety grows best in a wet environment, especially where the soil base is waterlogged in the winter and drains rapidly in the summer. They are the sod-forming plant species, whose reproduction occurs through underground stems called rhizomes. In certain places, the thick mass of rhizomes helps create a rich soil base known as sod. When the rhizomes decay in the rich, black soil, a further step occurs to form the material known as peat.

Pay attention to the depth beneath your keel as you round the point; the tips of granite lie just beneath the surface and may scrape your hull if you are not vigilant.

Rounding the point, slow down to scan the cove's surface for any birds, especially Great Blue Herons *(Ardea herodias)*, the shy Common Merganser *(Mergus merganser)*, and her brood of down-covered chicks; watch for any sun-bathing Western Pond Turtles (*Clemmys marmorata*) that may bask on a rounded boulder or on an emerging tree limb.

Point your bow to the next rocky point with its islands of barren granite that project from the water.

Make your approach, and be wary for signs of wildlife on the jutting points of granite, and you may spot the profile of the California Gull *(Larus californicus)*. The Latter Day Saints or Mormons honor this same bird with monuments and praise, because it arrived in time to eat the hordes of crickets that threatened the harvests. This bird breeds on the islands found on several of the Great Basin lakes, specifically, Pyramid Lake (east of Reno, Nevada) and the Great Salt Lake (outside of Salt Lake City, Utah) as well as the former volcanic islands that are part of Mono Lake, California. Other birds that use the barren granite for a rest area are the colorful common merganser males with their handsome black and white markings and, of course, the ubiquitous Canada Goose *(Branta canadensis)*. Because this cove is situated farther from the road and campground and is protected from wind, it is not uncommon to spot the American Bald Eagle *(Haliaetus leucocephalus)* or its sometime target of opportunity, the Osprey or fish hawk *(Pandion haliaetus)*.

A gently sloping white granite beach, with gulls and diving ducks, lies to the left of the granite protrusions.

The Pond

Beach your boat, and hike up past the willows and the row of single-standing conifers to the top of the glacially polished berm of granite, for a view of a small melt-water pond.

Approaching the Pond

From the shape of the highly polished, north south trending granitic trough in which the pond sets, it appears that the area was once the floor of a glacier. Other evidence lies in the plentiful patches of glacial polish that cover the area, as well as the willy-nilly piles of odd-shaped boulders, called erratics that litter the bed of the trench. Some sheets of glacial polish are quite large, measuring two to three feet across.

A closer look at the smooth surface of the granite will show tiny scratches aligned in a row, not unlike scratch marks of a cat. Grit, mixed in the ice of the glacier as it moves across the rock's surface, creates these striations. Their alignment indicates the direction the glacier was moving as it polished the granite.

This unique evidence of ice scouring is less common as the weather in the Sierra mountain range and other erosional agents attack and remove this thin glacial sheen. Even here, on top of the granitic bedrock, one sees where former sections of polish erode away, leaving a rough and pitted surface.

Young fisherman with a good-sized trout.

Paddle Note:

To obtain the best view of the surface areas that contain the glacial polish, and, therefore, obtain a good photograph as well, hike upward along the bedrock past the pond. Stand on one of the granite ledges to be higher than the bedrock. Be sure that the sun is at your back. The polished area will reflect the sunlight, not unlike the surface of well-burnished chrome.

Veins of cream-colored mineral known as, aplite cut across the same bedrock, in lines of various width and length. These veins, or dikes, as they are called in geology-speak, are a common feature in a granitic environment *(See: Region I, Paddling Area 10: Kirkwood Lake and Paddling Area 8: Twin Lake).* Looking closer on the surface of some of the granitic boulders, especially those that make up the knoll above the pond, you see what at first appears to be a bad case of rock acne. Protruding bumps of various sizes, shapes, and shades of black literally pockmark the entire surface of the slabs of eroding granite. Where the granitic rock lies as bedrock, these same grayish-black discolorations appear as blemishes within the granite. The geological explanation for this is rather interesting. The grayish sections are part of inclusions, the so-called country rock that the molten granite intruded through on its rise to the surface. Inclusions found in igneous rock (rocks created from a molten state), include rocks of a granitic nature, and are also known as xenoliths. The xenoliths that pockmark the surface of the boulders are more resistant to erosion than the surrounding granite; therefore, they project outward until the surrounding matrix of granite is eroded and the xenolith tumbles down to join the other debris at the base of the boulder. The blemishes are obviously xenoliths that have not been subjected to the degree of erosion as their more exposed counterparts.

The Pond

It is quite possible that this small body of water originally was formed from a glacier scouring the bedrock to a depth whereby melt water flowed from later snow packs forming this now lovely pond. If so, then the pond may be called a glacial tarn; "A small lake created by glacier erosion or deposition."

Stately pines and firs guard the outer rim of the pond and mats of manzanita, willow clusters, and a spreading carpet of sedges create a vegetative rim around the shoreline. Due to the pond's placement, in a depression surrounded by rock and cover, not so much as a ripple from any breeze that blows overhead mars its surface. The stillness of the pond creates a mirror reflecting the guardian trees, blue skies overhead, and any clouds that sweep across. Several polished, granite boulders of various volumes and shapes sit in the water; their placement adds a Zen-like character to the entire scene. A young pine struggles to gain a foothold in a fissure that slices diagonally across the length of one of the granite slabs that rests in the pond. Lining the length of this fissure is a miniature growth of shrubs, wildflowers and sedges. The entire slab gives the appearance of a bonsai garden, further accentuates the serenity of this place.

You may surprise a couple of Mallards (*Anas platyrhynchos*) as they rise vertically in a spray of water produced as they beat their wings. Startled, their loud quacks echo off the granite.

If you are fortunate to arrive at the pond and have it to yourself, take advantage of the solitude; enjoy the quiet beauty and embrace its tranquility.

The Cove and Inlet

Look across the narrow cove where your boat is beached, and spot a flat sandy surface with circles of Willow Shrubs (*family Salicaceae*) growing in odd patterns the length of the meadow. Although you cannot see it, a stream snakes its way through this sandy deposit. The meadow is being formed by the continuous deposit of sediments laid down by the flow from this stream. Your nose will begin to tingle from a delightful scent as you paddle closer to the inlet in the late spring. This heady bouquet emanates from the thick carpet of Brewer's Lupine (*Lupinus breweri*) that covers the entire surface of the meadow. The scent intensifies as you pass into the inlet with lupine blossoms bordering

From a nearby ridge this overhead view clearly shows three kayakers entering a small inlet of Upper Blue Lake.

both sides and spilling over the sidewalls of the drowned streambed.

As you paddle further into the inlet, the openness of the meadow gives way to the dense thickets of willow, clumps of grass and stands of wildflowers, particularly the paintbrushes. The two most common paintbrush found in this environment are Applegate Paintbrush *(Castilleja appelgatei)* and Indian Paintbrush *(Castilleja miniata)*. Of the two, the Indian paintbrush favors a moister environment. Work your way deeper into the streambed, and note the fine clarity of the water that easily allows you to follow the large trout that dart away from your approach. Occasionally, you spot the movements of Crayfish *(Pacifastacus leniusclus)*, with their reddish-brown shells, as they lumber down the sediment covered slopes of the underwater embankment. Eventually, after several bends in the stream, you reach the end where a logjam blocks any further passage.

Take the time to beach your boat and hike through the forest before your return. *(See map for guidance and In the Eddy on a description of what you will find.)*

Note: If you decide to paddle along the western shoreline paralleling the ridge, do not paddle adjacent to the shore, because the silts and mud deposited from spring runoff, have made this side of the lake extremely shallow in places. Either paddle in the more open portion of the lake, or put in at the upper northern end and working your way down.

The Northern End

Access

Unlike the southern or lower end of the lake, with its easily accessible boat ramp, the northern section has only two areas to launch from, although you can paddle in from the lower lake.

Your first put-in choice is from the upper lake campground. Unfortunately you must have a campsite in order to launch your boat; even so, you will have to portage it from your campsite to the beach. But, even if you do have a campsite, you will still need to portage your boat from it to the beach. The second choice also involves a portage, although a shorter one than from the campground.

Midway between the lower lake campgrounds and upper lake campgrounds on Blue Lakes Road is a pullout, large enough for either four standard-sized vehicles or one large RV. The portage trail is located across the road and down the embankment to the gravel beach. The trail is approximately 100 yards long. From this site, you have easy paddling to the upper lake and less distance to the lower lake than from a put-in at the upper lake campground.

Exploring the Upper Lake

The north or upper end of the lake is less protected from the wind than the lower end and, therefore, provides the paddler with a bit more challenge in the afternoons when the winds pick up. There is no prevailing wind; instead, it is more capricious in nature as the breeze appears suddenly blowing from one end of the lake to the other.

You can truly capture the entire vista of the lake and its surrounding basin on a calm morning or late afternoon. Osprey, occasional White Pelican *(Pelecanus erythrorhynchos)* and the common merganser use the lake as their fishing grounds. From your boat, you have an unobstructed view of the osprey's dives, its fish-catching ability, and the head-bobbing antics of the pelican as it fishes for its meals or follows the high-speed flight of a string of mergansers. I am in awe of the diving gooses' ability to literally skim the lake's surface at what appears to be supersonic speed and then gracefully brake before skimming on the water in one smooth motion. Their flight pattern will do the Navy's Blue Angels proud! If you are at the far northern end of the lake where the stream enters, and before the campground becomes heavily used, look for a great blue heron or even a Great Egret *(Casmerodius albus)* as it silently stalks frogs along the braided streambed.

Past the shoreline that leads to the campground, you will encounter a small cove where a series of streams empty into the lake. From your boat, you can also spot the lakeshore trail that has been created by countless fisher-folk and hikers. The trail is not an official one, but has evolved as an easier alternative to hiking the ridge above the lake. This section of the upper lake is also where you beach your boat for the hike into the forest or up to the ridge beyond. If a hike is not on the agenda, the wide expanse of beach, with the forested meadow beyond, serves as a great location for a picnic or a break to stretch those legs.

Paddle parallel to the ridge along the northwestern shoreline as you leave behind the meadow with its tall conifers and enter the narrow strandline dominated by rockfalls on one side and the lake's lapping waters on the other. The main vegetation consists of sedges and low-growing willow shrubs. If you venture too close to these clumps of willow in the summer, you are guaranteed to become a target of every territorial Red-Winged Blackbird *(Agelaius phoeniceus)* guarding its nest.

Note: *Similar to the depth conditions of the south end, be wary of paddling too close to shore as you approach the mid-section of the lake due to shallow mud banks that are only partially visible on the surface. Unless you plan to paddle to the lower southern end of the lake, turn around and beat the rising breeze back to your take-out and campsite.*

Sources and References:

Smith, Genny, Ed., *Sierra East Edge of the Great Basin*. Berkeley: University of California Press, 2003.

Schoenherr, Allan, A., *A Natural History of California*. Berkeley: University of California Press, 1995.

Guyton, Bill, *Glaciers of California, A California Natural History Guide*. Berkeley: University of California Press, 1998.

Horn, Elizabeth L., *Sierra Nevada Wildflowers*. Missoula: Mountain Press Publishing Company, 1998.

Maley, Terry, *Field Geology Illustrated*. Boise: Mineral Land Publications, 1994.

Storer, Tracy I. and Robert L. Usinger, *Sierra Nevada Natural History*. Berkeley: University of California Press, 1963.

In the Eddy:
Hiking the Western Ridgeline of Upper Blue Lake
Section I: The Southern End

A pproach this hike from either end of the lake, as the complete hike starts from the meadow at the south end or from a small cove at the western edge of the north end. The hike follows the ascending terrain to the north-south trending ridge that dominates the southwestern shoreline of Upper Blue Lake. Ascend to the top, and hike the ridgeline to the opposite end of the lake, or explore the forest area abutting the ridge.

To fully describe each of the two approach areas, I have created two sections. Section I describes the area that surrounds the lower or southern end of the lake and Section II covers the approach from the upper or northern end.

Your best approach for exploration is to start from the flat beach that borders the inlet described in the text; from there, begin a gradual ascent by hiking in a westerly direction through the willow thicket before passing through a thin stand of conifers. Reach the cleared slope where a rock pile is visible, and follow the small streambed to where the clearing ends and the forest begins.

View of the small tarn with its screen of conifers.

Take a break when you reach the tree line, and enjoy your first lake view with its surrounding topography.

Continue on exploring the wet meadows and the surrounding forest or hike to the base of the ridge that you have been paralleling and scramble to any of the ledges that form the ridge.

The Ridge

Investigate the ridge, and scan for game trails that lead through the dense willow thicket bordering the streambed. Negotiate your way across the stream and look for clusters of Tiger Lilies *(Lilium parvum)*, whose bright orange flowers may be hidden by the willow's branches. Once you reach the ledges that are part of the ridge, rely on the game trails for the best route through the maze of rock. Follow these trails to the top, or be content to locate a shady, level bench of granite with striking views of Upper Blue Lake, The Nipple (9,342 feet), and both Markleeville (9,415 feet) and Jeff Davis (9,065 feet) Peaks.

The evergreens surrounding you are a mixture of pines *(Genus: Pinus)*, Firs *(Genus: Abies)*, and Mountain Hemlocks *(Tsuga mertensiana)*.

Listen for the harsh, grating *kraaa,* a call signifying the presence of a Clark's nutcracker *(Nucifraga columbiana)*, which is best described as "a chunky gray bird with black wings and black central tail feathers." The nutcracker resembles a jay, but exhibits the mannerisms of a crow. Its importance to the ecology of the American West far outweighs its size and weight. In his wonderful book, *Made for Each Other,* Ronald M. Lanner states:

> *"The Western Landscape owes much to these feathered cultivators of our rocky highlands. . . . In these corvid-established [the nutcracker is a member of this family] forests, a tree grows where a bird planted it . . . "*

The nutcracker's primary diet consists of pine seeds, mainly from the Whitebark Pine *(Pinus albicsulis).*

I was able to observe a couple of Clark's nutcrackers ply their trade. They strip cones from a White Fir *(Abies concolor),* shred them, and devour or store the seeds. In less than five minutes, the bird was able to completely shred a cone of all its seeds before discarding the remains onto the duff pile forming around the pine *(See: In the Eddy: The Trail to Hawkins Peak and Vicinity, Burnside Lake Paddle for additional description of this bird).*

The Forest and Wet Meadow

Continue upward and follow the shallow stream to the forest. Quietly enter the conifer-covered woods and tune your senses to activity, and to the details of trees and plants. Explore the edge of a wet meadow viewed straight through the trees. Approach quietly, and take the time to orient yourself to the dim light; you may spot a family of Mule Deer (*Odocoileus hemionus*) browsing on the tender new growth or just rising from their grassy beds to check you out. The sight the bulky shape of the Black Bear (*Ursus americanus,*) as it forages through the meadow, should not be a surprise, as I have spotted one bear and seen evidence of others, specifically, droppings, scarring on trunks of conifers, and the ripped-apart deadwood where a bear was seeking insects and grubs.

Both this and the adjacent meadows are popular with many species of animals because of the variety of food that grows and lives here. Follow the stream as it meanders through the meadow to understand how many kinds of animals use the meadow, and look for the miniature mud bars that build up at the bends in the stream. Here, you will find paw prints, hoof imprints and bird tracks of a host of different species. By the way, this is the time to pull out your seldom-used field guide on animal tracks and scat piles!

Avoid hiking directly through the center of the meadow, as it will be wet, muddy and slippery, but also because you can damage the fragile plants that grow here. Follow the southerly edge of the meadow to your left for a better approach. Catch the scent of mint as you pass. The sudden whiff from the wild Mint (*Mentha arvensis*) that resides in wet soils of marshes and meadows is a joyful surprise. I pick a few leaves and put them into my water bottle for an extra zing!

As you intersect the stream that feeds the meadow, cross over it to the granite and pine island. This oasis from the wetness around you provides a comfortable dry spot for taking a break, and also gives you the opportunity to look back and view the meadow in its entirety from higher ground.

This break spot also allows you to decide to explore further beyond the meadow—where you can intersect a pack trail leading from Middle Creek Campground to Granite Lake and beyond, or follow the meadow's stream back toward the lake.

The Meadow Stream

Follow the streambed back for an opportunity to study and view the diverse plants of forest and stream. Myriad wildflowers grow all along the wet banks of the stream. Lupines, paintbrushes, lilies, phloxes, and

This scene resembles a life-sized bonsai garden in its serenity.

members of the sunflower family are all hardy flowers that grow in the damp as well as the drier soil of the forest proper. Three flowers of note growing along the streambed are: the aforementioned small Tiger Lily *(Lillium parvum)*, Red Columbine *(Aquilegia truncata)*, and Scarlet Gilia *(Ipomopsis aggregata)*. Of the three, the Scarlet Gilia exhibits several interesting traits. In the early summer, the red blossoms attract hummingbirds that help pollinate the plant. By late summer, when the hummingbirds migrate to lower elevations, the plant's flowers undergo a coloration change from red to pink or even white. This adaptation occurs because the pollinator shifts from bird to the Sphinx Moth *(Sphingidae)*. The moth seeks nectar from plants at night, and the lighter coloration of the blooms makes them more visible. In addition, studies show that plants grow heartier and produce more stems, flowers and fruit, from deer nibbling their tops.

Follow the winding path of the stream, and look for crayfish and tadpoles in the clear water. Occasionally, you will spot the stealthy, slithering, brownish-colored Garter Snake *(Thamnophis)*. They are sometimes called water snakes because of their presence near and in the water.

Hike through the ground away from the stream before you arrive at the edge of the forest. You will find some interesting fungi that grow on decaying matter, everything from the common Shelf Fungus *(Ganoderma lucidum)* that grows primarily on pines, to the colorful Sierra Puffballs *(Calbovista subsculpta)*, whose fleshy globular white body grows out from the duff of the forest.

Make your way past the fallen and decaying trunks of conifers, and look for evidence of bear activity. You may spot the claw marks on the harder inner wood or the irregular pattern of the strewn bark and chunks of wood spread out around the fallen tree.

Eventually, you make your way to the edge of the forest where you can spot your boat on the beach below.

Sources and References:

Field Guide to the Birds of North America. Washington, D.C.: National Geographic Society, 2nd. Ed., 1996.

Lanner, Ronald M., *Made For Each Other A Symbiosis of Birds and Pines.* New York: Oxford University Press, 1996.

Lanner, Ronald M., *Conifers of California.* Los Olivos: Cachuma Press, 1999.

Schoenherr, Allan, A., A *Natural History of California.* Berkeley: University of California Press, 1995.

In the Eddy:

Hiking the Western Ridgeline of Upper Blue Lake

Section II: The Northern End

Whether you start your hike from your boat or from the upper lake campground, your entry into the forest, and subsequent access to the ridge above, originates from the same section of the lake. Begin your hike along the small vegetation-covered stream that meanders its way into the lake, by way of the short boxy-looking inlet just south from the campground beach area.

Make your way past the conifers that border the shoreline, cut across the lakeshore trail described earlier, and follow the stream up towards the forest. Cross as the stream bends to the south and continue to hike upward and keep the stream on your left and the ridge to your right.

Pass through various wildflowers as you hike the grassy meadow adjacent to the stream. One of the more colorful blooms is that of the Anderson's Thistle *(Cirsium andersonii)*. This perennial, with its scarlet blossoms, was named after a nineteenth century Swedish Botanist, Nils Anderson, who collected plants in California. The genus name, *Cirsium*, is an ancient Greek name meaning swollen vein and refers to the extract

The drainage visible in this photo is the access to the meadow hike as well as the way to the top of the ridge visible on the right.

from thistles that's used to treat the condition. Here in North America, some Native Americans ate parts of the plant (either raw or cooked) as we do today, and called them artichokes. The second flower that grows nearby is a flashy pink annual, Copeland's Owl's Clover (*Orthocarpus cuspidatus ssp. Cryptanthus*). Like many of its relatives in the Figwort family, particularly the paintbrushes, Owl's Clover is a parasite because it attaches its roots to the roots of nearby plants for nourishment. Mountain mule's ears (*Wyethia mollis*) is a hearty perennial plant whose blossoms appear to cover the entire meadow; it is also considered one of the icons of the Sierra mountain range. The bright yellow disk-shaped blossom brightens many a mountain meadow. The plant was named in honor of Nathaniel J. Wyeth, an early nineteenth century explorer, by another famous botanist of that century, Thomas Nuttall.

Be sure to give yourself and your partners a good visual tick check before you enter the forest, as those little varmints are hard to spot, and the bushwhacking you just went through is prime country for that nasty little arthropod. With the threat of Lyme disease, or the lesser-known Relapsing Fever, it is imperative to check yourself and partners for a tick's presence.

Once the tick check is complete, your entry into the shadowy and cool realm of the pine forest should be welcome after the hours spent paddling in the morning sun. Negotiate through the downed limbs, and feel the softness of the pine duff under foot, look for freshly gnawed pinecones and the litter associated with the cones' demise. These piles of cone scales, called midden, will accumulate either directly under the trunk of a pine or in a neat debris pile on a stump or rock outcrop. They are the work of either the Western Gray Squirrel (*Sciurus griseus*) or its nosy and nosier cousin, the Douglas Squirrel, better known as the Chickaree (*Tamiasciurus douglasii*).

Eventually, you reach a section of high ground that slopes upward toward the base of the granitic outcrop and marks the location of the ridge to be climbed. On your way to the rocky outcrop, look around at the conifers that grow in the area. Depending on the time of year, you may see cones growing upright from the tip of the drooping limbs. These handsome barrel-shaped cones are distinctive of the Red Fir (*Abis magnifica*), also known as the Silvertip. John Muir called it the "Magnificent Silver Fir." Examine a cone on a branch close to the ground and look for a mature purplish-brown one approximately nine inches long, oozing a whitish crystalline-like pitch from the cone scales.

The Ridge

Go up the game trail, through the break in the rock wall, to reach the top of the ridge on your hike. The climb is not difficult and is more of a scramble than a climb.

Once you reach the top of the ridge, you are pleasantly surprised to find yourself on a gently sloping ground that consists of grus, a thin crunchy soil base. Grus is the name for weathered granitic particles broken down from the exposed bedrock (*See: Region II: Paddling Area 1, In the Eddy: A Hike Through a Glacial Landscape*). The grus covers an area extending the length and width of the ridge. Before you move on to absorb the anticipated view, take a moment to appreciate the beautiful symmetry of the ridge you just trekked up, as it bends southward toward the meadow. (*See In the Eddy description.*)

You are now ready to take the last few steps upward for that well-earned view. Approach the edge of the ridge top and your first glimpse of the panorama presenting itself makes you realize this hike was well worth the effort. But this is just the first of two surprises in store for you today. It is hard to break away from this majestic sweep of lake, mountains, forest and sky, but you have only a few hours left to explore the rest of the ridge. A solution is to hike parallel to the lake as you trudge upward toward the center of the ridge. Work your way through the wind-sculpted pines and notice the slightly orangey, rust-like, tint of the trees' thin-scaled bark. You have paddled past the taller versions of the Lodgepole Pine (*Pinus contorta ssp. Latifolia*) before, but maybe with scarcely a glance at the densely packed stands lining the shore of the lake. Two other species of conifer provide a contrast to the dun-colored rock and sweep of deep blue sky. Growing in small thickets of three or fewer, or as lone sentinels, are Mountain Hemlocks (*Tsuga mertensiana*), which John Muir rhapsodizes about in his *The Mountains of California*, where he describes it as:

"*The most singularly beautiful of all the California coniferae.*"

The hemlock is easily identifiable by its characteristic droopy tip. This tip, or leader, bends gracefully, as do the branches that lead from the main trunk. Clusters of cones in various stages of maturity hang at the ends of limbs, high in the crown of some of the trees.

The third member of this rarified conifer group is the Whitebark Pine (*Pinus albicaulis*). We meet this sturdy dweller of the timberline as we watch the Clark's nutcracker attack the tree's cones with such gusto.

Shrubs carpet the floor where the conifers grow: vegetation such as Manzanita (*Arctosaphylos*), and members of the Oak family (*Fagaceae*),

Whimsical natural art courtesy of Mother Nature.

the bushy Huckleberry Oak *(Quercus vaccinifolia)*, whose small acorns are a sought-after food source by rodents and other animals, and the occasional Bush Chinquapin *(Castanopsis sempervirens)*, recognized by its burred fruit and evergreen leaves with a golden undercoat.

As you reach the apex of the ridge, you stand breathless from the thin air as well as the stunning panorama that unfolds before you. Your second well-earned surprise now dominates the horizon. Stretching from one end of your vision to the other lies the massive rock wall of the Devil's Corral, a perfectly formed glacial cirque, carved off the northeast side of Deadwood Peak (9,846 feet). The grandeur and scale of the cirque's massive face is difficult to comprehend. Mature conifers, with a height of 100 feet or more, grow on the ledges and rim of the cirque, and appear to be the size of matchsticks.

In the broad valley floor below, flows the sun-drenched Devils Corral Creek.

Find a shady comfortable bench of granite and sit down to enjoy your reward and be glad of your decision to climb the ridge.

Sources and References:

Lanner, Ronald M., *Conifers of California*. Los Olivos: Cachuma Press.

Blackwell, Laird R., *Wildflowers of the Sierra Nevada and the Central Valley*. Edmonton: Lone Pine Publishing, 1999.

Grater, Russel, K., *Discovering Sierra Mammals*. Yosemite Association and Sequoia Natural History Association, 1978.

Storer, Tracy I., and Robert L. Usinger, *Sierra Nevada Natural History*. Berkeley: University of California Press, 1963.

Thomas, John Hunter, and Dennis R. Parnell, *Native Shrubs of the Sierra Nevada*. Berkeley: University of California Press, 1974.

Wiese, Karen, *Sierra Nevada Wildflowers*. Helena: Falcon Publishing, Inc., 2000.

REGION I: LAKES OF THE HIGH COUNTRY
PADDLING AREA 10: LOST LAKES

Position: 38°38.50'N, 119°56.45'W

Difficulty: Both lakes are small and may be paddled by boaters of all skill levels.

Trip Length: These high country lakes are too small for any time frame; however, due to the traveling distances and time on the road, plan on a weekend at this location.

Portage: None for the first lake, but approximately a 100-yard carry on a former access road to the second Lost Lake.

Paddling Distances: No measurable distances.

Season: Late spring through fall, before the first snows.

Lake Size: Each lake is approximately 0.25 mile long.

Elevation: 8,652 feet.

County: Alpine County.

Lakeside view of the first Lost Lake from the main campsite. The view is north toward the dam, and the start of the West Fork, Carson River.

107

National Forest/Wilderness Area: Although the lakes straddle the combined boundaries of El Dorado and Humboldt-Toiyabe National Forests as well as the Mokelumne Wilderness Area, the Lost Lakes fall under the jurisdiction of the Carson Ranger District of the Toiyabe National Forest and the Mokelumne Wilderness Area boundary.

Maps:

USGS 7.5-Minute Quadrangle Topographical Map Series: Pacific Valley, CA and Carson Pass, CA.

National Forest Service/Wilderness Area: Humboldt-Toiyabe National Forest (Carson Ranger District) and Mokelumne Wilderness Maps.

Road Maps:

Compass Maps, Inc: Alpine, Amador and Sacramento Counties.

California State Automobile Association (AAA) Maps: Central California – Bay Area to Lake Tahoe.

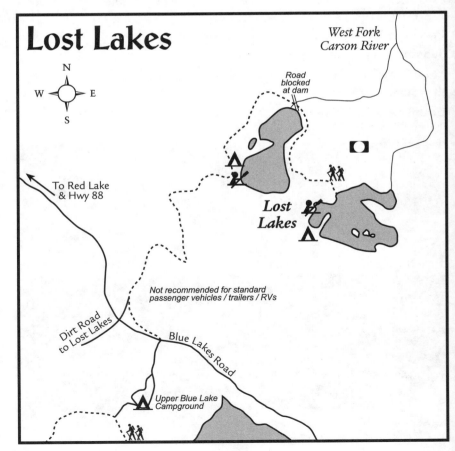

Historical Background:

The water rights to Lost Lakes reservoirs were purchased in 2001 by the Carson Water Subconcervancy District (CWSD), a multi-county, bi-state agency. The water is released in the fall to augment the flows in the West Fork of the Carson River.

Access:

From State Hwy. 88, exit onto Blue Lakes Road, located approximately 6 miles west from Pickett Junction (Hwys. 88 and 89). Stay on the recently paved Blue Lakes Road for an additional 12 miles. You will pass both Lower Blue and Upper Blue Lakes.

The paved portion of Blue Lakes Road ends at the Upper Lake Campground, and the unpaved portion begins. Continue to climb past the campground for approximately one mile. Look for a Forest Service sign depicting the turnoff for Lost Lakes. The turnoff will be on your right.

From the turnoff, follow the dirt road to a small knoll overlooking the first Lost Lake.

To reach the second lake, hike on the former access road or paddle across the first lake, before hiking on the former access road to the second lake.

The former access road parallels the north shoreline of the first lake and crosses over the dam before continuing around the lake. You can spot the road from your vehicle on the opposite shore looking easterly. The road enters a saddle between two knolls that block the view of the second Lost Lake, before ending on top of the berm separating the natural drainage between the lakes.

Note: The access road to the second lake has been blocked. Do not attempt to drive to the second lake; there is NO turnaround at the blocked area.

Heads-Up:

The section of road from Upper Blue Lake to Lost Lakes is a steep, narrow two-lane non-paved road. High-clearance vehicles are best suited for the drive (four wheel drive is not necessary).

All camping is dispersed and primitive. There are no toilet facilities; consequently, bring your own portable toilet (*See Volume 3 of this series, Introduction, Wilderness Ethics, for sources on the subject*). Finally, PLEASE, if you pack it in, pack it out!

- The best campsite is located under a stand of conifers with a view of the lake and dam. Other smaller sites are available along the north shore of the first lake.
- Bring your favorite brand of bug repellent. . . you will need it!
- The road that used to lead to the second lake has been blocked off at the dam.

The forested west shoreline of Lost Lake, with the volcanic plug known as the Nipple (9,342 feet) visible in the background.

- If planning on boat camping at the second lake, bring a boat cart to transport boat and gear to the lake (*See Up the Lake with a Paddle, Volume 3, pp. 13-17 for information on packing, portaging and carting canoes and kayaks*).
- Do not attempt to drive the road leading up to the adjacent crater on the northern end of the first lake; the free fall is sure to be exciting, but only as a one-way event.
- The second lake is located due south over the small berm visible across from the first lake.
- If you get the opportunity, make the hike to the top of The Nipple, the volcanic plug that dominates the southwestern side of the area.

Description:

The Lost Lakes may be well hidden, but they certainly are not lost! This is a good thing if you seek privacy or want to camp in a more intimate setting. The Blue Lakes are below the Lost Lakes and are fascinating and beautiful, but their size and majesty preclude any personal empathy to their setting. Not so with the Lost Lakes! Their small size and accessible location allows you to embrace their presence on a more personal level.

To hike around each of the lakes is easily accomplished within a short period of time. This unhurried walk-about allows you to acquaint yourself with each lake's personality. Unlike the huge expanse of rock and sky that dominate the horizon of the Blue Lakes, here the vistas are hidden until you approach them. Your first views insure a treasured memory.

At each of the Lost Lakes, placing a canoe or kayak in the water is not so much to accomplish a long-distance paddle, as it is to soak up the peaceful presence of the place.

Note: The best way to fully appreciate these lakes is to take your boat out in the night and let it drift under the full moon or the star-lit sky. The Milky Way will always be memorable.

The First Lake

Nestled in a small basin surrounded by pines, the first of two Lost Lakes looks like a typical Sierran lake. This first view, however, is deceiving. If you spend any time at this lake, you realize that it is a lake of multiple personalities.

The first time, the glassy calmness of the lake delights you, as its surface casts a reflection of the surrounding forest. Barely able to contain your excitement, you cast your boat into its waters and place yourself comfortably in it. Then this lovely lake initiates a mood swing. Gone is the mirror reflection; instead frothy wavelets from a wind-whipped fetch stir the entire lake into an angry tempest. Struggling awkwardly with the boat's movements in the

A good view of the second Lost Lake, the Nipple and its adjoining ridge form the background; located in the saddle between the Nipple and the ridge on the right, are two small picturesque tarns.

wind, you ultimately drag it onto the shore and curse your timing and luck. No sooner is the boat safely secured on shore, and you begin to set up camp, then the wind dies, the fetch slowly subsides, and a gentle breeze stirs the lake's surface. Not to be fooled by Mother Nature again, you continue with your camp chores. Soon you have built up a sweat while the lake maintains its innocent charm and beckons you onto its surface. You grab your craft and head for the lake. This time you paddle past the shoreline, the breeze holds, the sun shines and all is well. You paddle out to the snags that stand like sentinels in the center of the lake; their presence, so incongruous in the water, is photogenic. As you dig for that camera, the lake suffers another mood swing. Gone is the sun, and in its place a series of dark clouds slowly, ever so slowly, drift overhead. That Kodak moment is gone in an instant!

These multiple mood swings at Lost Lakes will guide your actions and test your resolve during your time here.

With that said, the stark beauty of the lake is worth every shift in its appearance.

The best way to appreciate the beauty is to explore each lake on an early morning paddle, before the capricious winds spoil the morning calm. The small, oval-sized lake allows you to explore the little things along the shoreline. The steepness of the banks on the upper end of the lake prevent you from getting out of your boat, but as you glide through the deeper water, you spot some of the stocked trout swimming lazily among the drowned trees. The conifers that grow along the shore are Western Hemlocks *(Tsuga mertensiana)*, some young firs, and an occasional Sierra-Cascade Lodgepole Pine *(Pinus contorta ssp. Murrayana)*. Lodgepoles are often called tamarack pines, and prefer moist damp places, such as the banks of creeks and margins of wet meadows.

Listen for birds that dart from conifer to conifer in search of seeds and insects, or spot a small flock of Mountain Chickadees *(Parus gambeli)* as they flit from the tops of the high hemlocks in search of food. These birds have an interesting foraging technique, and that's their ability to use small twigs as tools to probe cracks in bark and limbs for insects. Another bird, whose flashy presence will attract your attention, is the Western Tanager *(Piranga ludoviciana)*. This brightly colored bird, with its reddish face, yellow shoulders and breast under a dark back, is a common sight in the open or mixed conifer forests during the summer months. The birds breed in the high country, building their nests in the tall pines, firs and aspens. Their diet consists of insects and berries. Look for them in the tops of trees, particularly the conifers.

Piles of fallen rocks create the steep shoreline and are volcanic in origin. The entire ridge above this end of the lake makes up the remnant of the volcanic plug called The Nipple (9,342 feet). Consequently, most of the rocks are weathered andesite and basalt, along with granitic rocks that are common to the Sierra mountain range.

The andesite found at Lost Lakes is a light gray, porphyritic, igneous rock that contains small, white phenocrysts of plagioclase. Some of the rocks display an orange coloring due to iron staining from the oxidation of certain minerals in the rock. The term andesite is derived from the Andes Mountains, along the western edge of South America.

From the edge of the steep shoreline, paddle toward the standing snags, which give the lake a certain aesthetic appeal. As you make your way closer to them, look for swallows *(Family: Hirundinidae)* that use the cavities in the snags as nesting sites. Observe the tops of the snags to spot the swallows as they fly in and out of the cavities that dot the trunks of all three snags.

When your neck begins to ache from staring at the birds, give it a break and look downward into the depths of the lake surrounding the snags. Once your eyes are accustomed to the shadows and soft light, you will spot the languid movements of trout as they pass under your boat. Alas, these fish are not true natives, but like many of us, have been transported here, probably by truck, as part of the stocking program that has been going on for many, many years. Small rainbow fish are called fingerlings because they are as long as your fingers and also as dinkers.

From the standing snags, point your bow southerly toward the brushy low point that separates the steep ridge on your right from the barren one on your left. Paddle over to where the large snags parallel the shoreline. As you make your approach, keep an eye out and one ear cocked for the sight and sound of a Canada goose. Small families like to feed on the green sedges, which carpet the ground of the swale you are paddling toward. One goose always stands as a sentinel for the flock and, consequently, your approach will produce a loud *honk* as a warning to the rest of the birds. If you stand off, the rapid, repetitive honks may cease or die down to a few nervous mutters. If, for some reason, the sentinel considers your approach a threat, the honking will rapidly increase, just before the birds spread their wings and take flight.

A lonely grave under the spreading bough of a hemlock, located on a berm straddling the two lakes.

Along with the geese, this section of the lake is a popular feeding area for Great Blue Herons (*Ardea herodias*) and the occasional Great Egret (*Ardea alba*). Both species stalk the sedges for small frogs, garter snakes, and other game that live in and around the swale.

> "The terms 'heron' and 'egret' are somewhat interchangeable, as shown by the fact that the Little Blue Heron is an undoubted member of this genus (Little Blues are closely related to Snowy Egrets). Birds that are called egrets are medium-sized herons, and most are white."
>
> —Kenn Kaufman, Lives of North American Birds. Houghton Mifflin Company, New York, 1996, p. 53.

If you think that the loud honks of a Canada goose are disturbing, wait until you are startled by the prehistoric cry of an offended heron! The bird's stillness, along with its nondescript coloration, blends well into the shadows along the shoreline. Usually, your first inkling that a great blue is in the area comes from a guttural call that contains a distinctly disgusted tone. The cry is followed by a slow, yet majestic rise of the large bird, as it beats its broad wings and languidly disappears over the tree line. If no birds are present, beach your boat on the coarse gravel. Look for the myriad frogs and small brown-colored garter snakes *(Thamnophis)*, often called water snakes, which frequent the shoreline. If you have a moment, sit back in your boat and observe the slice of life playing out between the frogs and snakes. A young garter snake slowly moves among the sedges hunting for its prey—one of the young frogs. It chooses one, and slowly begins its stalk. With slow movements, concealed by sedges, the snake approaches. When the distance is right, the snake strikes, and grasps the small frog in its mouth. As the frog disappears down the reptile's gullet, its legs continue to jerk. Observing the harsh reality of nature's life cycle makes you aware of the diversity and sanctity of the many life forms that inhabit our planet.

From this sedge-covered area, hike up and over the berm, which upon closer inspection is a small dam that separates the two Lost Lakes.

Lower Lake

Paddling toward the dam of the first lake takes you out of the trees and into a more open and windier section of the lake. Even the vegetation's appearance is modified by the extreme exposure on this end of the lake. Just after you pass the conifers that protect the swale, look upward, across the roadway onto the light green belt of vegetation. You are looking at a grove of stunted Aspens *(Populus teremuloides)* that remains a shrub instead of growing into a tree. Harsh temperatures and wind at this open section of the lake have arrested the shrub's growth. One clue to the severity of the winds is seen on the barren trunks of the conifers that grow near the dam. Their entire western side appears to be sandblasted by the prevailing wind.

Across from the dam, and parallel to the shoreline, is the former jeep road that terminated on the dam of the second Lost Lake. Now it serves as a hiking trail, due to the blocked access in the center of the first lake's dam.

From this section of the lake, as you paddle parallel to the dam, the view in front of you, beyond the shoreline belt of conifers, is of a former cinder cone. The adjacent ridgeline is a former ash field that covers an old lava flow. The reddish tint on the cone's rim is due to oxidation from the high iron content of the igneous rocks that make up the cone and adjacent ridge. The orange and yellow coloration visible on the surface of the rocks comes from the growth of crustose lichens called Flame Lichen *(Caloplaca ignea)*, which is the flaming orange growth, and *Acarospora,* the bright yellow lichen. In the late afternoon sun, their colors become so intense, they appear to take on a neon glow.

Although not visible from the lake, a portion of the Pacific Crest National Scenic Trail follows the military crest of the cinder cone's western ridge. The trail then comes around the southern flank of the cone, before intersecting the access road leading to the lakes. Once it crosses the road, the trail rounds the southern shoreline of the first Lost Lake before ascending the ridge that borders the northern flank of The Nipple. The trail skirts this geological feature and eventually makes its way into the Sunset Lakes region of the Humboldt-Toiyabe National Forest.

The last leg of your paddle carries you past the tree- and brush-covered shoreline that borders the base of the ridge and leads to the cinder cone. This narrow corridor is where the road that leads to the dam cuts through the brush and rocks. Several small campsites are near the water's edge, along the length of this shoreline. The lack of a breeze invites hordes of mosquitoes, and the thick brush, along with jumbles of boulders that fell and rolled from the ridge, do not make this stretch of shoreline an inviting place to camp.

It is a quick paddle past this conifer-covered section of the lake, and within a few minutes you are at your starting point, ready to take-out and enjoy the comforts of camp.

The Second Lost Lake

To make the portage to the second Lost Lake, paddle across the first lake, take-out at the aforementioned swale, and portage the length of the swale to the top of the artificial berm and down to the lake below.

A second approach is to cart the boats on the old access road up to the dam that separates the lakes and down onto the shoreline of the second lake. Both ways have equal plusses and minuses. I personally enjoy using the paddle and portage approach because it breaks up the labor and makes the whole task an adventure rather than a tedious grind. This is true despite having to pack gear for an overnight stay, because the actual portage is so short that by the time a sweat breaks out, you're standing at the shore with wavelets lapping over your toes.

Unless you plan to camp across the second lake, a choice camping spot exists near the standing snags on the southwest edge of the lake. The Pacific Crest Trail runs alongside your campsite and you have a spectacular view of the lake and the adjoining Nipple.

As you portage your boat, you pass a small, lonely grave, almost hidden by the lower branch of a nearby conifer. The headstone is too weathered to read any inscription, but from its appearance, it seems to have been there for some time.

Paddling the second lake is best done in the early morning or in the late afternoon. Otherwise, the wind makes it difficult to explore the shoreline or enjoy the view.

The open exposure of this second lake produces a barren and rocky shoreline with only a few small stands of stunted pine growing along the lake's southern edge. However, from the middle of the lake, you have a spectacular view of the steep, multi-hued walls of the volcanic dome called The Nipple. From the lake, the reason for the name becomes clear as you view the prominent, round point that so accurately resembles a nipple. From the side of the Blue Lakes, this rocky protuberance is not clearly visible, so the name does not seem to make much sense unless you hike or paddle the northern exposure.

Three islands of differing sizes are part of the lake. The three line up in a row on the southeastern end of the lake, with the largest facing northwest. It is past the last and smallest island that a cove, protected by a small screen of conifers and with a small gravel beach, is visible. If you are willing to make the effort, this cove makes an extremely memorable campsite, as it is the only protected campsite on this end of the lake. At night, your view of the heavens is unparalleled. The ridges behind you blocks off any ambient light, allowing you to see the heavens as you seldom have before. The depth of the dark night sky, along with the cold crisp air, cause the stars to appear in such sharp relief you are tempted to reach up and touch them. Stay up late to see the Milky Way with its multitude of stars clustered into a dense mass that provides the illusion of a puddle of milk spilled across the night sky.

Before you leave for the first lake to unpack and prepare for your journey home, paddle across this second lake to the barren, rocky bluff that dominates the western edge of the narrow cove where a dam controls the flow of the headwaters to the West Fork of the Carson River. This particular paddle is best done in the late afternoon of a sunny day, in order to see the outstretched landscape under the best light conditions. Beach your boat and scramble to the top of the bluff. To not spoil the surprise. . . all I will say is that your trip out here will be worth it just for this view alone. Oh yeah, don't forget the camera!

Sources and References:

Kaufman, Kenn, *Lives of North American Birds*. Boston: Houghton Mifflin Company, 1996.

Lanner, Ronald M., *Conifers of California*. Los Olivios: Cachuma Press, 1999.

REGION I: LAKES OF THE HIGH COUNTRY
PADDLING AREA 11: KIRKWOOD LAKE

Position: 38°42.20'N, 120°04.55'W

Difficulty: Paddlers of all skill levels may paddle this small resort lake safely.

Trip Length: The lake may be paddled in its entirety in one hour or less.

Portage: None required.

Paddling Distance: The small size of this lake precludes any meaningful distances.

Season: Campground is open from June to September.

Lake Size: 2,100 feet long.

Elevation: 7,640 feet.

County: El Dorado County.

National Forest / Wilderness Area: Eldorado National Forest.

The limited primitive parking area for Kirkwood Lake. The information board and phone (in oval container) are visible to the left of the photo.

Maps:

USGS 7.5-Minute Quadrangle Topographical Map Series: Pacific Valley, CA and Carson Pass, CA.

National Forest Service/Wilderness Area: Humboldt-Toiyabe National Forest (Carson Ranger District) and Mokelumne Wilderness Maps.

Road Map:

Compass Maps Inc.: Alpine, Amador and Sacramento Counties.

California State Automobile Association (AAA) Map: Central California – Bay Area to Lake Tahoe.

Historical Background:

The lake was named for Zachariah S. Kirkwood who first built a rough wooden stage house and inn adjacent to the lake in 1864. In 1895, travelers through the area reported a post office and dairy ranch.

Kirkwood Lake

Access:

Off Hwy. 88 between the community of Martin Meadow and the turnoff for Kirkwood.

Note: The road leading to the lake is a very narrow, winding, two-lane road with limited turnaround at its end. Not recommended for large RVs and trailers.

Heads Up:

- The campground contains 12 sites with water, vault toilets, tables and a fire pit. Pay phone at entrance. No RV or trailers. No reservations. Daily fee.
- Bear country—pack and camp smart!
- Small beach near campground.
- Limited access for boat launch.
- Ideal location for family camping with small children.

Description:

When the winds blow strong over nearby Caples Lake, the surface of tiny Lake Kirkwood displays scarcely a ripple. The lake sits in a natural valley surrounded by granite walls and is protected by a pine forest. Although the lake is small, its size is perfect for families with small children, or people with their first canoe or kayak wishing to familiarize themselves with their boat prior to paddling on larger more open waters.

You can gauge the popularity of the lake by the filled campground, the ring of summer homes, and, of course, the ubiquitous scout camps, such as Camp Two Sentinels or Girl Scouts of America. In the peak of summer, this lake vibrates with laughter and good times. To launch your craft, walk it to the water from the parking area off the entrance road of the campground, or drive and put-in from the lakeside parking area, if space is available.

Once on the water, practice your strokes by paddling the length of the lake, or take a few strokes to reach deeper water before casting out your fishing line. Whatever your choice, the tranquility of the lake will lull your stress levels to zero and allow you to relax thoroughly. As you begin to admire the scenery, the first feature to draw your attention is the sheer wall of granite that covers the entire northwestern side of the lake. This wall displays several interesting geological features.

The shape of the granitic mass is due, in part, to the work of early glaciations, which occurred in the Sierra mountain range within the last Ice Age, between 1.5 million and 10,000 years ago. Once the glaciers removed the overburden that covered the granite now visible before you, the granite began to expand, or in the words of the writer, Stephen Whitney, in his classic Sierra Club guidebook, *The Sierra Nevada*:

> ". . . [The granitic rock breathed] a magnificent 'sigh' of relief."

West shoreline with a portion of the granite roche moutonee, forms the ridge in the background.

The expansion creates or follows existing stress fractures, causing the granite to crack and break along huge fracture zones. The granite expands at various rates as it rises to the surface. This creates a series of pressure-release points, on top or on the sides of the exposed granite. As the pressure within the rock is released following the emerging fractures, particularly on the top and sides, these shells literally pop loose. This phenomenon is unique to granitic landscapes and is known as exfoliation. Weathering agents such as water, wind, ice, and the chemical actions of certain plants, such as lichens, insure the rounded dome-like shape to the granitic rock.

A final testament to the work of the former glacier is the unique overall shape of the entire exposed dome. The westerly-facing section is a heavily fractured steep-face wall, followed by a relatively slick sidewall, and a tapering easterly back wall. This unique shape has all the characteristics of a glacial feature known as a *roche moutonneé* (a French term translated as rock sheep). The term was coined by Horace Benedict de Saussure, an early French mountaineer and geologist from the eighteenth century, because the similar, but smaller, rock shapes reminded him of sheep standing in a field.

Gaze onto the sides of this excellent example of glacially worked, exfoliated granitic rock to see many of the fractures or joints as they crisscross the sidewall of the rock. Plants and trees gain a foothold within these fractures, causing them to expand even more. Eventually, sections break loose and slide down onto the bench below as talus piles. Some of these apronlike rock piles are partially visible behind a row of cabins built at the edge of the lake.

The dark stained patina covering portions of the sidewall are actually lichens *(See: In the Eddy: A Hike Through a Glacial Landscape, Bear River Reservoir [Lower Bear Lake])*.

For a continuation on the glacial geology of this area, spin your boat around until the bow is facing south. Examine the sculpted wall of the granitic ridge before you. If the sun angle is just right, usually in the afternoon to early evening, you will be dazzled by sections of the rocky surface as they reflect the sunlight. Paddle up to the wall where it dips into the lake to view the cause of all this reflection. Panels of rock are polished, some to an extremely slick finish. Miniature scratches that parallel each other and run in the same general direction are imbedded in the finish. You are gazing upon excellent examples of glacial polish. The scratches are formed when small bits of gravel or sand are dragged across the rock by the moving glacier. The pressure from the ice mass, combined with the coating of detritus within the ice, produced a surface polish that is still visible today. Running parallel with, and cross-angled to, the mass of granite are lines of a cream-colored mineral. These bands or lines are sometimes referred to as veins but are correctly called dikes. A dike is formed when minerals are injected into igneous rock (rock that forms through melting beneath the earth's surface) along weak lines or fractures. These particular dikes contain minerals of various sizes. The sizes determine its composition. Fine-grained, light-colored ones are called aplite dikes, and the coarser grained (a half-inch or more) are referred to as pegmatite dikes. The white-colored dikes appear to be fine grained and, therefore, aplite.

By this time, the beginning of a breeze carries you up lake past the granite and into the belt of pine where cabins sit hidden among the trees. Excited voices and a commotion on the deck indicates the presence of a Girl Scout troop readying their boats, either for a rowing class or just casting off for a morning of fishing. Passing the camp's boat dock, you go by several small sedge-covered coves where Canada geese, Mallards *(Anas platyrhynchos)* or even a Great Blue Heron *(Ardea herodias)* feed.

Around the upper end of the lake, the mouth of the feeder stream empties into it. As part of its origin, this stream may be fed from the waters of Kirkwood Creek flowing above this valley. The water from Kirkwood Lake is released at the dam near the campground and joins the main Caples Creek located below the lake.

Cross over to the northern shore and come upon a family of Common Mergansers *(Mergus merganser)*. These shy, diving ducks seldom tolerate humans and are quick to take flight. If you are in a position to watch, their high-energy take-off, followed by an almost jet-like streak across the lake, is a gorgeous sight.

On your return, paddle by a line of summer cabins and note that some of the homes sit on a magnificent granitic ledge whose sloping side dips cleanly into the lake. Just past the last house, you reach a gravel beach protected by a stand of Jeffrey pine *(Pinus jeffreyi)*. This beach provides a nice spot for sunbathing and has a trail behind a screen of willows that leads back to the campground. Paddle on, passing the dam, to reach the main take-out and the end of your day on the water.

Sources and References:

Durham, David L., *Place-Names of California's Gold Country*. Clovis: Word Country Press, 2000.

Guyton, Bill, *Glaciers of California*. Berkeley: University of California Press, 1998.

Hill, Mary, *Geology of the Sierra Nevada*. Berkeley: University of California Press, 1975.

Wessels, Tom, *The Granite Landscape*. Woodstock: The Countryman Press, 2001.

Whitney, Stephen, *A Sierra Club Naturalist's Guide: The Sierra Nevada*. San Francisco: Sierra Club Books, 1979.

REGION I: LAKES OF THE HIGH COUNTRY
PADDLING AREA 12: CAPLES LAKE

Position: 38°42.25'N, 120°02.55'W

Difficulty: Caples Lake is known for its winds. This large open body of water can change at a moment's notice from dead calm to frothy whitecaps. These changes are especially prevalent in the afternoon and continue to affect the lake until early evening. Beginners should stay away from the open lake and be wary of crossing unless they are willing to wait for a late afternoon return.

Trip Length: To appreciate Caples Lake, paddle it in stages. To attempt a one day paddle of the entire lake will involve wind, waves, and prolonged sun exposure. For a better time, pick a section of the lake and explore it at leisure.

Portage: None (although if you put-in at the dam site located at the western end of the lake, there is a short walk over the berm adjacent to the dam before reaching the shoreline).

Lake Size: 2 miles long, 600 acres.

Public put-in at the southern end of lake at the dam.

Paddling Distances:

From the SW corner of the lake near the dam:

0.8 mile to the Caples Lake Resort;

1.1 miles to the entrance of Emigrant Bay;

2.12 to the southern end of Emigrant Bay.

From Caples Lake Resort boat ramp;

1.5 mile to the end of Emigrant Bay.

From the NW cove of Caples Lake;

2.9 miles to the end of Emigrant Bay.

Elevation: 7,798 feet.

Season: Spring after the snows melt, through fall.

County: Although the lake is in Alpine County, it borders El Dorado County to the north and west, and Amador County to the south.

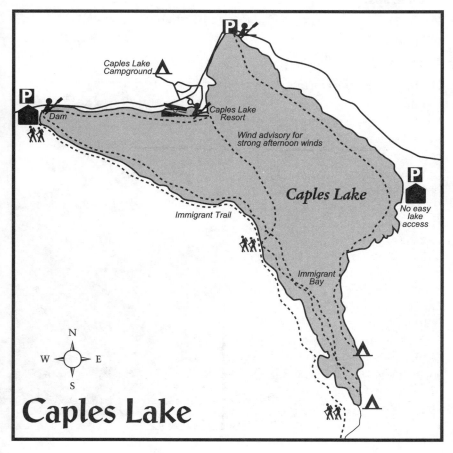

Caples Lake

National Forest: Except for three small sections located at the southern and eastern ends of the lake, the entire area is within the jurisdiction of Eldorado National Forest.

Ranger District: Amador Ranger District, 26820 Silver Drive, Pioneer, CA 95666 (209.295.4251).

Wilderness Area: The southern boundary of the lake falls within the border of Mokelumne Wilderness; the eastern section, except for one small private holding, is part of the newly formed Carson Pass Management Area.

Maps:

USGS 7.5-Minute Quadrangle Topographical Map Series: Pacific Valley, CA and Carson Pass, CA.

National Forest Service/Wilderness Area: Humboldt-Toiyabe National Forest (Carson Ranger District) and Mokelumne Wilderness Maps.

Road Maps:

Compass Maps, Inc.: Alpine, Amador and Sacramento Counties.

California State Automobile Association (AAA) Maps: Central California – Bay Area to Lake Tahoe.

Historical Background:

Originally named Lake Valley by the early emigrants, it became known as Twin Lakes, two connected lakes with an adjacent marsh sometime after 1850. Other names for the area were Clear Lake, Summit Lake and Twin Lakes Reservoir. The lake is named after James "Doc" Caples, a delegate to the 1849 California State Constitution convention, which wrote the constitution under which California was admitted to the Union in 1850. Caples settled in the area in the late 1850s. He started a way station for travelers on the old Carson Valley and Big Trees Road near the present path of State Hwy. 88.

One of the cabins overlooking the lake at Caples Lake Resort.

View from the water of Caples Lake Resort, State Highway 88 runs through the tree line. The bluffs visible in the background are composed of volcanic debris.

Access:

The entire northwestern shoreline abuts Hwy. 88.

There are three routes to the lake. From the west, you may take state Hwy. 88 out of Jackson for 63 scenic miles. From the north, take U.S. I-50 to Pollock Pines, exit onto Sly Park Road south (E-16). Continue until you reach the fork for Forest Road 5 (Mormon Emigrant Trail).

Stay on this road until you reach Hwy. 88. Turn left onto Hwy. 88. The first lake you pass will be Silver Lake; Caples Lake is another 14 miles or so.

From Tahoe or the Nevada side, you can pick up Hwy. 88, either by way of Hwy. 89 out of South Lake Tahoe, or by taking the Hwy. 88 exit from U.S. 395 at Minden, Nevada.

Heads Up:

- The only open area for dispersed camping is along the shoreline of Emigrant Bay. No other camping is allowed on the lake except at designated campgrounds.
- A free campfire permit is highly recommended for ANY dispersed camping.
- Bear country—pack and camp smart!
- The lake is known for its cold, cold, afternoon wind.
- Stay off the main body of the lake; best places to explore are either Emigrant Bay or the coves and islands of the southeastern shore.

- Fishing is excellent, stocked with a variety of trout: rainbows, brook, browns, and mackinaw, beginning with sizes in the 10-12 inch range.
- USFS, Eldorado National Forest, maintains the Caples Lake Campground, located on the northwest side of upper lake across the highway from Caples Lake Resort. The campground opens around June 1st and remains open through the middle of October, depending on snowfall.
- Campground has a total of 34 units consisting of drive-in campsites, RV sites, walk-in tent sites and 2 family units. For additional information, contact the Amador Ranger District (209.295.4251).
- As an alternative, Caples Lake Resort (209.258.8888) offers either lodge rooms, or individual cabins for overnight guests.
- The resort has a restaurant, marina for launching as well as canoe or kayak rentals, and a small store for groceries, fishing tackle, and other whoops, I-forgot-it items.
- Further south and down the road a bit is another alternative lodging at Kirkwood, a year-round resort; call 209.258.8888 for additional information.
- If the wind is up, consider hiking the historical Emigrant Trail or drive up toward Carson pass and hike the trails of the Carson Pass Management Area.

Description:

Despite the size and openness of Caples Lake, there are two sections of the lake where canoeists or kayakers can enjoy their day on the water. The island-dotted eastern shoreline and the Emigrant Bay area, provide ample coves, islands and other wind-protected areas of interest to satisfy any curious boater.

Unfortunately, this side of the lake does not contain any accessible locations for an easy put-in or take-out. The one parking area located via an exit road off Highway 89 on the northeastern edge of the lake (See map), requires a short but tree-covered portage to the nearest shoreline. Once on the water, you are within easy paddling distance of the islands and coves located south of Woods Creek and the entrance into Emigrant Bay.

The second closest launch spot is a small beach located below a turnout on the lakeside immediately after crossing the dam if heading east on Highway 89; or, if you are approaching from Carson Pass, heading south, it's where State Highway 89 makes a final bend before it crosses over the Woods Creek Dam.

The put-in is located immediately below the highway berm on a small and cobble-strewn beach. Once on the water, hug the shoreline, or dare a direct crossing toward the entrance of Emigrant Bay or the islands adjacent to Woods Creek, visible due east across the lake.

Whatever route you take, explore the islands and coves below Woods Creek first and then, when the winds lift, you are in a perfect position to enter into the wind-protected arm of Emigrant Bay.

The water table of the lake is high in the early spring and it is a treat to explore many small coves and islands that cover the entire shoreline beginning at the mouth of Woods Creek and leading into the east entrance of Emigrant Bay. The wind-protected coves provide shelter for the young of many water birds that nest in the area. Some of the species that share the water are the common merganser with her brood of fuzz-covered chicks all paddling in a row, the noisy but regal Canada geese, with gray-downed goslings paddling in controlled confusion, and the assorted sizes of young ducklings whose protective mothers will attempt to steer them away from the wake of your boat.

Hide in the shaded areas and keep a sharp lookout for great blue herons and great egrets hunting for frogs, snakes or any other prospective meals, including an unwary duckling, or gosling if the opportunity arises. Don't be surprised if you come across a family of Raccoons *(Procyon lotor)* working their way methodically, the length of the shoreline. Using their paws like hands, they reach into crevices to turn over cobbles in search of anything edible, particularly, the crayfish *(Pacifastacus leniusculus)*, a favorite food.

The diversity of the trees that grow on the shore and on some of the islands makes for a picturesque scene as you work your way through the narrow passages and glide past the coves that lead to other narrow inlets.

Two male Common Mergansers, one keeping a wary eye out on the passing canoe, while the other preens his feathers.

You will recognize the cove that marks the entrance into Emigrant Bay by the single rounded erratic, sitting aloof on a rounded ledge of glacially carved rock.

Emigrant Bay

Be sure to allow plenty of time to explore the area surrounding the bay, as paddling Emigrant Bay is just one of the interesting activities to do while on the lake.

Enter the bay by way of the islands and Woods Creek and paddle to the opposite side, where the T-marker for the former Carson River Route of the Emigrant Trail is located *(See: In the Eddy, Paddling Area 4: Red Lake).* Give yourself plenty of time to hike at least the first ridge of this leg of the Emigrant Trail. You will come to appreciate the hardships that early pioneers endured, making this climb in heavy clothing, with cumbersome, travel-worn wagons with all their possessions inside. An awesome view from the ridge crest of Caples Lake below, and Black Butte (9,031 feet) framing the lake to the north, awaits you.

The dark, gravelly trail surface is comprised of ash and cinders from an old ash flow, technically known as a pyroclastic flow. You will encounter a nice outcrop of this deposit as you reach the first ridge of your hike following the former Emigrant Trail. Study the chunks of rock embedded in their cement-like matrix, and note that all the individual rocks have sharp edges and appear in different shapes and sizes. Their edges demonstrate that the rocks were tossed and tumbled, causing them to break up as the flow carried the entire deposit down slope, away from the main vent. Although the bits of ash and cinders are embedded in their natural cement, it doesn't take much to break them free, thereby creating an unstable hiking surface. Imagine the affect this friable surface had on wheel traction on wagons being pulled by tired, undernourished draft animals.

Snowfields from a wet winter can cover portions of the trail causing instability even in late spring or early summer.

Be careful not to step on the colorful flowers growing out of the small base of soil established around the margin, where the pathway leads to the top of the ridge. These pretty pink blooms are called Rock Fringe *(Epilobium obcordatum)* and they are members of the Evening-Primrose family; their species' Latin name means heart-shaped, which refers to their petals.

Now is the time to catch your breath and reap your reward for completing this climb. Upper Caples Lake stretches out before you with its shimmering blue water. Turn slightly westerly to make out the Caples Lake Resort structures that look like tiny Legos® set around the forested shoreline. Behind the lodge, and spreading majestically to the left and right, is the forested base of Little Round Top (9,590 feet), which dominates the background. From your vantage point on the ridge, follow the dark green

Rocks, pines, and a contrail sky.

mantle of conifers that form a patchwork of individual stands. These stands are thicker in the drainages, but when the forest encounters the rounded, glacially formed granitic domes, the trees thin and disappear, exposing odd-shaped islands of grayish-weathered stone. Follow this quilt-like maze of forest and granite upward to where a thin grass carpet overtakes the trees and granite, the angle of repose becomes too steep to hike and only barren, rocky ground is visible. Follow the peak's ridgeline to the northeast to clearly view Highway 88 where it leaves the Caples Lake shoreline and begins to ascend the wide, forested saddle of Carson Pass. Refer to the diagrams in Frank Tortorich's book on the Emigrant Trail, to visualize where the former Emigrant Trail descends into the pass, closely paralleling the existing highway, before veering off and crossing the meadow that is now inundated by the lake. The trail continues on up the ash- and cinder-strewn ridge before snaking its way to the top of West Pass (9,600 feet). Frank Tortorich describes the pass as, ". . . the highest point wagons ever reached . . . in the westward migration."

The last clear view lies to the east, with the impressive mass of Black Butte (9,031 feet) rising in the foreground and the stately shapes of Round Top (10,381 feet), followed by the Sisters (10,045 feet and 10,153 feet) completing the background to your visual tour.

Descend from the ridge to study the individual trees that make up the forest surrounding the lake. Lodgepole Pines *(Pinus contorta)* make up

131

the majority of the conifers, followed by Sierra Juniper or Western Juniper *(Juniperus occidentalis)*, White Fir *(Abis concolor)*, the occasional Jeffrey pine *(Pinus jeffreyi)*, the regal Sugar Pine *(Pinus lambertiana)*, with their distinctive long and narrow cones hanging from the ends of their branches, to the occasional Mountain Hemlock *(Tsuga mertensiana)* with its nodding top and graceful silhouette. Thin belts of the deciduous Aspen *(Populus tremuloides)* form groves in which their bright green leaves quake in the slightest breeze.

At one time the wagons rolled past this point and continued up the ridge toward West Pass. The Emigrant Trail Rail Marker is visible in background.

Locate your boat and cast off, to enter the inner portion of the bay and confront the spectacular geologically and historically significant panorama. The view is all encompassing as your boat glides deeper into the bay with Black Butte on the left, followed by a small portion of Round Top, and the prominent Sisters. Your eyes slide down the left portion of the saddle that forms the right Sister and rides up its right side onto the profile of Fourth of July Peak (9,536 feet). Another smaller saddle connects Fourth of July Peak to the forepeak leading to Melissa Coray Peak (9,763 feet). The low saddle visible between Melissa Coray and the next prominent peak is called the Thimble (9,805 feet) and marks West Pass (9,600 feet), the highest point reached by those who traveled along the Emigrant Trail on their western migration to the California goldfields.

As the expansive scenery unfolds in the distance, it would be easy to disregard the local points of interest that continue to pass by your bow. Islands of various sizes appear as you paddle into the lower portion of the bay. Common mergansers, snoozing on the rocks of the sheltered coves, are caught off guard by your stealthy appearance; they sit up, spread their wings and beat the water with their feet in a desperate attempt to fly away.

Just before you round the cove, three islands appear. The largest is rather picturesque with its small, mixed grove of pine, aspen and willow standing guard over the rocky shoreline.

View of Black Butte in foreground, Elephants Back, first peak to the right of Black Butte, and The Sisters—the two pointed peaks to the right of Elephants Back.

At the tip of the cove, you see the mouth of Emigrant Creek that empties into the lake. The eastern shoreline bordering the creek contains many sandy beaches that are just right for sunbathing or a picnic lunch.

This small section of the lake is also the only area that is not part of the Mokelumne Wilderness Area and is designated as non-Forest Service land; therefore, boaters can come in and camp overnight in established campsites behind the screen of pines. Please use one of the established sites, only 50 yards inland from the lake. Leave early so you are not caught in the gusty afternoon winds that blow over the lake.

Sources and References:

Storer, Tracy I. and Robert L. Usinger, *Sierra Nevada Natural History*. Berkeley: University of California Press, 1963.

Tortorich, Frank, Jr., *Gold Rush Trail A Guide to the Carson River Route of the Emigrant Trail*. Pine Grove: Wagon Wheel Tours, Revised 2002.

Wiese, Karen, *Sierra Nevada Wildflowers—A Falcon Guides*. Helena: Falcon Publishing, Inc., 2000.

REGION I: LAKES OF THE HIGH COUNTRY
PADDLING AREA 13: SILVER LAKE

Position: 38°40.05'N, 120°07.15'W

Difficulty: Boaters of all skill levels may paddle this lake. Novices, however, should pay attention to the wind if attempting to cross the lake. The afternoon winds on Silver Lake may become strong enough to tire out a beginning paddler or generate a fetch large enough to broach the boat.

Trip Length: It is possible to circumnavigate the entire lake in one long day. However, to fully appreciate the lake and its setting, two days minimum is recommended.

Portage: None required.

Lake Size: 2 miles long.

Paddling Distances:

1.5 miles from Plasse's Creek to Put-in at Sandy Cove Picnic Area;
0.78 mile to Southeast cove of Treasure Island;
0.78 mile to Waterfalls of Summit Meadow Lake Creek;
1.86 miles from Ferguson Point Put-in to Plasse's Creek Put-in.

Elevation: 7,261 feet.

Season: This lake is best paddled in the late spring or early summer, before the water draws down and the crowds of summer visitors arrive at the surrounding resorts.

County: Although the lake is within Amador County, it is adjacent to El Dorado County to the west, and Alpine County to the east.

National Forest: Eldorado National Forest.

Ranger District: Amador Ranger District, 26820 Silver Drive, Pioneer, CA 95666 (tel. 209.295.4251 or fax 209.295.5998).

Wilderness Area: Although Silver Lake is not located within the boundaries of any Wilderness Areas, the southern boundary of the Mokelumne Wilderness Area follows the military crest of nearby Squaw Ridge.

Maps:

USGS 7.5-Minute Quadrangle Topographical Map Series: Pacific Valley, CA and adjoining Carson Pass, CA.

National Forest Service/Wilderness Area: Humboldt-Toiyabe National
  Forest (Carson Ranger District) and Mokelumne Wilderness Maps.

Road Maps:

Compass Maps, Inc: Alpine, Amador and Sacramento Counties.

California State Automobile Association (AAA) Maps: Central California
  – Bay Area to Lake Tahoe.

Historical Background:

In 1850, the lake was first dammed with brush, to provide water for miners
employing the destructive methods of hydraulic mining. In 1871 a permanent dam replaced the brush dam and by 1884 hydraulic mining became
illegal. Early pioneers who came by the thousands through here in their
wagons recognized the lake's appeal. When the first California Geological
Survey, led by William Henry Brewer, came through the area in 1863, Brewer
penned these words:

First view of Silver Lake heading east on State Highway 88, just before the turnoff for Plasse's Resort and Upper Lake.

"Here we descended into the valley of Silver Lake, a lovely little sheet of water, very deep and blue . . . "

At present, Silver Lake is part of the hydroelectric project known as Project 184, managed by the Eldorado Irrigation District.

Access:

Silver Lake is located approximately 52 miles east of Jackson on State Hwy. 88.

You may also reach Silver Lake via State Hwy. 89 out of South Lake Tahoe over Luther Pass to Pickett Junction where you pick up State Hwy. 88 West. Continue on Hwy. 88 over Carson Pass. Silver lake is located approximately 12 miles west, past Caples Lake.

A third route is the drive from Pollock Pines, located off Hwy. 50, onto Forest Road 5, better known as the Mormon Emigrant Trail Road, to Hwy. 88 at the Iron Mountain Snow Park. Upon entering Hwy. 88, turn left and continue on Hwy. 88 for approximately 8 miles. You view the lake as you descend the grade around Tragedy Spring.

Unless you are staying at the campgrounds or resorts located at upper lake, take the first exit marked for Plasse's Resort and Stockton Municipal Camp.

For those wishing to stay for a day paddle, park alongside the southwestern shoreline. Several shaded roadside parking areas are located past the quaint wooden church with its adjacent parsonage.

Heads Up:

- Silver Lake, being a resort lake, the adjacent parking around the lake is primarily for day-use only.
- The nearest campgrounds are Silver Lake Campgrounds, run by the Amador Ranger District of the Eldorado National Forest. There are 62 units, some for tents, some with RV access, still others are walk-in tent sites, and there are two family sites.
- The second campground is Silver Lake West, operated by the Eldorado Irrigation District, EID. For additional information on their camping fees and other information, call 530.644.2545.
- Camping is also available at the private resorts that border the lake (*See Appendix III, Region I, for names and phone numbers*).
- Many private cabins circle the lake; please respect the postings of the property owners.
- Bear country—pack and camp smart!
- A free put-in/take-out is located at Ferguson Point, off the old high-way, adjacent to the dam, north of Kay's Resort; otherwise, you will have to pay a fee to launch from Kay's boat ramp.
- All the resorts rent canoes and kayaks, Kay's kayak rentals, however, are higher-end Necky models.
- If paddling on the lake in late summer, pay attention to weather changes; you do not want to be caught on the water during a summer thunderstorm!
- When exploring the surrounding granite landscape, keep an eye out for rattlesnakes, bears and other predators higher than you on the food chain.

Description:

Bill Brewer certainly got it right when he described Silver Lake as,

" . . . *a lovely little sheet of water, very deep and very blue* . . . "

The only change to that original description is that Silver Lake is no longer a little lake.

When the permanent dam was constructed in 1871, and enlarged in the early 1920s, the lake's capacity increased in size to its present shoreline. As a result, thousands of visitors come and leave, enchanted by the lake's beauty and charm. One of the more pleasant aspects of Silver Lake is its easy access, as you can drive up to its shore, step out, and touch the water. Of course, this happens only in the springtime when the water table is high; however, the access is not difficult in late summer either.

Unless you are staying at one of the three resorts that border the lake (*See Appendices for details and websites*), there are only two free access points

The chapel at upper lake and Plasse's Resort. The road leading to your put-in is visible to the right of the chapel, with Silver Lake in the background.

to the lake. The good thing about these sites is that they are on opposite ends of the lake.

Lower Lake, The South End

The most picturesque and visitor friendly put-in is located at the southern end, where a section of the southwest shoreline has been allocated for free day-use. Arrive early to obtain one of the few spaces along the narrow road that parallels the shoreline. The pines provide shade and the sweet scent comes from the Sierra-Cascade Lodgepole Pines *(Pinus contorta ssp. Murrayana)*. These trees prefer wet places like the surrounding terrain of the lake bank. Intermixed with the pine, is the familiar Quaking Aspen *(Populus tremuloides)*. Growing up from the moist earth in the shape of little green cigars are Corn Lilies *(Veratrum californicum)*. These striking plants are well named, as they remind us of the tall corn plant of the Midwest. Unlike corn, however, *corn lilies are extremely poisonous plants and should be kept away from small children or pets.* The short portage distance from your car to the water brings a big smile to your face because you are immediately off on your adventure with a quick stroke of your paddle. Paddle in a counter-clockwise direction. Start on the southeastern shoreline and complete the paddle on the western side. You will be protected from the major wind gusts, as well as have more shade from the afternoon heat. Cross the shallows where the marsh is, and observe the Canada geese, watching you because you have entered their territory. The lush marsh grasses and willow thickets at this end of the lake make it a well-sheltered goose-nesting heaven. Over a hundred geese congregate here in social flocks throughout the late spring, so look for goslings of various size and cuteness tagging alongside their parents.

Notice small inlets created from weathered granite and surrounded by brush as you paddle past the mouth of Plasse's Creek. Here is where you find the shy common merganser asleep on a barely exposed boulder top, or herding her brood of young to a choice feeding area. Unlike the other ducks that visit the lake, mergansers are divers, built for speed under water and equipped with long-serrated bills to catch and hold their prey, such as small fish, crustaceans and mollusks.

Enter the narrow passage that separates the southern tip of Treasure Island and the southeastern shoreline a short distance up from the marsh area. The water is shallow in spots with many barely submerged rocks. With a calm surface and proper light, you can spot the obstacles in the water, before you reach them, but if you do not have the proper conditions, slow down and stay in the center where the water is deeper.

You can explore the island before you continue.

Treasure Island

Look for a small beach approximately 200 yards from the willow-covered end. A deck built onto the trunk of an old snag marks the location. At one time, you could camp on the island; however, it is now for day-use only. The many old fire rings attest to camping's popularity here.

Blowing air into the IK (inflatable kayak) for a day on the lake.

Lather yourself with mosquito repellent before venturing farther into the shaded pine grove, as those voracious blood suckers will hone in on your body heat in no time.

The densely packed conifer forests consist primarily of lodgepoles and red firs, whose limbs and under story teem with birds. Sitting patiently on a small branch near the water, a member of the Flycatcher family, the handsome Black Phoebe *(Sayornis nigricans)*, makes short flights off its perch to catch small insects in mid air. Higher up on the branches, Mountain Chickadees *(Parus gambeli)* forage enthusiastically for insects. The sound of rustling among the pine duff reveals a small group of Pine Siskins *(Spinus pinus)* with their flashy patches of yellow standing out against the drab, dead pine needles.

Standing snags, with their silver trunks, reveal cavities of various size and depth. Many show characteristics of fresh excavation. The rhythmic tapping from somewhere in the grove identifies the probable culprit—a member of the Woodpecker family *(Picidae)*.

Near the fire rings is a lightly used trail that crosses over the ridge, to the highest point on the island, before ending at the exposed bedrock of weathering granitic rock.

Proceed with your paddle where the gap between the island and the main shore is narrow, and you are protected from any wind. Cross this part of the lake early in the day, rather than later in the afternoon, when the wind begin to blow. Once on the lake, proceed directly to the cove where a series of small waterfalls in the creek cascade, into Silver Lake. The water source for this creek comes from the small alpine lakes within the west-facing cirques of Squaw Ridge (9,200 feet and 9,100 feet, respectively) and Thimble Peak (9,805 feet).

Camp Minkalo

Upon approaching the cove, use your binoculars to quietly search the limbs of the dead snag standing sentinel near the shoreline, and to the right of the creek. With luck, you share your visit with a bald eagle, whose presence is common around the lake.

Beach your boat and follow the stream to hike up toward the ridge hiding behind a screen of junipers and pines. Look for a lone brick chimney among the trees. This impressive chimney is all that is left of what was once a meetinghouse, or a large building, that predates the current Camp Minkalo Boy Scout Camp. So, how do you tell if you are near a scout camp? Look for the ubiquitous pathways, lined with cobbles, leading in all directions. To verify this clue, I was fortunate to meet two former Boy Scout leaders who actually helped build some of the pathways and were here for a nostalgic campout at this once vibrant camp. Today, the camp is abandoned by the Scout Council. Walk around the buildings, and stand and imagine the dim voices of the young boys who gave this camp purpose.

One of the older stone cabins on the west Shore of Silver Lake.

Happy companions pass Ferguson Point.

Just to the east of the dirt parking area in the center of the camp is a trail that intersects the main trail leading to Granite Lake, a small alpine tarn *(See http://www.enfia.info/silverlake.htm and http://kevingong.com/Hiking/ThunderMountain.html for a description of hiking around Silver Lake).*

Upper Lake

Paddle away from the Boy Scout cove, round the small point and enter a shallow cove with several cabins standing on barren granite. Immediately to the right of the first cabin, look for an aspen grove that borders the entrance into a cozy inlet.

Hidden within this grove is a small but energetic creek whose rushing water you clearly hear as you make your way into the inlet. The source for this unnamed stream is the dominant peak of Thunder Mountain (9,408 feet).

Unlike the surrounding bedrock composed of granitic rock, Thunder Mountain is all that remains of a former volcano, as are the entire series of peaks that make up Squaw Ridge. Water percolates through the volcanic debris and flows out as streams, springs and seeps.

The granite outcrop that forms the small point surrounding the inlet makes for a nice stop. Take a swim in the lagoon, or climb the granite and bask in the sun as you enjoy the view. Hike among the granite to find several small clearings where others have taken advantage of the protective rock and soft grassy floor to construct fire rings and camp.

Don't be surprised to come across a family or two of Canada geese,

142

cropping the grass as they feed or raising their goslings. This quiet out-of-the-way cove makes for an excellent location for geese to nest.

From the inlet, you pass the last outcrop of granitic rock, with its trio of cabins, and the site of Camp Silverado, an active Boy Scout camp.

You are now paddling under the shadow of Thunder Mountain and the darker rock of volcanic origin. Here, the forest hides many cabins, and the escarpment of the mountain rises vertically behind the forest.

On the water, before you enter the bay with the dock belonging to Kit Carson Resort, look for two small, craggy islands guarding a small cove. Paddle up to these islands and examine the rock. This is the same material as the bluffs of Thunder Mountain. If you examine it carefully, you see cobbles, rocks and chunks of rock jumbled together in a cement-like matrix of smaller pebbles and coarse granules. The larger, angular rock and cobble fragments are called breccia (Italian for broken rock). The cement-like matrix consists of smaller pebbles and the breccia binds it together to create tuff.

Various shrubs and lichen begin the task of slowly eroding the welded breccia into smaller pieces that forms the weathered surface of the larger island.

Ferguson Point

Pass by the cluster of rental cabins to paddle between two small islands with their growth of lodgepoles pines and manzanita ground cover. These islands mark the entrance to Ferguson Point, a popular day-use picnic area. Round the point to see the dam that controls the water flow into the Silver Fork of the American River, known locally as Silver Creek.

The small section of road that runs across the top of the dam is a remnant of the old highway before it was re-routed onto a new bridge downstream from the present dam. It has free public parking and lake access. For a while, this newly constructed bridge enjoyed a historical footnote due to its style of construction:

> *"This new bridge involved the use of the longest pre-cast girders ever placed on a California bridge – almost 40 meters [132 feet] long, weighing more than 70,000 kg [77 tons]"*

The group of buildings to the left of the dam belongs to Kay's Resort. With the exception of the cabins, these refurbished structures have stood on this portion of the lake as a traveler's way station and a summer haven for the rich and famous of Stockton and Sacramento since the resort was established in 1874. As the main lake expanded, it covered over the original hotel and horse race track.

The entire complex historically has been named after the individuals

Tonya at the falls from Summit Meadow Creek.

and families who operated the store and resort; first, it was Fagan's, then it changed to Caminetti's. In the 1930s, the Kay family gained ownership and it has been known by that name ever since. Presently, Mona White owns and maintains the family-oriented resort.

Before paddling further down the lake, stop in at the resort and satisfy your hunger or thirst at its well-stocked grocery store.

Sandy Cove

Armed with goodies from the store, load your boat and paddle out to the Sandy Cove picnic area. Located in the cove just south from Kay's, this protected area offers an opportunity to enjoy a swim, relax under a shady pine grove or picnic overlooking the lake and the peaks bordering the eastern shoreline. The pines that surround the cove are not dense and crowded but separated by small green meadows, giving it an open airy look. Picnic tables are strategically placed in various open spaces.

The cove itself has a beach with clean sand in which you can wiggle your toes with delight. The sun warms the shallow waters for a refreshing swim. Sandy Cove makes an excellent destination for families who do not wish to paddle on the more open lake, or who prefer a short paddle from their put-in at the southern end of the lake.

West Shore

From Sandy Cove, the shoreline becomes less forested and more cabins appear along the side of the lake. The granite appears as broad slabs with the occasional conifer or juniper growing out from a bench or eroded joint. Paddle past Treasure Island and notice the difference between the rugged rocky shores on the western side, versus the forested, gentle slope of the eastern shore.

As the breeze freshens, there are many small coves to paddle into and take a rest before tackling the rising headwind.

Eventually, you will spot the tall lodgepoles that mark the site of your put-in, catch the telltale flash of sunlight off the windshield of your vehicle, and dip the paddle one last time before beaching your boat.

Sources and References:

Browning, Peter, *Place-Names of the Sierra Nevada: from Abbot to Zumwalt.* Berkeley: Wilderness Press, 2nd. Ed., 1992.

National Geographic Society, *Field Guide to the Birds of North America.* 2nd Ed., Shirley L. Scott, Ed., 1996.

" . . . A man feels at home with a paddle in his hand, as natural and indigenous as with a bow or spear. When he swings through a stroke and the canoe moves forward, he sets in motion long forgotten reflexes, stirs up ancient sensations deep within his subconscious . . . There is magic in the feel of a paddle and the movement of a canoe, a magic compounded of distance, adventure, solitude, and peace. The way of a canoe is the way of the wilderness and of a freedom almost forgotten. . . . When a man is part of his canoe, he is part of all that canoes have ever known."

—*Sigurd F. Olsen, The singing Wilderness, 1956*

Shaded camp with a blue canoe.

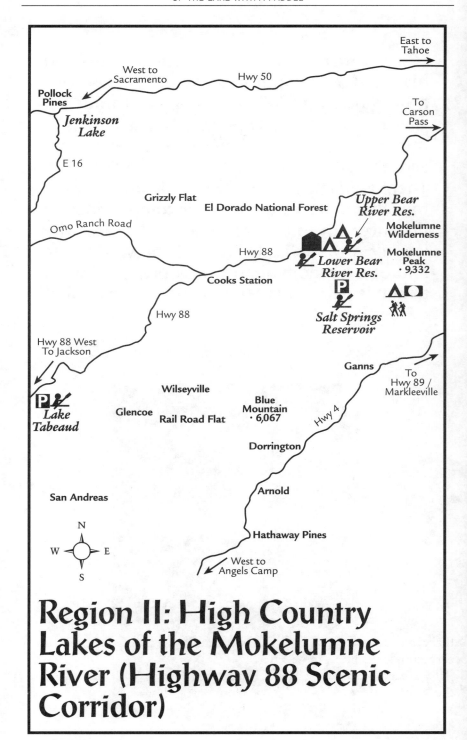

East to
Tahoe

West to
Sacramento

Hwy 50

Pollock
Pines

To
Carson
Pass

*Jenkinson
Lake*

E 16

Grizzly Flat

El Dorado National Forest

*Upper Bear
River Res.*

Omo Ranch Road

Mokelumne
Wilderness

Hwy 88

*Lower Bear
River Res.*

Mokelumne
Peak
· 9,332

Cooks Station

Hwy 88

Salt Springs
Reservoir

Hwy 88 West
To Jackson

Ganns

To
Hwy 89 /
Markleeville

Wilseyville

Blue
Mountain
· 6,067

*Lake
Tabeaud*

Glencoe

Rail Road Flat

Hwy 4

Dorrington

San Andreas

Arnold

N

Hathaway Pines

W ⊕ E

West to
Angels Camp

S

Region II: High Country Lakes of the Mokelumne River (Highway 88 Scenic Corridor)

Region II: High Country Lakes of the Mokelumne River (Highway 88 Scenic Corridor)

Four man-made reservoirs lie sandwiched between lakes formed by the damming of water from the Carson River to the north and the Sierran lakes created by the free-flowing expanse of the Stanislaus River to the south. Each reservoir occupies a niche within a different eco-system governed by altitude.

Drive up State Highway 88 east to the charming setting of Lake Tabeaud Reservoir, as the heat from the low-lying Sacramento Valley partially abates. Located at a modest elevation of 2,000 feet in a park-like setting, Tabeaud straddles several life zones: a riparian community, a chaparral belt, and the plants of the higher elevation of the yellow pine forest.

Exit the highway onto the road leading to the lake and pass under a canopy of black oaks with stringy fingers of lichen hanging from their limbs. As you approach the reservoir, manzanita and chamise thickets surround the hardy digger (or grey) pine, whose presence is more familiar to travelers of the lower foothills.

The familiar species that make up the trees of the higher-elevation, mixed conifer forest are also present. Big-leaf maples and Pacific dogwood grow along the moister shoreline that makes up the mixed forest under story. Farther up from the shoreline are stately Ponderosa Pines (*Pinus ponderosa*), also known as the western yellow pine, which are the defining tree of the mixed conifer forest. Clusters of the ubiquitous incense cedar grow alongside the ponderosa and are considered to be the weed of the conifer family.

Paddle this small, but intimate, reservoir to appreciate its setting—high enough to be away from the stifling heat of the valley, yet temperate enough that the heavy snowfall of the higher Sierra does not preclude a late fall or early spring paddle.

To reach the hidden basin of Salt Springs Reservoir, first drive up into the heart of the yellow pine belt before descending into a mixed bag of biotic communities that make up the intermixed zones surrounding the reservoir. The last leg of the journey includes a drive under a belt of ripar-

Looking down into the Mokelumne River Drainage from Highway 88.

ian under story that protects the flowing waters of the North Fork of the Mokelumne River.

Your paddle on the reservoir takes you through a canyon whose steep walls are covered by stands of deciduous black and canyon oaks. Dangling vines of California wild grape and poison oak intertwine among the oaks' branches—an incongruous sight in the depths of a Sierran mountain canyon. When you look up to the gorge's rim, the more familiar biotic setting of the high country is evident. While the gorge floor radiates from temperatures that allow vines, flowering plants, and acorns to thrive, the rim harbors the stern, snow-tolerant stands of pine, cedar, and hemlock.

Located above the singular domain of Salt Creek are the Bear River Reservoirs (one name for two reservoirs separated by dam and portage). Tall pine specimens with various names guard your entrance into Lower Bear Lake. Everything from the large-trunk sugar pine with its handsome long cones, the admirable ponderosa pine with characteristic jigsaw-puzzle bark, the Jeffrey pine, whose "Bark smells like pineapple[s] . . . ", to the robust stands of incense cedar that grow in a more moisture laden environment provide visitors with a firm sense of place.

Paddling the length of Lower Bear to the take-out for Upper Bear Reservoir, you begin to notice another transition within the biotic community, from stately conifers to shaggy junipers with their craggy wind-shaped cousins, the mountain pines. This shift in the plant community is by no means abrupt or even noticeable to the casual passerby. Only when you study the lichen-covered domes that make up the granitic walls of the reservoir do you see tall pines gradually give way to the Sierra juniper, lodgepole pine and western hemlock.

Complete the portage onto the shoreline of Upper Bear Reservoir, and once again you stand in the familiar presence of the tall conifers; however, the elevated destination adds a few more species to the forest. In the distance, along the far shoreline of the reservoir, shimmering, bright green leaves, almost luminescent, mark the presence of the quaking aspen, a tree that thrives in high dry places near clean rushing water. Mixed stands of white and red firs grow above the aspen belt. The latter denotes a moister climatic zone and the former marks the transition to a higher elevation.

Paddle any one of these four reservoirs to appreciate the beauty and diversity of California's life zones without having to drive distances or find the extra time to view this same slice of California's Sierra Nevada.

Sources and References:

Gary Snyder, "The Foxtail Pine," *The Backcountry*, from p. 12 of *Graced by Pines*, Alexandra Murphy, Missoula: Mountain Press Publishing Company, 1994.

Bakker, Elna, *An Island Called California*. Berkeley: University of California Press, 2nd Ed., 1984.

Lanner, Ronald M., *Conifers of California*. Los Olivios: Cachuma Press, 1999.

Conifers, ridges of bare rock, and expanses of blue sky are all part of the scenic vistas of the lakes along the Mokelumne River Drainage.

REGION II: HIGH COUNTRY LAKES OF THE MOKELUMNE RIVER
PADDLING AREA 1:
BEAR RIVER RESERVOIR (LOWER BEAR LAKE)

Position: 38°32.15'N, 120°15.15'W

Difficulty: Unpredictable wind gusts especially by late morning. These winds may blow either up-lake from the dam (southwesterly) or from the upper Bear River Gorge (northeasterly).

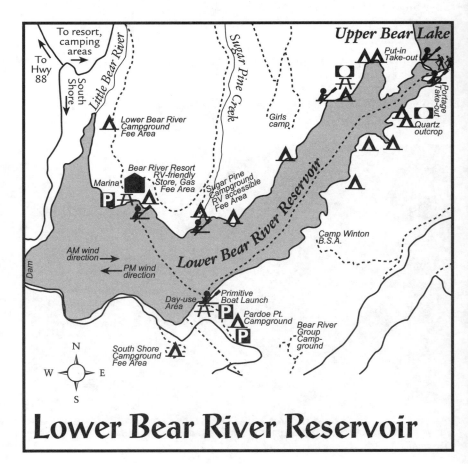

Lower Bear River Reservoir

View of Lower Bear Lake from the dam.

Trip Length: Lower Lake may be paddled in one long day, but it is best to give yourself at least two days to explore the many coves and inlets.

Portage: None for Lower Lake.

Paddling Distance:

0.73 mile from Bear River Resort Marina to day-use boat launch across the lake;

1.94 miles from the Marina to take-out for the portage to upper lake from day-use area boat launch.

Season: Late May through early June insures high water and uncrowded conditions. Weekends are notoriously crowded and busy.

Lake Size: 725 Acres.

Elevation: 5,818 feet.

County: Amador County.

National Forest Service/Wilderness Area: Eldorado National Forest.

Maps:

USGS 7.5-Minute Quadrangle Topographical Map Series: Pacific Valley, CA and Carson Pass, CA.

National Forest Service/Wilderness Area: Humboldt-Toiyabe National Forest (Carson Ranger District) and Mokelumne Wilderness Maps.

Road Maps:

Compass Map: Alpine Amador and Sacramento Counties.

California State Automobile Association (AAA) Maps: Central California – Bay Area to Lake Tahoe.

Historical Background:

A Pacific Gas and Electric (PG&E) hydroelectric project. Lower Lake was completed as an add-on in 1952 to the original Bear River Lake located above this larger and newer reservoir.

Access:

The primary highway access to Bear River Lakes (Reservoir) is via State Hwy. 88 east from Jackson, CA.

The Bear River Lakes Reservoir turnoff is the third right exit after passing Hams Station (Bear River Road at the Forest Service Road 08).

The resort is to your left at the junction, approximately 1 mile from the turnoff.

To reach South Shore Campground and Pardoe Point with its campground and use area, continue on Bear River Road; cross over the dam and turn left.

South Shore (fee) Campground is approximately 0.5 mile on your right. Pardoe Point Campground and adjacent features are located a short distance beyond South Shore Campground on your left.

The marina from Bear River Resort & grocery store.

Heads Up:

- Easy Access off Hwy. 88 (all roads paved).
- RV/car trailer accessible (Bear River Resort, South Shore Campground).
- Bear River Resort (tel: 209.295.4868 or fax: 209.295.4585 or visit www.bearriverlake.com).
- The resort marina and general store sell fuel, ice and groceries.
- Campground reservations: Sierra Recreation Managers 209.295.4512
- Late spring and early summer insures high water.
- To beat the crowds, arrive midweek.
- Many lakeside primitive campsites to choose from (see map).
- High Sierra scenery at its best.
- Excellent fishing. Trophy sized rainbows stocked every summer, German brown and mackinaw trout.
- Campfire permit (free) required if camping outside of designated campgrounds. Must obtain permit in person.
- The nearest Forest Service Office to Bear Lakes is in Pioneer. Amador Ranger District, 26820 Silver Drive, Pioneer, CA (209.295.5996)
- Bear country—pack and camp smart!

Description:

Rounded domes of glacially polished granite surround the glistening blue water of the lake. This simple descriptive statement only just begins to describe the beauty of the Bear River Lakes. In addition to the towering granite, the green hues of conifers provide a vivid contrast against the bluish tint of the lower lake shoreline of weather-stained rock. This contrast between rock, lake, and forest is more apparent as you drive across the dam. Look down toward the Bear River Gorge and see how the granite predominates and only a thin shimmering line marks the path of the tumbling river.

Don't be surprised if your drive across the lake is buffeted by a strong breeze. This section of the lake, closest to the dam and the gorge below, attracts more wind then the upper end of Lower Bear Lake.

As soon as you drive across, park in the large open space on your right, and walk back across the dam for a spectacular view down the gorge. The gorge provides a visual reference to gauge how much water is impounded behind the dam, which is dramatic and deep.

Be careful not to stand too close to the edge; if the wind gusts while you peer down the gorge, you will be paragliding before you learn the art.

Finally, look at the rock layers that make up the ridge rim across the gorge and to the west. Notice their various colors, ranging from yellow and orange to brown. Scan across the multi-colored ridge to the lake and note the demarcation between the colored rock and the beginning of the granite. These colors represent minerals of former volcanic origin. Further proof of this volcanic activity lies all along Highway 88 and the main road leading to the lake. As you drive up the highway, you see chunks of volcanic rock within in a cement-like matrix that forms the road-cuts on both sides of the roadway. These exposed cuts are remnants of former lava and volcanic mudflows, called lahars. They thundered down from now extinct volcanoes or flowed out from deep fissures in the ground. *(See Area Sources and References.)*

Cross the dam, turn left and parallel the lake. A short distance from your turn, you get your first glimpse of the lake's expanse. In the far distance, where the lake narrows, you can make out the horizontal line that marks the dam separating Lower from Upper Bear Lake. Approximately one mile down the road, you come to a sign and information board that mark the entrance into South Shore campground. Although sites are available on a first-come basis, reservations during June and July are recommended.

Your fee includes use of a cinder-block toilet, running water, picnic tables and a fire pit. There is room for RVs and tent trailers; however, it is best to bring stabilizers.

Budget-minded tent campers, or those wishing to be closer to the lake, may want to drive farther down to the no-fee Pardoe Point (also known as the Bear River) campground. This primitive campground has only two port-a-potties, along with some picnic tables and fire pits.

If you are boat camping or going on to Upper Lake, use the parking area adjacent to the turn leading down to Pardoe Point and the day-use area. Before you reach the day-use area, where the road deadends, a primitive earthen boat launch cuts off from the road on your right.

The Lodge, Adjacent Marina and Lower Lake

Note: Payment required for launching all car top boats.

The best time to launch and enjoy a pleasant experience paddling the lower lake is in the early morning or late afternoon, because the wind and motorboat activity are down and the lake's surface is calm. Plan your paddle around the prevailing wind, using the wind direction to assist your travel direction on the lake. The lower lake, especially the open bay around the dam, is subject to strong, shifting wind gusts.

To enter the cove that borders the beaches along Sugar Pine Campground, paddle along the western shoreline toward upper lake, and you will pass a couple of small islands, actually the tops of barren granite knobs. *(See map).*

If any Sugar Pine campsites that border the southern shore of the lake are available, grab one, but make sure you officially sign-in at the lodge. The lake view from these campsites is spectacular and you get a wind-free cove

Lone pine and dark granite of lower Bear Lake.

with a private beach for your paddle craft, too. These fee-area campsites have picnic tables, metal fire-pits, and vault toilets. The sites also accommodate RVs and tent trailers.

South Shore

The shoreline on the southern end of the lake is steeper than the northwest shore and is hidden by stands of pine and brush. The small structure standing on the shore adjacent to the rocky shore, houses a pump that pulls water between Bear River Reservoir, Cole Creek and Salt Springs Reservoir.

A short distance from this structure is the primitive boat launch strip, the site of the day-use area and Pardoe Point Campground.

Northwest Shoreline Sites

If you plan to camp on the lake's northwest side, the best campsites are at the far end past the cabins that belong to the Mormon Girls Camp *(See map)*.

Paddle past the high granite wall that marks the location of the camp cabins, and look for the rope suspension bridges and climbing ladders that are used to reach the camp's boat dock. A climbing class conducts a series of belays off the nearby shear granite walls that form the base on which the cabins are constructed.

Shortly after paddling past the camp dock, you pass a blocky, dark-stained granite wall rising out of the lake. On the granite façade's weathered surface is a patchwork of vertical and horizontal cracks within the rock. The process of rocks weakening and shattering through this weathering action, produced in part by the effects of water turning into ice, is called frost riving. Specifically, weak zones in the rock face allow water to enter, either as rain or snowfall. When it freezes, it expands, exerting outward pressure (as high as 1,000 pounds per square inch) within the crevice.

Through time, these crevices widen causing more of the granite to fall away.

Several excellent campsites are located on the left bank just as you enter the deep-set cove located on the north end of the lake, a short distance past the girls camp and the frost-riven cliff. (*See Sections 8 and 9 on a Bear River Reservoir 7.5-Minute Quadrangle Topographical Map*.) The sites consist of a series of beaches within small coves that form the shoreline of a granite bench. The bench extends upward, away from the water, and contains level areas suitable for a freestanding tent and a *thick* sleeping pad. Actually, the level areas where a vegetation-free soil base has built-up may provide for a comfortable sleeping site.

Even if you do not camp overnight, the area is worth the stop for the nice view of the lake with the surrounding granitic landscape and profusion of wildflowers. And, let's not forget the wonderful rock diving and sunbathing off the granite slabs.

In The Eddy:
A Hike through a Glacial Landscape

Study the Sierran-glacial landscape up close and personal by taking a short hike around the area.

Many of the odd boulders, lying about like a child's scattered marbles, appear to be of a different mineral composition than the terrain on which they rest. These boulders are the dropped remains of glacial debris; some were transported many miles from where they now reside. Geologists refer to the rocks that are different, and do not fit into the local landscape, as erratics.

Walk up to an erratic and notice the various sizes, shapes and colors that appear to stain the boulders. These colorful designs are formed by the growth patterns of tiny organisms known as lichen. Most lichens are composite symbiotic organisms and not true plants. This means that their survival depends on a working relationship between members of as many as three different kingdoms: fungus, algae and bacteria. The *Fungi* kingdom forms the body and is the dominant partner. The fungus provides shelter, absorbs moisture from the air, and extracts mineral salts that are necessary for healthy plant life. Sometimes, the partner is from the *Protista* kingdom, better known as algae. The algae are capable of producing food for themselves and their partner through photosynthesis, a complex interaction of sunlight on a green substance within the algae called chlorophyll. The third possible relationship may occur with *Cyanobacteria* kingdom *(Monera)* bacteria. Together, these organisms take nitrogen gas out of the air and turn it into useful compounds necessary for a healthy soil. Lichen that grows on and forms tight crusts on the surface of a granite boulder is known as crustose lichen. The lichen cannot be removed without damaging the boulder's infrastructure.

Lichen grows very slowly, less than a millimeter a year, and is among the oldest living things on earth (along with bacteria). Lichen grows on areas considered too harsh by other living organisms, and is considered a pioneer plant, surviving on bare rock, desert sand, live bark, dead wood or bones. Lichen with known growth rates is being used as a date indicator of glacial retreat and rockslides caused by former earthquakes.

Please be careful where you walk and place your gear now that you know these facts.

Step back from your inspection of the erratic to see if the boulder is lying in a trench-like groove carved into the granite floor. These glacial grooves are wider than they are deep and are formed by the rocks

159

imbedded in the bottom of the ice sheet that scrapes across the granite. Look for smaller scratches, usually in conjunction with a mirror-like feature found throughout the surface of the granite slab. When the sun's rays hit this surface feature at the correct angle, you have a reflection not unlike a mirror dazzling your eyes. This slick surface is called glacial polish and the small straight scratches are glacial striations. Fine grains of sand, mud and clay, embedded in the ice as it moved through the area, form polished surfaces. The striations are the work of larger rocks intermixed with fine silt. It is interesting to note that these glacial scratches show the direction of the glacial flow.

On barren granite, free of soil and debris, look for crescent-shaped depressions of various sizes and numbers. A line of single crescent-shaped depressions, not unlike the hoof marks of a one legged horse, are referred to as chatter marks. Rocks in the moving ice are forced through a repetitive up and down motion similar to hammer blows, and thus create rock divots. The crescent's size is proportionate to the rock that made it; consequently, the line indicates the direction of the glacier's movement, with the crescent points facing in the opposite direction from the travel.

When you kneel to examine the chatter marks, your knees touch the soil and you hear a distinct crunch sound. This gravel is composed of small pieces of granitic debris that resemble a larger version of Grape-Nuts® broken down into the final stage for soil building. These same coarse-grained crystals that you are holding in your hand, give granite its name from the Latin word meaning grain (*granum*). The largest of the crystals determines the overall color of the granite, be it white, gray or pink. The white, opaque crystals are most likely feldspar, which comprises the majority of the granite. The next most common is quartz, the glass-like shiny crystals. The dark, iron-containing crystals are either mica or hornblende.

Gruss is the assemblage of the various minerals that make up granitic gravel.

Stand at the edge of the granite bench near the water and look north toward its sloping top where you'll see that the bench is just one of a series of step-like layers with rounded edges that eroded at different levels. The highest point of the bench is actually the top of a low dome whose base is hidden beneath the lake's waters. Use your imagination to compare the layers of the granitic dome to the cross-section of an onion you've peeled and sliced.

When the huge amount of overburden that covered all this granitic landscape that makes up the present Sierra Nevada Mountain Range was eroded away, the once buried granite heaved a sigh of relief and expanded. In the process, the granite developed a series of curvilinear fractures called expansion joints. When water seeps into these fractures or joints, it freezes. The ice expands, breaking off portions of the granite along its weak point, the expansion joint. This erosion process, unique to granitic landscapes, is called exfoliation. Since the expansion joints are naturally curved, their exfoliation creates dome-shaped topography. After glaciation, the process of exfoliation is one of the primary-weathering agents of the Sierra mountain range. *(Refer to Wessels, Tom,* The Granite Landscape, *pp. 34-39.)*

Bear lake Reservoir

Round the point and pass one of the best of the campsites in this area. When the lake is full, look for a huge, squared block of weathered granite (erratic) near the water's edge. The beach and campsite are to the right of the boulder. Slightly inland are a picnic table and fire-pit in a pine grove. Other localities, but without the amenities, are available along the shoreline that is part of this gently sloping bench.

Another ideal site on this side of the lake is at the far end of the same large cove that you entered. This site can accommodate more people in a tree-shaded environment. From either area, hike to the dam that separates the two lakes.

Campsite along the southeast shore of Lower Bear Lake.

Waterfall of the Bear River separates Lower Bear Lake from Upper Bear Lake.

Lower Bear Lake (From Pardoe Point to Upper Bear Lake Dam)

From Pardoe Point, point your bow eastward toward the dam. Once you pass the cove of the Boy Scout's Camp Winton, all kinds of small coves and interesting beaches await exploration.

On this southeast side of the lake four campsites stand out from the many others that dot the lake. In order of appearance, from south to north, the first is a small cove with an inlet on its northeastern end, located past Camp Winton as you round the bulbous point at the northeast tip of Section 17 on the Bear River Reservoir Topographic map. The cove is protected from the wind and has a fine swimming area. Explore the sloping granite above.

The second site is located just a short paddle past the tip of a small point one cove over from the first site. This area contains a level granite bench with many small camping areas from which to choose. A long-time visitor to the area mentioned this location because of the many potholes and inlets created by erosion. As the day progresses, the sun warms the holes and in-lets, thus creating excellent bathing areas or, as he put it, *"Mother Nature's own hot tub(s)."*

The last two sites are the largest of the four, holding two or more couples plus their boats.

One is tucked into the southern most side of the deep cove immediately north of the second of these two sites, and you can hike between the two. You also can hike to the third site from the second site mentioned above. If you approach the cove from the south, you will not spot it until you enter the cove or paddle past its southern point. Once you see it, it has the appearance of a classic camping site with a sandy beach extending into the tree line onto a grassy meadow surrounded by forest. Located strategically around a stone fire pit are several field-made benches and tables constructed from driftwood. The site has a cozy and homey look to it.

The fourth site is similar to the third but without the meadow. It is tucked in at the far end of the cove adjacent to a granite bluff.

Paddle past the fourth site to see other small, single-person or maybe single-couple sites, but you won't find any additional camping areas until you cross to the other shore.

A small but interesting natural feature that, at first glance, fools many passing boaters lies ahead. Paddle toward the inlet that leads into the lagoon located below the dam and look for a shimmering white patch partially hidden beneath a manzanita bush growing at the water's edge. Your first thought is, "What is that patch of snow still doing lying beneath the bushes?"

Upon closer examination, you see it's a large band of milky quartz; its sheen is similar to a snow bank that has turned to ice due to the constant wash of the lake.

Upper Bear River Lake Dam Area

Before crossing to the west side of the lake, explore the lagoon that forms below the dam and separates the two lakes. It is worth the short hike to view both lakes from the dam, even if you do not portage over to Upper Bear Lake. If the spillway at the upper dam is open, paddle into the small cove to the right of the lagoon to view the picturesque waterfall. In the early morning, the rising sun highlights the cascade and its bonnet of spray.

Paddle from the waterfall into the lagoon that forms the tail of lower lake. The take-out for the portage trail that leads to the top of the dam is at your right. Paddle to a granite ledge at high water, and step out to hike the short distance to the dam. At the top, the spillway creates the waterfall you admire from below.

Hike over the pile of granite boulders lying to the left of the pine to reach the dam.

Look at the polished surface of the granite at your feet as you hike along the sloping granite ledge and toward the cement walkway of the dam. This is an excellent example of glacial polish created by one of the glaciers that covered this valley.

To reach the concrete lip of the dam, use the stepping-stones on the gravel fill adjacent to the spillway. Walk the 100-foot gravel trail at the base of the concrete lip and then boulder hop to the pathway located on the opposite end.

From the dam's lip, take in the dramatic southeast exposure of the lagoon and the lake's main body. Turn towards Upper Bear Lake for an equally spectacular view of this smaller original reservoir with its islands and surrounding granite walls.

Let your eyes follow the northern shoreline to the islands to see the waterfall's shimmering cascade.

The small tower with attached wheel is the control mechanism that opens and closes the spillway. To meet hydroelectric needs as the summer progresses, the upper lake is drained first, then the larger lower lake.

Stroll across the lake on the concrete walkway for an unparalleled view of both lakes and their glacially scoured terrain. At the opposite end of the walkway, walk over several flowering yellow blossoms of the Woolly Sunflowers (*Eriophyllum lanatum*), which belong to the aster family. These daisy-like flowers grow in the rocky crevices that surround both lakes. Walk around the dam and keep an eye out for the occasional cream-colored blossom growing alone in the open spaces. The subtle beauty of this lily, known as Leichtlin's Mariposa Lily *(Calochortus leichtlinii),* can easily be overlooked. The common name mariposa comes from the Spanish and means butterfly.

On your descent, note the iron remnants from the dam construction. Some of the metal here dates back to the 19th century, particularly the riveted pipe sticking out from the rock at the base of the dam. The iron rails lying twisted near the pathway were probably used to carry ore hoppers containing rock for the dam.

REGION II: HIGH COUNTRY LAKES OF THE MOKELUMNE RIVER
PADDLING AREA 2: UPPER BEAR RIVER LAKE

Position: 38°33.25'N, 120°12.55'W

Difficulty: The portage to the lake is the most difficult part to this paddle.

Trip Length: Definitely an overnighter.

Portage: Requires a short but steep trek from Lower Bear River Lake over the dam to Upper Lake.

The portage entails take-out at the upper right end of the lagoon below the dam, then portaging the boat and gear up a rough-hewn granite path onto the concrete pathway at the lip of the dam.

The put-in and take-out for Upper Bear River Lake is on the opposite side of the dam (northern end) at the base of a granite slope.

Note: Although you may want to use the gravel path at the base of the concrete, and skip having to pitch your boat and gear up to the concrete walkway, I advise against it. A portion of the pathway has been eroded, requiring boulder hopping to the opposite side.

Paddling Distance:

0.46 mile from the dam's put-in and take-out to second island and waterfall;

0.98 mile to third island campsite;

1.18 miles to campsite at far end of lake.

Season: Spring, after the roads are open, to late June before the lakes draw down. Call the Amador Ranger Station or the Bear River Lake Resort for current lake levels.

Lake Size: Approximately 1 mile long.

Elevation: 5,876 feet.

County: Amador County.

Maps:

USGS 7.5-Minute Quadrangle Topographical Map: Bear River Reservoir,CA and Peddler Hill, CA.

National Forest Service/Wilderness Area: Eldorado National Forest Map.

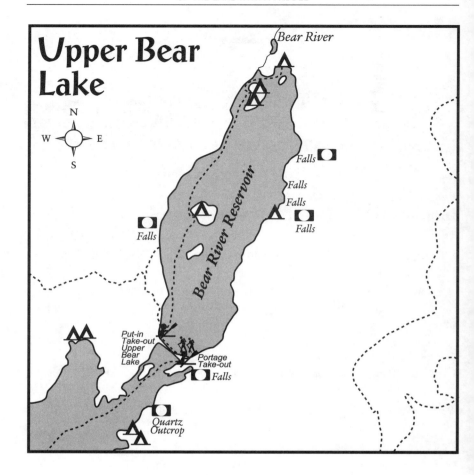

Road Maps:

Compass Maps, Inc: Alpine, Amador and Sacramento Counties.

California State Automobile Association (AAA) Maps: Central California – Bay Area to Lake Tahoe.

Historical Background: This PG&E Reservoir was built in 1905 and is the original reservoir of the two lakes.

Access: *(See Lower Bear River Lake Access.)*

Heads Up:

- Campfire permit (free) required for camping in non-designated campsites.
- Bear River Resort general store has groceries, ice and other needed items.
- Gas and other fuel may be purchased at the Bear River Resort Marina.

The lagoon below the dam with take-out. The portage trail is visible in the foreground.

- Lake best paddled in spring and early summer before draw-down of water.
- Complete the portage early to insure a good campsite.
- Bear country—pack and camp smart!
- Excellent fishing, especially at the mouth of Bear River.

Description:

The hardship of a portage is well worth the sweat it takes to paddle and camp on this gorgeous reservoir. Situated above the busy and active lower lake is Upper Bear River Reservoir; it is a quiet oasis for solitude and a taste for the wilderness experience. The sound of waterfalls and your paddle through water are the predominate sounds on the lake. Occasionally, the honking of Canada geese breaks up the rhythmic swishing sounds that mark your boat's passage.

As the day rolls on, a muted growl of an outboard from below makes its way to your ears, but this is a sometime sound and not the norm.

As you paddle farther up the lake, especially during the calm of a morning, you encounter a yellow pollen sheen covering the lake's surface. Your boat's bow wake causes the surface to undulate, creating a phosphorescent-like shimmer to the water passing by.

Not a bad way to start your morning, eh?

Lower Lake: Islands and Waterfall

Once you catch your breath from that last tote of gear and load your boat, take a moment to look around and enjoy the panoramic view. The shadows that hide the details of the southeastern shore do not take away from their grandeur. That entire side of the lake seems to contain no genteel beach or friendly cove; instead, the entire shore rises directly off the water in craggy, dissected domes, with conifer-covered slopes.

At first glance, the sun-lit northern side, which is partially hidden by two islands, appears no better. The sight of the long, thin ribbon of the waterfall in the distance is intriguing, so you maneuver your boat toward the sound of falling water.

As you leave the portage site and approach the shoreline, which is hidden from view behind the base of the dome that abuts the dam, small intimate coves with gravel beaches or clean rock that are sheltered by stands of conifer and black oak are readily available for camping. As more of these potential campsites come into view, you realize that this lake hides its campsites from the casual viewer. The problem, however, is that the majority of these sites will hold only one or two boats; larger groups have to look farther on the lake for a site . . . not necessarily a bad thing!

The sound of the waterfall is more pronounced as you approach the islands. The first of the islands is nothing more than a rounded granite

The take-out for the portage is in background where the sloping granite meets the water's edge. Once at the lip of the dam, use a concrete walkway (not visible) to reach your put-in (at the debris pile) for Upper Bear Lake.

dome with a few conifers growing in the crags. Ah, but the second island looks very promising! The opening to a small sandy cove is made for a canoe or kayak, but you're immediately faced with a dilemma—check out the island first or visit the waterfall? The sweat built up from the portage, plus the warmth of the mid-morning sun strengthen the vote in favor of the waterfall. A few strong strokes of the paddle(s) and your boat is bobbing up and down at the base of the falls. What a grand view! Your eyes are directed straight up the cascading water as it streams down from the granite heights. The falls are not one, but many streams falling at different intensities. Behind the sunlit watery curtain, you make out a lovely grotto of ferns, mosses and wildflowers. A flicker of movement on one of the granite faces attracts your attention. An American Dipper (*Cinclus mexicanus*) sits on a knob of granite and enters the falls without hesitation for a choice insect. The dipper flies off to a well-hidden nest in a moss-covered rocky niche with a struggling morsel in its beak.

Secure your boat and carefully make your way on the sloping granite to the base of the falls. Once on the ledge, where the falling water splashes onto the granite, locate a cascade to suits your needs.

Clothing is optional as you stand under the falling water. The sudden chill takes your breath away! Goosebumps, the size of robins eggs spread rapidly over your body. The shock of it all forces a hearty yell from deep within your chest, and the sound echoes off the basin walls.

You let the poor man's shower cleanse your body before rapidly exiting the falls. Standing and shivering in the morning sun, your wet body displays the ultimate definition of the word, *COLD!* Ah, once you dry off, you are full of energy and vitality. A feeling of refreshment brings contentment to your sore muscles and sun-baked skin.

Perched on a sun-warmed slab of polished granite, you slowly absorb the view. Refreshed, you step into your boat and paddle toward the island with its attractive cove.

The Island

A small cove protected by boulders and vegetation on the southwest end is the best take-out. The beach consists of small, pea-sized gravel with a few rocks, which can scratch the underside of your boat.

The startled cry and erratic flight of a small brown bird running away surprises you as you step ashore. The Killdeer (*Charadrius vociferous*) protects its nearby nest with its famous broken-wing display. She hopes to distract you from her nest by mimicking a bird with a broken wing, so that you follow her rather than locate her nest. At the same time, from the corner of your eye, you catch a fast moving object aiming for your head and it does not look like it will divert. As you turn to see what it's all about, you meet an angry Red-Winged Blackbird (*Agelaius phoeniceus*) and its mate beak-to-face.

It turns out that you are in an active nesting area and are being greeted by its inhabitants.

Retreat quickly inland away from the nesting area; as the birds quiet down, you now have an opportunity to study the island.

At ground level, a riot of color from the variety of wildflowers produces a visual display that you miss while attempting to dodge the black bird. Carpets of orange-red Applegate Paintbrush *(Castilleja applegatei)* cover the more open spaces, while the shaded areas contain dense strands of pale blue lupine, probably Brewer's Lupine *(Lupinus breweri)*. As you study the flora of the Sierras, the name *brewer* comes up often. William Brewer was a professor of agriculture at Yale and worked on the botany of California in the late 1800s. He also was the first botanist in the U.S. Geological Survey (also known as the Whitney Survey) in a four-year study of California's natural resources from 1860-1864.

The beauty of the wildflowers is enhanced by their subtle scents that drift in the warm, still air. Interspersed with these delicate aromas, comes a more pronounced scent of pine and vanilla. Did some careless camper leave their pudding cup behind?

Following the scent to its source, you almost smack your head into a huge pine whose girth and height dominate the island. Permeating all around the pine, are the delicious scents of butterscotch and vanilla. Putting your nose up to the deeply furrowed bark and breathing deeply, you are on sensory overload as the wonderful chemistry created by oils within the tree's resin releases its magic.

As the heat of the sun increases, the resin warms and releases oils called terpenes; the hotter the day, the more fragrant the pine scent. The vanilla-like aroma is also characteristic of a Jeffery pine. The Jeffrey is the predominate pine growing throughout the areas bordering the two lakes.

The ground around the tree is also the site of a former campfire ring, and no wonder!

The area is open, so a breeze will keep the site free of mosquitoes. The ground is soft enough for your sleeping bag and tent, and it affords you a delightful view of the lake.

As you make your way to the shrub-covered northern shoreline, you startle two Common Mergansers who were sunning themselves on a nearby log. Adjacent to the log is a pile of smooth granitic boulders. One of them has a naturally smooth slope that seems tailor-made for sunbathing. The water of the upper lake is warm for a refreshing swim. Soon you put that sloping boulder to the test.

If you explore the shaded shoreline on the north side of the island, peer close to the ground at the miniature world of the spongy moss. The moss provides a green carpet bordering piles of small stones and rocks that make up the beach along the shoreline.

View of Upper Bear Lake.

The individual chain of green is a small cell called *protonema*. From these cells, buds develop into shoots. The shoots resemble miniature asparagus with spiral-shaped leaves. The smaller stalks, topped by a cup-shaped capsule called a *seta* contain thousands of spores. When grown, they are released and scattered by the wind.

Main Lake

Stretching outward from the island, the main body of the lake beckons for exploration. Braving the gauntlet of bird indignities, you quickly enter your boat and cast off toward the far end of the lake. Cross towards the southeastern shoreline and parallel its granite ledges. The now familiar sound of falling water draws you to a shaded crevice within the rock. There, a cascade sprays down from a thin ribbon of water and splashes from one jutting rock to another before dropping into the lake. Flowers, moss and small shrubs surround the falls. A hummingbird flits from blossom to blossom, gathering energy from various nectars in each bloom. Before you reach the campsite at the end of the lake, you pass at least four such falls with their islands of blooming gardens.

Interspersed between the falls are ledges where the exfoliating granite has eroded to create an open space. Some of these ledges are accessible and deserve investigation, especially the ones containing a streamlet or waterfall. Many animals and birds seek out the colorful display of wildflowers in a park-like setting for food and shelter. Canada Geese *(Branta Canadensis)* use the area to feed and raise their young. It is possible to come upon a deer (or

The falls make an excellent shower, in which to cool off, after the portage.

Campsite with a view.

two) taking a drink or simply resting in the shade of a strand of Mountain Alder *(Alnus tenuifolia)* or Lemmon Willow *(Salix lemmonii)*. Perched on a dead branch of a standing snag, a bald eagle or its cousin the osprey observes every move you make.

Geologically, many of these fairly level ledges show ample signs of past glaciations. Most of the streamlets that wind their way from the upper granite toward the lake are captured by long crevices and are called glacial grooves. These grooves, created by boulders being dragged by former glaciers, are common and mar the slick surface of the granite ledge. Shallower cracks or joints, created by the release of pressure on the granite when it became exposed through erosion, show their path by the straight ruler lines of flowers or grasses crisscrossing the bedrock. There are piles of boulders in various size, shape and composition everywhere. These erratics are the leftover burden from retreating glaciers. Now they are claimed as the territory of either the Western Fence Lizard *(Sceloporus occidentalis)* or the Sagebrush Lizard *(Sceloporus graciosus)*.

Mouth of the Bear River

If you approach the upper end of the lake from the eastern side, it is easy to miss the mouth of the Bear River due to the jutting mass of granite that divides the upper end of the lake. If you are fortunate to be on the lake at its fullest, you can paddle around this island and approach the river mouth

The early morning sun silhouettes islands of Upper Bear Lake.

through a stand of lake-covered conifers. The mouth of the Bear River is partially hidden by an outthrust finger composed of rock and brush. The best approach is from the northern side where you can easily spot the river's entry into the lake.

If you seek a campsite and the island is available . . . take it. The best put-in for the island is in a small cove on the southwest side within a grove of conifers. The pre-built fire pit and log table make up the amenities for your comfort and use. Zachary and his father who have been coming to this lake since the 1960s erected them. I met the father and son on the portage to the lake, and later we shared a convivial tote of very fine brandy over a crackling good fire in that same firepit. Please appreciate the camp, and leave it in the same or better condition for others to enjoy.

Use the upper branch of one of the nearby conifers as a food tote to keep the bears out. Bears are active on this side of the lake, so be careful of your food habits and clean all fish away from camp.

If you fish, the upper pools of the river contain trout, but they are very wary, so approach quietly and sneakily.

If this campsite is unavailable, try to find one on the other side of the same island *(See map)*, or paddle to the northeastern end of the lake. Whatever site you locate, be sure it has a sufficient breeze to keep the mosquitoes at bay.

For an excellent cap to your stay, bring some light (glow) sticks for a night paddle. Mark the location of your camp with one or more sticks, and attach one to the back of each boat. Place some coffee, cocoa and other snacks in one of the boats and paddle out for a memorable time on the water under the stars. *(See: Paddle Note in* Up the Lake Vol. 3 *for a complete description of preparing for a night paddle, pp. 88-90).*

Sources and References:

Blackwell, Laird R., *Wildflowers of the Sierra Nevada and the Central Valley.* Edmonton: Lone Pine Publishing, 1999.

Durham, David L., *Place-Names of California's Gold Country.* Clovis: Quill Driver Books and Word Dancer Press Inc., 2000.

Konigsmark, Ted, *Geologic Trips Sierra Nevada.* Gualala: GEO Press, 2002.

Murphy, Alexandra, *Graced by Pines: The Ponderosa Pine in the American West.* Missoula: Mountain Press Publishing Company, 1994.

Storer, Tracy I. and Robert L. Usinger, *Sierra Nevada Natural History.* Berkeley: University of California Press, 1963.

Wessels, Tom, *The Granite Landscape: A Natural History of America's Mountain Domes from Acadia to Yosemite.* Woodstock: The Countryman Press, 2001.

REGION II: HIGH COUNTRY LAKES OF THE MOKELUMNE RIVER
PADDLING AREA 3: SALT SPRINGS RESERVOIR

Position: 38°29.55'N, 120°12.50'W

Note: Not to be confused with Salt Spring Valley Reservoir, also located in Calaveras County, but in the foothills below, approximately 7.5 miles from the village of Jenny Lind.

Difficulty: The Lake itself presents no obstacles or other paddling constraints. The greatest danger comes from the extremely strong winds that blow each day. This lake has a formidable reputation for the intensity of the wind. The narrow, high rock walls surrounding the reservoir create a funnel that intensifies the wind. Usually the wind blows from west to east beginning to intensify mid-morning and maintaining its strength until the evening. Due to the steepness of the reservoir's basin walls, few adequate takeout spots exist the length of the reservoir *(See map)*. If you are caught by the wind, the northern shoreline is less steep and can be a temporary take-out.

Trip Length: Under normal circumstances, a reservoir this size may be paddled in one full day. The intensity of the wind, plus the agitated state of the reservoir, will dictate how far and for how long your paddle will take.

Portage: None required; however, no public ramp or other access is provided to the reservoir. ALL gear and boats have to be lifted up and over the dam's portal.

Lake Size: 3.5 miles long by 0.5 mile wide.

The road down to the gorge of the Mokelumne River and the location of Salt Springs Reservoir.

176

Salt Springs Reservoir

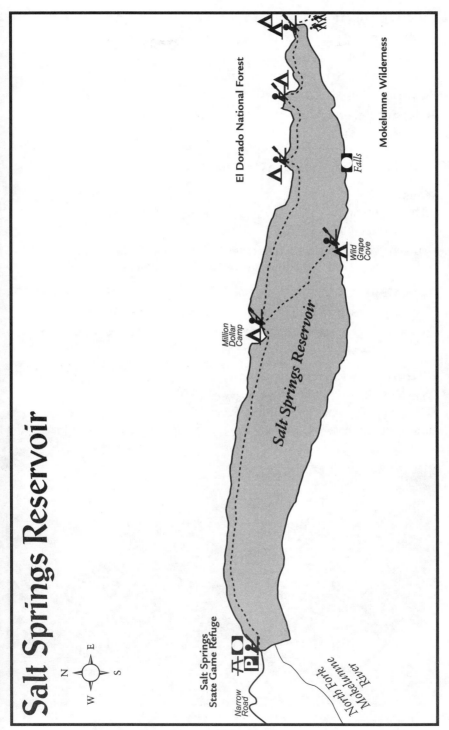

Paddling Distance:

2 miles from the put-in and take-out to Million Dollar Camp;

2.5 miles to Wild Grape Cove;

3.5 miles to Salt Springs Campground.

Elevation: 3,949 feet.

Season: Late spring through early summer, before heavy draw-down of the reservoir occurs.

County: The reservoir is a dividing line between two counties: Amador County to the North, and Calaveras County to the South.

Maps:

USGS 7.5-Minute Quadrangle Topographical Map Series: Bear River Reservoir, CA and Calaveras Dome, CA.

National Forest Service/Wilderness Area: Eldorado National Forest, Stanislaus National Forest, and Mokelumne Wilderness Maps.

Road Maps:

Compass Maps, Inc.: Alpine, Amador and Sacramento Counties.

California State Automobile Association (AAA) Map: Central California – Bay Area to Lake Tahoe.

Historical Background:

Completed in 1931, Salt Springs Reservoir is one of the reservoirs built by PG&E as part of the Mokelumne River Hydroelectric Project that encompasses approximately 45 miles of the North Fork and main stem Mokelumne River.

Portage over the gate leading into the main body of the reservoir.

On the water and ready to paddle.

Before PG&E, the river valley was a major trade route between the Miwok Indians living on the west side of the Sierras and the Washoe and Paiute on the east. Located at the upper end of the reservoir is evidence of an extensive salt gathering operation *(See In the Eddy)*. The Natives constructed salt traps and traded the salt for obsidian, used in the manufacture of tools and weapons.

Access:

State Hwy. 88 is the primary route to the turnoff for Salt Springs Reservoir. Take the Ellis Road turnoff (Forest Service Road 92) located between Hamm's Station and Bear River Road. The turnoff is marked by a small sign and is also the location for Lumber Yard Campground.

Continue on Forest Service Road 92, as it descends into the Mokelumne River Gorge. The road stays paved the entire way but becomes very narrow at the end.

When you reach the river, you will also pass the string of Forest Service campgrounds named Mokelumne River, Moore Creek, and White Azalea.

The first two are wide and open enough to handle a trailer or RV. You may also camp in areas adjacent to the river within the national forest that have not been posted. Please note, however, that ALL camping will require a campfire permit *(See the Heads Up section)*.

Continue past the last campground until you reach the gated entrance of the PG&E Powerhouse. The road makes a sharp bend to the left, narrows even more before ascending the last mile to a sand and gravel parking area at the foot of the dam.

Note: Be cautious of driving onto the sandy areas located at the far western end of the parking area. Some of the spots contain deep patches of loose, tire-swallowing sand.

If possible park next to the signboard adjacent to the rock wall nearest the dam, and coincidentally, the location of your put-in and take-out.

From the parking area, walk to your put-in and take-out located on the opposite side of the wooden portico (gate) at the far left end of the dam. This side is also the trailhead for the pack trail that follows the northern shoreline of the reservoir into the Mokelumne Wilderness. From the trailhead, you can see over the dam or gate and spot the new ramp as it descends toward the depths of the lake.

Heads Up:

- A campfire permit (free) is mandatory prior to camping outside of designated campsites. The nearest Forest Service Office to Salt Springs Reservoir is in Pioneer. Amador Ranger District, 26820 Silver Drive, Pioneer, CA (209.295.5996).
- A wilderness permit (free) is mandatory if camping within the boundary of Mokelumne Wilderness (*See map*). You may pick one up at the same location as the campfire permit.
- At certain times of the year, usually midsummer, campfires are prohibited even with a valid campfire permit. Call ahead for closure dates. See the signboard located at the edge of the parking access.
- NO trailered or motorized boats allowed.
- The earlier the start, the less problems with wind.

This magnificent dome of granite guards the approach into Salt Springs Reservoir.

- If seeking a wilderness experience with no other people, try a mid-week time frame.
- Mosquitoes are less of a problem on the mid-lake campsites, which are more open and breezy.
- The campsites at the end of the lake are mosquito prone — no other camping alternative, so bring repellent.
- Poison oak is everywhere, so watch where you tread.
- Due to the lower elevation, rattlesnakes are more active than at the higher elevation reservoirs.
- Bear country—pack and camp smart!
- Bring hiking boots; the loop trail *(See In the Eddy map)* around Salt Springs Pond to Blue Hole is worth every step.
- Fishing, especially fly-fishing, is excellent, particularly on the river and at Blue Hole.

Description:

This is the next-best scenery (short of paddling on Tenaya Lake in the heart of Yosemite Valley), but without the entrance fee or the crowds! Does that spark your interest?

To the south, dominating the entire skyline is Calaveras Dome, a massive exfoliating granite dome. Easterly, the expanse of Salt Springs Reservoir shimmers in the sunlight before receding into the distant glare of glacially polished Sierran peaks. All around you, massive walls of granite, capsulate your view to either the lake in the foreground or the river gorge slicing deep to the west.

It takes a long time to come to terms with the awesome grandeur surrounding you. Every turn of your head brings a new vista of majestic proportions to be savored.

You can spend a good 20-minutes sitting at a nearby picnic table staring at the mass of granite that makes up Calaveras Dome.

The Dam and Parking Area

Before you begin the task of unloading and preparing for your paddle, be sure to glance at the granite wall that makes up the northwestern section of the parking area. Notice the deep, straight grooves that run the width of the wall. Drill bits carved these grooves as they cut deep into the granite during the construction of the dam. Shorter grooves are visible along the road as you drive up the last section leading to the parking area. Facing away from the dam toward the south, is a clear view of the waterfall as it cascades down to the powerhouse at Deadman Flat. As mighty as the falls are, in early spring after an exceptional winter, that entire wall from the dam outward is one solid sheet of churning water!

Take a moment to walk across the dam and view the spillway with the powerhouse located below.

In the late afternoon, the picnic table makes for a nice lunch area with a view. Primitive cinder block restrooms provide a good comfort margin before or after your journey.

The Loading Ordeal

Prior to dropping your gear over the top of the gate, have someone there to catch any errant bag or gear. The only level area for gear is at the base of the portico; the rest of the ramp slopes toward the water. The top of the cement dam casement is wide enough for bags and other gear, but do not place anything there that is light enough to blow over. Use the wooden gate as a base over which to slide your canoe. The wood is a lot easier on the gunnels than the surrounding cement.

When loading your boat, canoe, or kayak, load it bow light, so if the wind comes up, you have maneuverability on the bow and less danger of the bow broaching on a wave.

On the Water

Once the boat is loaded and you are underway, paddle on the north side of the reservoir and close to the shore. If the wind comes up, you stand a better chance of finding a small cove or beach to take shelter. Although the wind usually blows from west to east and will be at your back, stay close to shore to decrease the chance of an unfortunate accident. Also, Million Dollar Camp (*see map*) is on the same north side of the lake, making it easier to reach.

No matter which side of the lake you paddle, take a close look at the vegetation that grows along the shoreline. You've become so accustomed to seeing conifers as the primary forest tree, that the sight of oaks, vines and various shrubs replacing the pines surprises you. Your descent from the higher slopes of the mixed-evergreen forest has brought you to the transition zone between foothill riparian woodland and the mixed-pine belt. Look up to the top of the gorge and follow the evergreen forest down slope until the pines give way to the deciduous Black Oaks (*Quercus kelloggii*), Canyon Oak (*Quercus chrysolepis*) and tall dense stands of Manzanita (*Arctostaphylos*). Along the water's edge are the Willows (*Genus Salix*) and occasional Black Cottonwood (*Populus trichocarpa*). Growing in luminous green tangles within the shaded under story of the oaks, and a true indicator of a woodland environment, are vines of California Wild Grape (*Vitis californica*). Poison Oak (*Rhus diversiloba*) grows everywhere. This widespread shrub is seen as a single erect plant, low bush, or vine on nearby oaks.

As a matter of fact, you find poison oak is a common plant throughout the shore and backcountry of the reservoir. Take necessary precautions to prevent contact with any part of the plant (*See Paddle Note*).

Paddle Note:

Poison Oak, (Toxicodendron diversilobum or Rhus diversiloba): Information You're Itchin' to Know
(Translated from Latin as, the poison tree with leaves of different shape.)

Description

Poison oak is a highly diverse plant. It appears as an individual upright shoot, a small shrub, dense brush of various heights, or as a climbing vine. The plant's most identifiable feature is its individual leaves growing in groups of three which gives us the old adage, "shiny leaves of three, let it be; flowers of white, run in fright."

There is no set characteristic shape to the plant's leaves. Some of the leaves will be oval, others pointed, while still others, especially the older leaves, may be lobed and more rounded.

In the spring through early summer, the leaf surfaces are a shiny green, and new foliage is a deep florescent burgundy color. The flowers are whitish, hanging off the end of a leafy stalk in dense droplets. They range from 1-2 mm in length and have five petals and five sepals. The fruit are small berries either white or greenish-white, growing in small clusters. Each berry is approximately 5 mm long.

Poison oak is a deciduous plant and its leaves undergo a colorful fall display.

The poison tree with leaves of different shape is commonly called poison oak.

Range

Poison oak is one of the most common plants in California. Officially, the plant is found west of the Cascade and Sierra Nevada mountains from southwestern British Columbia, south through the Puget Trough to Northern Baja California. It is also found in the Virginia Mountains to the west of Pyramid Lake in Nevada.

In the Sierra Nevada Mountains, it grows below 5,000 feet.

Some authorities separate the plant into two categories: western poison oak found along the Pacific coast, and an eastern, low-growing shrub variety from New Jersey to Texas.

Its Toxin and Preventive Remedies

The volatile oil found in *all* parts of the plant that causes so much irritation to us, is *urushiol*. The plant's defense mechanism against insects produces the oil. Unfortunately, we get a severe rash when we come in contact with the discharge of this potent antigen.

It doesn't take much to initiate the release of the oil. Everything from a cut to the stalk, pressure on a leaf or the scraping of any part of the plant will induce a surface coating of urushiol. It takes anywhere from 12 to 48 hours for the characteristic linear rash to develop. Before this happens, you have approximately 10 minutes to wash the oil off with copious amounts of water. After 15 minutes of contact, the urushiol binds to skin proteins.

Contrary to many folk tales and remedies,

> *"Once the antigen is fixed, the antigen cannot be washed off or transferred to other areas. Scratching or oozing blister fluid cannot spread the antigen to other areas of the body or to other persons.*
>
> *New lesions that appear a few days after the primary lesions represent less sensitive areas or areas where less antigen was deposited, not spreading of the antigen."*

The entire sequence of exposure, contamination and reaction (immune response) usually lasts 12 to 15 days. As for wishing for a quick cure or remedy, the hoary response is: *if untreated, it'll last two weeks, but with treatment it'll go away within 14 days.*

The best remedy is to stay away from the stuff . . . but should you become exposed, wash the area as soon as possible with rubbing (isopropyl) alcohol, which removes the urushiol. Next, wash the area with generous amounts of water of any temperature to wash off the oils. Don't use soap at this time because the soap will pick up and move any urushiol the alcohol failed to remove around your body. Finally, if the opportunity presents itself, take a regular shower with warm water and soap. Remember to wash the clothing you were wearing when you came in contact with poison oak.

With luck, but don't count on it, you removed the oil in time, or are one of the very small percentage of people with an immunity to the antigen.

Once the reaction begins, the best course of action is to treat the itching skin with dressings of calamine lotion, Epsom salts, or bicarbonate of soda.

Million Dollar Camp

The sound of water rushing down rocks greets you at the entrance into the shelter of a cove that forms the rocky finger of Million Dollar Camp. As you paddle around the point, watch for partially submerged rocks along the shoreline. The sight of a mature black oak will mark the lovely gravel beach; the campsite is beyond the oak.

According to local lore, the camp was named, not so much for it's setting (it's definitely worth the million bucks), as it is for its crucial mid-lake location. The site is a welcome harbor for paddlers and fishermen who get caught on the lake during a big blow; hence, the phrase, "I'd give a million dollars for a safe camp right now . . ." provides the motto for the aptly named camp.

Approaching Million Dollar Camp from the water.

185

Unless you are pressed for time, spend at least one night at this campsite. At the very least, stop long enough for lunch and a swim. You are sheltered from the strong winds that blow in either direction, and there is enough of a breeze to keep the bugs at bay. The cove's shallow, warm water provides a perfect swimming area, and the deeper cove located next to the stream outlet that you first approached makes a nice fishing spot.

If you are fortunate to be here in the spring when the flowers are in bloom, the trail crossing the width of the rocky finger harbors several species of lovely wildflowers.

You might have picked up on the presence of one species by the subtle bouquet of mint. Look for the stalks with their purple blossoms that denote the presence of the Giant Hyssop or Horsemint (*Agastache urticifolia*).

Growing nearby, the brightly colored Harlequin Lupine (*Lupinus stiversii*) is a colorful background to the bland, colorless granitic soil. The "can't miss 'em" bunches of yellow mountain mule's ears add a cheerful presence to the campsite. Standing sentinel at the base of the point where the forest meets the shoreline is stately Jeffrey pine, which is recognizable by its bark's reddish color, the pineapple-shaped cones, and the vanilla odor emanating from the furrows in its bark.

Paddle Note:
On Waterfalls

The topmost layers of rock that cap the gorge are volcanic. In some areas the soil base consists primarily of cinders or cinders mixed with debris, scooped then dumped by melting glaciers. In other places, the topmost rock layers are weathering remnants of former lava flows. One such example is visible on the left, a few miles from the turnoff onto Ellis Road.

Whatever the geologic conditions that initiated the volcanic activity, the results produced a porous soil base. As a result, water from snowmelt or rainfall percolates rapidly through these unconsolidated layers of mixed volcanic and glacial sediment and then collects at the next layer of granitic rock. The granite is far less permeable than the layers above and thus traps the water. Gravity and fissures in the granite provide the water with a route to the nearest low point where the water starts its journey down the sidewalls of the gorge in which you paddle.

The finest and more readily visible of these falls are actually two falls that braid around an outcrop of resistant granite. Their locations are marked on the map. On the 7.5-Minute Quadrangle Topographical

Second Haven (Wild Grape Camp)

If caught on the east side of the lake when the wind begins to blow, there's another site, smaller and less extravagant than the Million Dollar Camp, but available as the "any-port-in-a-storm" site. I have named this site Wild Grape Camp on the map because it apparently lacks a name, and the ample presence of the vine seems fitting.

This small nipple of granite, located just up lake on the opposite shore, approximately one-half mile from Million Dollar Camp *(See map)*, provides ample harbor against the prevailing southwesterly wind, the uncommon easterly wind, and the resulting choppy waters. Depending on the reservoir's level, a small level beach and dry gravel strand sits in the center of the small cove covered with overhanging vines of wild grape. Use any portion of the beach to pitch your tent. At low water, use this same (but now wider) area or move to the small clearing under the oak grove on the top shelf of the granite ledge above the beach. The higher campsite has a ready-built fire ring that you reach by scrambling up the rocky ledge facing due south when viewing the cove from the water.

If the wind is blowing from the east or up canyon, the opposite side of Wild Grape Cove also contains a small beach but no level or dry site

Maps of the Calaveras Dome, you will see their location is just at the lower right margin of Section 36. The strong cascades of the falls are a result of two streams joining prior to entering the reservoir. The falls on the far left, located in a grotto with a canopy of oaks, is the more dynamic of the two. However, you miss out on a hidden treat if you view only the first of the two falls. Although the cascading water is partially hidden by vegetation, on closer inspection, a profusion of wildflowers snakes a pathway up the bed of the stream. Growing on the drier slopes surrounding the streambed is red paintbrush *(Family: Figwort)*, Bush or Sticky Monkeyflower *(Mimulus aurantiacus)* and Red Larkspur *(Delphinium nudicaule)*. Along the banks, and on moist areas adjacent to the stream, is a mixed bouquet of Crimson Columbine *(Aquilegia formosa)*, Scarlet Monkeyflower *(Mimulus cardinalis)* and Large Leaf Lupine *(Lupinus polyphyllus)*.

Head out toward the center of the lake as you paddle away from the falls. Give yourself a few strokes, and then bring the boat around for a broad view of the falls and surrounding terrain. If you take a few more strokes out, be sure to take in the view down-lake toward the dam. The perspective of the oily-looking, slick, calm surface of the reservoir retreating ever smaller within the shaded silhouette of its granite walls is worth the price of admission.

Campsite at the mouth of the Mokelumne River, where it joins the reservoir.

for camp. Due to the prevailing southwesterly winds, almost the entire strand of this beach is littered, several feet thick, with driftwood and other flotsam.

Note: Be careful walking on these logs; some are unstable, others contain nails or spikes; furthermore, snakes, including rattlesnakes, like to hunt for prey hiding among the debris. If scrambling on the granite or seeking a privy spot, watch for poison oak growing profusely all along the ledge and shoreline.

Upper Reservoir

Follow the eastern shore if you are on the upper end during the morning hours and the reservoir is calm. Paddle along this side in order to view several of the waterfalls descending their steep beds from the ridges capping the gorge.

Upper Bay and Mouth of the North Fork Mokelumne River

Upon entering the upper bay, look to your right at the high wall of stained granite. The light-colored stains come from water flowing or seeping from the springs above the granite rim. Locate the eroded notch at the rim of the granite and trace its origin by following the thin line of green vegetation growing along the stream that leads up to the notch. This is your first destination point, should you decide to hike the trail as described in *In the Eddy.* To make it easier to hike the trail, head for the campsite on the partially screened point of land near the belt of manzanita, oak and conifers on the far right of the upper bay and below the stained granite Otherwise, you will have to make your approach from the river.

Other campsites are along the tail end of the reservoir where it meets the river's mouth and at the far left end of the cove. None of the campsites are visible from the water; some are run-down and some are cleaner than others. You need to put-in and walk to each site. Try to take a campsite that is not totally screened by the trees, thus allowing for a breeze. The mosquitoes and biting flies are numerous and pesky, so try to get a site farther away from the river's mouth due to the still water at the log jam that you see spinning in the eddy below the falls where the river meets the lake. The campsite at the far north end of the cove, below the stained granite, is the next best choice. Although you are away from the areas of interest and the fishing spots along the river, you gain privacy, an airy camp, and a grand view.

Sources and References:

Durham, David, L., *Place-Names of California's Gold Country*. Clovis: Word Dancer Press, 2000.

Hill, Mary, *Geology of the Sierra Nevada*. Berkeley: University of California Press, 1975.

Storer, Tracy and Robert L. Usinger, *Sierra Nevada Natural History*. Berkeley: University of California Press, 1963.

In the Eddy:
The Hike to Salt Springs Pond and Blue Hole

The best way to appreciate this end of the reservoir's grandeur is to hike the short but rugged one plus-mile loop up to the picturesque Blue Hole on the North Fork Mokelumne River by way of the Salt Springs Pond.

The starting point to the hike is the granite ledge containing the salt basins where the stream flows down from the notch visible upon entering the cove.

Before you begin your hike, take time to explore this shelf. Notice the bedrock mortars as you hike over the smaller ledge; they are partially hidden by the large manzanita shrub growing at the foot of the small ledge used to reach this larger rock shelf. Numerous *cupule* depressions

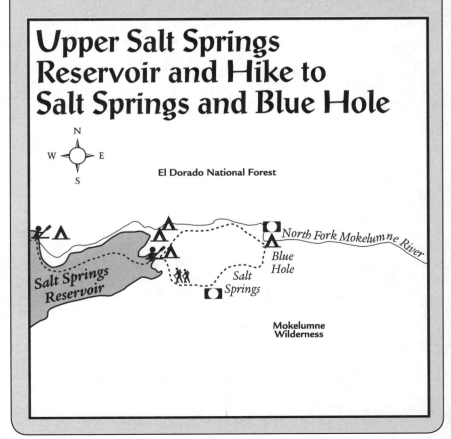

Upper Salt Springs Reservoir and Hike to Salt Springs and Blue Hole

The Native Americans living in the area later used these potholes, created through the action of water during the last glacial period, for the collection of salt, visible as the lighter colored stains surrounding the holes.

are cut into the rock to form cups; almost all are several inches deep and are aligned in parallel rows. Their depth is a good indicator of continued usage. Visible on the sloping larger ledge above the mortars are natural and man-made features unique to this area. Walk to the rock wall that faces southeasterly and you come upon the first of many drilled potholes. These excavated, round holes are scattered the length of the ledge, in a north-south direction and are examples of classic potholes, which were probably formed during the last glacial activity that carved this canyon. These potholes are described as:

> " . . . Circular holes with steep sides excavated into a riverbed by cobbles or boulders being spun around continuously in a circular turbulent eddy."—*Guyton, Bill,* Glaciers of California, *p. 169.*

Adjacent to some of these potholes, especially the ones close to the seep where water is slowly flowing and the salt encrustation is thickest, is a network of pecked, shallow trenches that lead to shallow man-made depressions resembling mortars described earlier. I suspect that former Native Americans facilitated the formation and collection of salt by pecking the smaller depressions along with the shallow trenches into the granite. This man-made system was used, in part, to allow water ladened with a concentration of salts and other minerals, a place to evaporate. As the water seeped from the larger natural basins or streamed into the carved trenching, the shallowness of the cupules allowed the water to evaporate quickly, consequently, leaving behind a salt residue, which was scooped into containers for trade or use by the gatherers.

To begin your hike, follow the stream as it flows down from the notch. If no water is flowing, just follow the bleached surface upward toward the V-shaped cut in the granite ledge above you. Once you reach the notch eroded by the flow of spring runoff, turn around and admire the view of the granite ledge below you and of the lake as it follows the shape of its former river gorge. Stay away from the streambed walls at the base of the notch as they are covered with poison oak. Continue upward with one last pitch over a small outcrop of granite, and you are soon standing on salt-encrusted gravel with an unexpected view of a pond overgrown with tule.

Salt Springs Pond

If you are carrying the Calaveras Dome 7.5-Minute Quadrangle Topographical Map, the body of water in front of you is listed as Salt Springs. This pond, which is a series of upwelling springs, is the source of the salt forming on the granite ledge below.

In the spring, when the accumulated snow begins to melt, the surface area of the pond overflows into the steep bed where you are standing. The water cascades through the notch, causing further erosion each season and flows onto the granite-wide expanse before spilling into the reservoir. When the water level recedes below the pond's natural spillway, the sun evaporates the water that bleaches the granite, leaving the

Salt Creek Pond, with the upper end of Salt Springs Reservoir partially visible in the background.

concentration of salts behind. This same melting snow helps dilute the salts gathering in the pond, allowing the Sedges *(Family: Cyperaceae)*, Tule or Bulrush *(Scirpus acutus)* and other vegetation around the rim of the pond to grow.

A trail of sorts follows the rim of the pond on your right and passes through the pines growing at the base of the granite ledge that borders the southeastern side. After a short walk on the trail, look for an exposed granite ledge whose surface is eroding as a result of exfoliation. *(See Lower Bear Lake, In the Eddy: Hiking Through a Glacial Landscape).* This exfoliated granite marks the entrance to a rock shelter. I did not spot any signs of habitation by either man or animal; on the other hand, I could roughly estimate how long the boulders lay here by looking at how the oak trunks shaped themselves around several of the largest boulders.

From here to where the trail ascends onto the granite, you pass through a duff-covered floor littered by debris from the dead pines that form a perimeter around the pond's shoreline. Many of the pine limbs contain round growths called *galls* and are symptomatic of a prevalent pine disease called Western Gall Rust *(Peridermium harknessii).*

Eventually, the duff-covered forest floor ends, and you climb to the granite outcrop at the northeastern end of the pond. From here, you gain a great view of the pond's layout, the surrounding vegetation and a small glimpse of Salt Creek Reservoir. In the spring, take a few minutes to study the nesting antics of the blackbirds. Many of the male birds have the distinct wing patch of the red-winged blackbird. The males vigorously defend their territories against fellow blackbirds and other predators or potential predators, such as a passing hiker. Do not be surprised if a plucky red-wing considers you a threat and attempts to drive you away with a series of high-angled dives that would make a fighter pilot proud. Any raven, song bird or any other animal species that unwittingly passes through the nesting area comes under attack by scores of these aggressive birds.

From your perch on the granite, the trail disappears and you now rely on the small rock *ducks* assembled on the granite to mark your direction of travel. Look for a clearing running in a southerly direction down slope past the oak and manzanita bordering the granite outcrop on which you stand. From the clearing, continue down, angling to the southeast until you intersect a creek bed. This is the Bellflour Canyon. Follow the creek bed until it intersects Mattley Creek, the main creek. You will recognize it by the strong flow and the many moss-covered boulders in its bed. Dodge the mosquitoes and follow the creek northward toward the river to Blue Hole.

Where the North Fork of the Mokelumne River enters the Blue Hole, *visible beyond the white water.*

Following the southern bank of the creek, you will find fewer hazards and obstacles than on the northern side. Hike over the creek bed bank, taking your time and watching your footing. The bank's cobbles are not only slick, but also unstable.

Where the ground levels out, you see a huge fallen black oak and spot several fire rings made by former campers. Before hiking through the last bit of forest and brush to the river, take a moment to view the beautiful varieties of wildflowers growing along the shady bank of the creek. Interspersed amongst the flowers are luscious clumps of Lady Ferns *(Athyrium filix-femina).*

The Blue Hole

Your first sight of the famous Blue Hole on the Mokelumne is all you've heard of and more. The dark- blue, circular-shaped basin of water, rotating counter-clockwise, as it is fed by a churning mass of water cascading down from a slick granite chute, is definitely a view to remember.

Picture a large bowl, like a dog's water dish. As you attempt to fill it using a hose, the jet stream entering the bowl causes the water to rotate in a circle as it fills the receptacle; in essence, the river is the hose squirting its water into the bowl, which is the Blue Hole.

The basin itself is approximately 200-feet long and considered a small lake that is fed from a combination of the North Fork of the Mokelumne River, and waters from Bellflour Canyon and Mattley

Creeks. The river's water does not just flow into this small lake, but arrives in a thunderous roar of white water directly from a constricted flume eroded into a nearby granite bench (the proverbial hose). The force of the inflow creates a giant eddy that provides a merry-go-round-like journey to any flotsam that is spit into the lake. As a result, huge piles of bark, polished driftwood, and assorted debris, cover the rocky shoreline. Sorting through the mass produces all sorts of interesting refuse and is fun to explore. My favorite items are the water-worked chips of tree bark. Some pieces are 6-8 inches in circumference and have a lovely patina showing off the bark pattern. Other favorites are the pieces of shaped driftwood that lie piled in heaps around the lake—everything from polished limbs of downed trees, to huge rounded burls are strewn into deep debris piles.

What's missing, mostly, is man-made debris, except for the occasional beer can or piece of plastic. The majority of the debris comes from nature and in a perverse way—this is refreshing to see.

The mouth of Mattley Creek, where it enters the hole, is worthy of inspection. Lining the upper bench just before the creek cascades down into the lake is a tangled jungle of willows, alders, vines, and ferns. Three or more varieties grow abundantly in the area. Magnificent fern clumps grow on rocky islands along the creek's banks. Peeking daintily through the overgrowth of alders and willows that line the upper creek bed are the California Maiden-hair (*Adiantum jordani*) fronds. Providing a bright green backdrop, not to mention a prehistoric look to the forest floor, are mats of Brake or Bracken (*Pteridium aquilinum*).

Growing along the mouth of the stream are various mosses and stalks of Common Horsetail (*Equisetum arvense*).

Climb to the lip of granite that overlooks the rocky chute to see a series of cream-colored veins in the granitic bedrock. These veins, or *dikes*, are intrusions of once molten minerals that were injected into the granitic bedrock by following weak cracks or joints in the granite. The dikes' interesting pattern is clearly visible due to the removal of the overburden followed by a scouring of the region through the work of prehistoric glaciers and the continued polish by the river.

To return to the lake and camping area, follow the trail along the bank of the secondary flood channel south of the main river channel, where a small side stream flows. Pick up the trail by hiking through the trees along the southern bank of the Blue Hole. The trail eventually drops down to the rock-strewn flood channel and meanders through the field of boulders to the area where the channel joins the main river. Stay to the far left, and look for a ledge of barren granite that parallels the main channel. Follow the narrow footpath eroded into the ledge to where the main river channel enters the lake. On the wide-sloping ledge below the small waterfall that enters the lake are numerous bowl-shaped potholes similar to the ones you explored at the beginning of the hike. Smaller and shallower mortar-like depressions, along with shallow trenches that lead from the natural bowls to the smaller depressions, are visible in the late afternoon sun.

To reach your starting point where you left your boat, hike over the lip of granite and drop down to the ledge leading to the oak glen that harbors the campsite. Where the trail enters the main clearing of the campsite, look down to your right onto a small granite boulder. The lone rock holds a single, deep cup of a bedrock mortar that is evidence of man's use of this area and provides a fitting touch to your day of exploration.

Sources and References:

Graf, Michael, *Plants of the Tahoe Basin*. Sacramento: California Native Plant Society Press, 1999.

Guyton, Bill, *Glaciers of California*. Berkeley: University of California Press, 1998.

Wood, David L., Thomas W. Koerber, Robert F. Scharpf, and Andrew J. Storer, *Pests of the Native California Conifers*. Berkeley: University of California Press, 2003.

REGION II: HIGH COUNTRY LAKES OF THE MOKELUMNE RIVER
PADDLING AREA 4: LAKE TABEAUD

Position: 38°20.35'N, 120°39.45'W

Difficulty: No major obstacles in lake; however, be careful paddling the area near the stream inlet. Avoid a partially inundated fence line; during heavy runoff, large eddies form at the mouth of the outlet.

Trip length: The lake is extremely small—you can comfortably paddle it in an hour or less.

Portage: None.

Paddle Distance: None.

Season: Because the lake is located in a transition zone, the weather conditions allow paddling from late winter through fall. As in all reservoirs run by utility companies, it is the water level that dictates availability for use.

Size: 0.5 mile long by 0.1 mile wide.

The Amador Canal, affectionately known by locals as The Ditch, *runs through the edge of the Lake Tabeaud picnic area.*

197

Elevation: 2,000 feet.

County: Amador County.

National Forest: None.

Wilderness Area: None. Lake Tabeaud Recreational Area is owned and operated by Pacific Gas and Electric Company (PG&E).

Maps:

USGS 7.5-Minute Quadrangle Topographical Map Series: Mokelumne Hill, CA.

Road Maps:

Compass Maps Inc.: Alpine, Amador and Sacramento Counties.

California State Automobile Association (AAA) Map: Central California – Bay Area to Lake Tahoe.

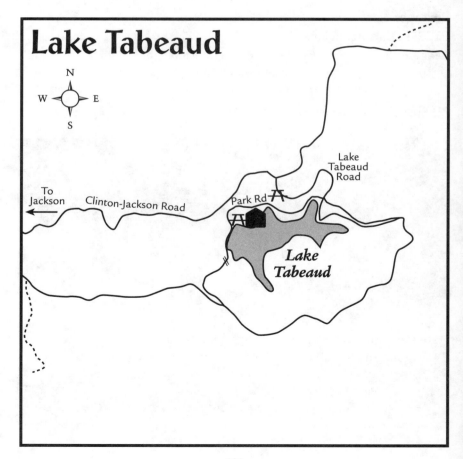

View of the Lake from the picnic area. Two fishermen enjoying the morning calm on the lake.

Historical Background:

Prior to 1934, the lake was listed as Tabeaud Reservoir. Another, smaller lake, listed as Petty Reservoir existed at or near the present location of Lake Tabeaud. In 1948, the reservoir was listed as Lake Tabeaud on the Mokelumne Hill 7.5-Minute Quadrangle Topographical Map.

Locals, affectionately call the historic Amador Canal The Ditch, as it runs 23.2 miles from Lake Tabeaud Reservoir to Tanner Reservoir. The canal provides raw water that is treated at Tanner and becomes part of the drinking water for Jackson, Sutter Creek, Ione and Amador City. Canal construction began in 1870 and was completed in 1874.

Access:

Lake Tabeaud is located east of Jackson off California State Hwy. 49.

From Hwy. 49 in downtown Jackson, exit on to Clinton Road heading east. Pass the Department of Motor Vehicles (DMV), and the new California Highway Patrol, (CHP) buildings. Cross Broadway and continue on Clinton Road for 5 miles. Exit right onto Pine Grove-Tabeaud Road. Continue for 2 miles and turn right into the Lake Tabeaud Picnic Area

Note: If you come upon a large happy face sprayed onto the trunk of an oak, you have driven past the entrance.

Upon entering the day-use area, follow the road past the first set of picnic tables and park at the first available spot overlooking the lake. If the area is crowded, or you want a more private spot, follow the road past the

The sign says it all!

spillway (unless it is full of water) and park in the cleared area on your left just before crossing the earthen dam.

Heads Up:

- Access is free; day-use only.
- Site contains toilet facilities, picnic tables and grills.
- A small yet pleasant family lake located high enough to enjoy the transition into pine, and be accessible in late winter and early spring.
- Bear country—pack and camp smart!
- No gasoline engines allowed on the lake.

Note: The nearby PG&E reservoir of Tiger Creek has a NO BOATING ordinance and does allow camping.

Description:

The paddlers living near Stockton or the south-central foothills have access to a lovely lake at no cost, other than the gas to drive there. Lake Tabeaud is situated in a valley that protects the lake from heavy winds and is at the right elevation to keep it from becoming snowed-in.

This is *the* spot to paddle if you want to introduce your new canoe or kayak to the family or test-drive it before undertaking a more ambitious paddle. The drawdown PG&E takes for its hydroelectric use is the greatest drawback to this lake. The drive to the lake is so picturesque that, no matter what the level of the lake, there is still plenty of hiking, biking and sightseeing to be enjoyed.

The very late stage of winter, usually around late February or early March is a great time to make one's way here. The hills are green and the air is clean and crisp, yet you still feel the sun's warmth as the day grows. Migrating waterfowl stop over on many of these small lakes near their routes. It is always a surprise to find small bands of duck or wild geese taking a break from their long flight. The resident mallards and farm geese also act as enticements for the wilder species.

Pack a picnic lunch and a fishing pole and you are set for an outing at the lake.

Make a slow paddle to the west shoreline and keep your eyes on the shadows over the coves for wild ducks feeding or just hiding out. Deer come out to drink or browse near the shore. Paddle toward the mouth of the stream where the resident ducks and geese sun on the bank near the green patch of grassy shore at the main launch point.

Make your approach closer to the inlet, but be wary of the sudden current and look for the submerged fence, or riprap, that lies concealed under the waters.

The small pier with pipeline off the upper east shore houses the pump that controls the lake's water level. Across the cove, on the eastside past the pump station, is a rounded point of shoreline that provides a nice shaded beach where you can take-out. This site has a grand view of the lake and forest extending below the dam, and is also a nice fishing area and picnic spot.

Eventually, the sun's warmth fades, the coots chase each other or a hapless mallard across the lake, and it is time to pack it all up and paddle back to load up the family steed. That new boat is now a treasured member of the family, and everyone vows to make Lake Tabeaud a family's yearly prelude to summer.

Sources and References:

Durham, David L., *Place-Names of California's Gold Country Including Yosemite National Park*. Clovis: Quill Driver Books and Word Dancer Press, 2000.

Stienstra, Tom, *California Boating and Watersports*. San Francisco: Foghorn Press, 1996.

"You can have your city job, and your clubs, and such; But I'll tell you now, I don't like 'em much. I'm a roughwater man."

— *Henry Elwyn Blake, Boatman,*
Colorado River Expeditions.

Summit Lake in the morning calm.

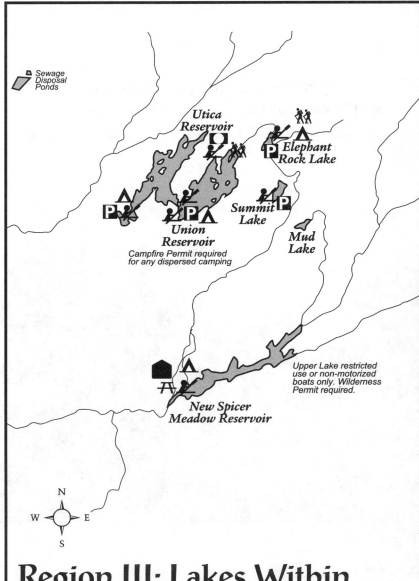

Sewage Disposal Ponds

Utica Reservoir

Elephant Rock Lake

Summit Lake

Union Reservoir
Campfire Permit required
for any dispersed camping

Mud Lake

Upper Lake restricted
use or non-motorized
boats only. Wilderness
Permit required.

New Spicer Meadow Reservoir

N
W • E
S

Region III: Lakes Within The Stanislaus River Drainage (California's Scenic Highway 4 Corridor)

Region III: Lakes Within
The Stanislaus River Drainage
(California's Scenic Highway 4 Corridor)

The sky is a deep shade of blue turning to black; afternoon puffballs slowly build into huge cloud patterns resembling nineteenth century battleships, sweep majestically overhead. A varied pattern of color in different shades of green mark stands of pines, fir, cedar, and on the higher slopes, the twisted trunks of juniper dominate the landscape. Vast stretches of glaciated, granitic rock glisten in the sunlight.

When the breeze picks up, you feel a chill, even in mid-afternoon. There is a crispness in the air not felt in the lower elevations and shortness of breath is common.

Arriving at Utica Reservoir, your first view of the lake is obscured by thick growths of conifers. Get out of your vehicle and walk to the lake's edge where the grandeur of the place strikes home. A long, narrow channel, bordered by rounded domes of granitic rock, catches your eye. Islands of various sizes and shapes are spaced randomly throughout a nearby cove. The first hint of a gentle breeze carries the tang of pine and wood smoke. Yellow-green patterns from wind-blown pine pollen swirl on the lake's breeze-driven surface. Somewhere in the distance a squirrel chatters and a jay responds.

Paddle beyond the channel to enter the Lilliputian-like bay covered with elongated islands, whose surfaces are bedecked with a mixture of conifers. Various-sized erratics, lying where retreating glaciers dumped them, are scattered about like loose marbles.

Caught in the maze of coves and inlets, you can easily become disoriented before locating the correct passage that leads to the portage site for Union Reservoir. Suddenly, a high-pitched noise, not unlike a moose in distress, echoes off the granite. This is your first encounter with the infamous Boy Scouts of America camp at Utica Lake, where the sound of the dying bugle awakens man, as well as beast.

All is not lost, however. By following the strident noise to its source, the disoriented paddler locates the portage route into the upper lake. A short carry-over through the Boy Scout fire circle leaves you gazing outward onto the lower end of Union Lake.

Arrive early for a choice parking space near the beach and your put-in.

If paddling Utica Lake resembles a fantasy land of elfin dimensions, then paddling on Union Lake approximates the solid, no-nonsense lakes in the North Woods of Canada. Yes, there are islands, but one can easily accept their dimensions, making them appear more true to form. Unlike the open, friendly and sun-sparkled granite country of Utica, walls of trees guard Union's shoreline. This adds to the mystery of what lies beyond the lake's shoreline. Hikes involve quickly scaling graduated domes of granite, rewarding the paddler-turned-hiker with stunning views of the two lakes or the Upper Gorge of the Stanislaus River.

A short driving distance from Utica and Union lakes, are Elephant Rock and Summit, two natural alpine lakes providing a more intimate setting for a canoe or kayak. Two pygmy lakes, nestled among the tall conifers, provide paddlers with an opportunity to relax, drop a fishing line and watch the trees sway to the natural rhythm of the wind.

Just a few miles farther, the treacherous waters of Spicer wait. Here lies the big dog of the reservoirs. While Utica and Union lakes give the paddler difficulty when the winds act up, the wind and wave combinations of Spicer Lake is downright frightening. With that said, however, these same waters provide the paddler with an early morning or late afternoon view that can be described only as breathtaking!

Here is a true body of water, with miles upon miles of shoreline, begging to be explored. Campsites are where you find them, and the views are extraordinary. At night, the heavens are filled with myriad stars, the constellations easily discernible, and during a full moon you can see the granite sparkle from the moonlight catching the individual crystals.

Sources and References:

Browning, Peter, *Place-Names of the Sierra Nevada*. Berkeley: Wilderness Press, 1992.

Durham, David L., *Place-Names of California's Eastern Sierra*. Clovis: Word Dancer Press, 2001.

REGION III: LAKES WITHIN THE STANISLAUS RIVER DRAINAGE PADDLING AREA 1: UTICA RESERVOIR

Position: 38°26.00'N, 120°00.00'W

Difficulty: Utica Reservoir is a major destination for kayaking and canoeing. Despite the strong afternoon winds that blow over the main lake, this is family boating and camping at its best. In the early morning, the beautiful alpine reservoir appears glassy as you paddle on the water.

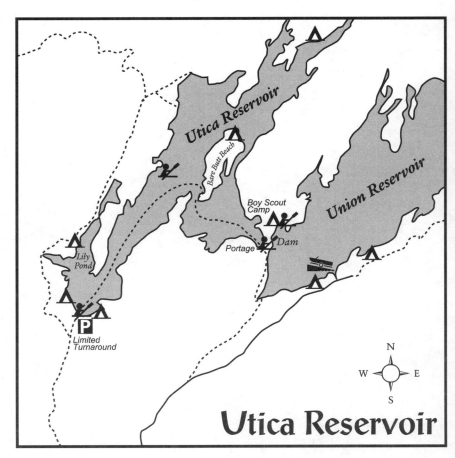

Utica Reservoir

The main put-in and take-out for Utica Reservoir.

However, as you leave, the prevailing wind is at your back; consequently, you face a strong headwind on your return.

As the summer progresses and the waters of the reservoir draw down, be alert for barely submerged granite outcrops that may damage your craft. These outcrops usually occur as you are rounding a point or nearing an island area.

Trip Length: An outing on Utica or the other nearby reservoirs is usually treated as a weekend trip due to the driving distances required. Therefore, paddling adventures can be either single- or multi-day outings.

Portage: None—unless you want to paddle Union Reservoir by way of Utica, if so, a short portage is required.

Paddle Distance: 0.5 mile one-way from the put-in to Bare Butt Beach;

1 mile one-way from the put-in to the dam at Duck Creek;

1.5 mile one-way from the put-in to mouth of south finger upper lake;

1 mile one-way from the put-in to portage site for Union Reservoir.

Season: From late spring when the snow melts, through summer. By late August, the water level is drawn down to the point where cattle and hikers roam where canoes and kayaks drifted earlier in the season.

Note: Due to increased popularity of this area, plan your trip around mid-week or a Sunday-Monday.

Lake size: 1.75 by 0.75 mile.

Elevation: 6,819 feet.

County: Utica Reservoir straddles the county lines of Alpine County to the north and Tuolumne County to the south.

National Forest/Wilderness Area: Stanislaus National Forest, Calaveras Ranger District.

Wilderness Area: The reservoir is adjacent to the Carson-Iceberg Wilderness

Maps:

USGS 7.5-Minute Quadrangle Topographical Map Series: Tamarack, CA and Spicer Meadow Reservoir, CA.

National Forest Service/Wilderness Area: Stanislaus National Forest, Calaveras Ranger District, Carson-Iceberg Wilderness (Stanislaus and Toiyabe National Forests). This map is the best one for the area.

Road Maps:

Compass Maps Inc.: Calaveras and Tuolumne County Communities, Alpine, Amador and Sacramento Counties.

California State Automobile Association (AAA) Maps: Lake Tahoe and Northern Sierra Map and Guide.

Historical Background:

Built in 1905 by the Utica Gold Mining Company, this was later owned by the Union Water Company. The dam was intended to provide ample water

One of the many picturesque granite islands that dot the lake.

210

for the parent company's mining and milling operations, as well as water for drinking and electricity for Calaveras County.

Cement for the Utica dams was shipped by rail to Angel's Camp, loaded into freight wagons and hauled by four- and six-horse teams to a storage site near present-day Lake Alpine.

Access:

Access California State Hwy. 4 East at Angels Camp, CA. Continue on Hwy. 4 for approximately 32 miles. Prior to your turn-off, look for a sign indicating Spicer Reservoir Road Exit. Turnoff at Forest Service Road 7N01 (Spicer Reservoir Road).

Follow the Forest Service road for approximately 8.5 miles before turning left onto Forest Service Road 7N75. This turnoff is easily missed. It is not clearly marked. Look for a wooden sign adjacent to a gravel road exit on your left. The gravel exit and sign will appear in the middle of a series of sharp bends.

Approximately 1 mile farther, the road forks. Take the left fork for Utica Reservoir. The right fork leads to Union Reservoir. Utica Reservoir is 2 miles farther.

When you reach the reservoir, take the first right leading down into the lake if you plan to off load your boat for either a day paddle or a multi-day trip. You will come to a small dirt parking area surrounded by campers. Look for the two signs that warn you of a 20-minute loading period. If there are any adjacent head-in parking spaces near the signs, park there and off load at your leisure (that way you are not blocking the turn-around, nor are you disobeying the 20-minute time period).

Heads Up:

- Last minute "Oops, I forgot" items may be purchased in Tamarack approximately 1 mile past the Spicier Reservoir Road exit off Hwy. 4.
- Located within the Calaveras Ranger District Hwy. 4 / P.O. Box 500, Hathaway Pines, CA (209.795.1381).
- A Fire Permit is required for dispersed camping. You may pick one up at the Calaveras Ranger District Office, or at the U.S. Forest Ranger Station off Hwy. 4 east of Dorrington.
- The three lakes—Utica, Union and Spicer—have become major canoe/kayak destinations. Be prepared for crowded conditions on summer weekends and holidays.
- As yet, there are no required fees or permits (other then the fire permit during the summer fire season). *No-Trace Camping* guidelines are the proper camping procedures for this region.
- Bear country—pack and camp smart!
- No potable sources of water—bring your own or use a filtration system.

- Many of the camping sites are on bare granite; bring a foam pad or other *tush cush*, as it keeps those aches and pains down to a tolerable minimum.

Description:

Until you walk to the lake's edge to take in the view, it seems like a long drive just to paddle another mountain lake. Ah, but that view certainly cleared the fuzzies from the drive and started the heart a-thumpin'!

Imagine a lake filling an elongated bowl of ice-carved granite, its surface aglow from sunlight sparkling off it. Islands of various size and shape containing spires of pine and juniper stretch to the horizon. In the far distance, enormous pillows of clouds are building and their whiteness is a sharp contrast against the cobalt blue sky. This sets the mood for your time on Utica Lake.

The only fray in this silver lining involves the timing to enjoy a peaceful paddle. You must be ready to go before the wind comes up in the morning or after it dies down in the late afternoon. The lake's location causes it to act as a funnel for the westerly wind that creates strong gusts, making boat handling and casual paddling very difficult.

Do not dismay. When you put-in with the wind a-blowing, you will have a tail wind to take you to the upper lake, and, once you're within the islands, the coves are in the lee of the wind.

Lower Lake

Immediately upon beginning your paddle, before you get carried away with wanting to explore the upper regions of the lake, take the time to familiarize yourself with the small bay at your put-in site. To your left (west), the bay contains several picturesque rock formations separated by the lake. Beyond the islets, the cove narrows onto a tight gap that serves as an entrance into a lovely lily pond. Paddle past the entrance and enjoy the sight of water lilies whose large leaves float on the surface. Occasional yellow flowers with long stems bob to the rhythm of the wakes produced by wind and your paddle.

Stop paddling, and as your boat floats on the surface you will see fish and giant pollywogs darting around the lily pads. If other parties have not disturbed the pond, look for the great blue heron standing motionless and attempting to hide in the shadows near the shore. Canada geese, along with their goslings, like to feed here on the sedges and other aquatic plants.

Notice several campsites tucked into the trees on the shore at the far end of the pond and at the shoreline of the larger cove. Dispersed camping is allowed around the lake and this is part of the reason for the area's

Utica resembles a land of elfin dimensions.

popularity. By summer, the entire lakefront adjacent to the road becomes a tent city. To escape the noise and confusion, your only hope is to paddle into the main lake, turn your bow up the lake, and let the breeze push you into the fairyland of granite and conifer.

Upper Lake

Even here, however, you will not escape the tents, boats, and gear partially hidden among the trees. But the numbers are reduced dramatically, and there is always that next island with that small glassy cove just a short paddle away.

Pushing up the elongated channel of the reservoir, you notice the broad width of the valley that harbors the reservoir and the granite ridges beyond. The grinding, plucking, and polishing forces, characteristic of glaciers, created all this. The broad U-shaped valley that you are paddling in was formed by the work of an ancient glacier. The familiar, narrow, V-shaped valley, created by the swift running river, has been drastically widened and straightened through intense grinding, polishing and plucking activities of the ice. This polishing is clearly evident by the reflective shimmer viewed on the sunlit granite walls. To see this up-close and personal, hike on any of the bare rock surfaces adjacent to the shoreline, and look for exceptionally smooth and brightly reflective granite sections. This glacial polish was created when mud-covered ice, under enormous pressure at the base of the glacier, slid or abraded over the surface.

As you make your way farther up the lake, resist the urge to pick a campsite until you have reached the mass of islands beyond the primary campsite at the dam. As you approach, and before actually seeing the dam's outline, you will spot an orange and white buoy line. The dam itself will appear on your left to the northwest.

This dam is important because it acts as a reference point for the first of two entrances into the cove that lead to the portage trail up to Union Reservoir. Just before the dam becomes visible, there's a narrow gap angling to the southeast. Look for this on your right; it is the first entrance leading into the cove separating the two reservoirs.

Immediately to your left is a large island with a broad sandy beach that surrounds the island. This is the largest open beach on both lakes. Its local name, Bare Butt Beach, is aptly named. Nowadays, because of the increased traffic, the beach serves as a great day-use area for families with kids. You may also camp here, but, because of its central location, visitors are constantly paddling by.

The second entrance into the portage cove, stretching easterly to your right, is known as Boy Scout Cove (for reasons to be discloses a bit later). It is located on the other side of the finger-like pine-covered ridge. If you plan to camp at Utica and paddle on Union Reservoir, you most likely will approach from this second channel.

Now, for that little bit about why the cove is named the Boy Scout Cove: A well-established Boy Scouts of America camp is located at the far end of that cove and, incidentally, this is the location for the portage trail and the site of Union Reservoir Dam. If you are lucky enough to be on the lake before camp opens, or between sessions, consider yourself very fortunate. How will you know if you're not? Well, the first clue is the resonance of what at first sounds like a dying moose; in reality, it is a well-used bugle. The second clue is the din of young males having the time of their lives, their chorus of voices reflecting the different pitches of their maturity. In their defense, the scouts rigidly follow the *good neighbor policy* and cease noisy activities by 9 p.m.

Consequently, unless you enjoy wholesome noise, you might want to camp elsewhere. If, by chance, you are blessed to be on the lake when the scouts are absent, stake a claim to the ridge tucked inside the entrance on your right upon entering the cove. Here, you have a campsite with a view of the cove, a portion of Union Reservoir, and on the far horizon, the tops of The Dardanelles (a former volcanic flow now guarding the southern boundary of the Carson-Iceberg Wilderness).

A series of smaller pocket coves are located at the southern end of the cove, near your site. Even during the height of the wind in the afternoon, these waters remain a glassy calm thanks to the forested ridge that cups the southern boundary. Here, you can enjoy a swim, fish for trout or just relax and enjoy the view.

If the site is already taken, continue paddling past the dam and look for a place either on one of the larger islands, or stake your camp on the shoreline bordering the upper regions of Utica Lake.

A well-learned hint on finding that perfect campsite: look for a site away from the woodsy areas and with some breeze to keep the mosquitoes at bay. It's not the bears you have to worry about (although you should take proper precautions) it's the rascally little rodents! At night, mice and the ground squirrels gnaw holes in your food packs to get your goodies. Either hang or stow your foodstuff before retiring for the night. By the way, don't make the mistake of thinking you are safe from Mr. Bear by camping on an island. Bears are excellent swimmers, and if they zero in on a satisfying scent . . . well, dinner is just a swim away!

Last, but not least, if an area looks appealing but no immediate camping site is visible, don't hesitate to beach your boat and check out the area on foot. Many excellent sites are not readily visible from your boat. Many of the campsites I have fond memories of are ones I found by actively searching them out. This also allows you to stretch your legs, take a break, and become familiar with the lay of the land.

Exploring the many nooks and crannies of the reservoir, you come upon several buoy lines marking off the small check dams that impound the waters of the reservoir. These short, concrete features are located at the drainages forming the upper boundaries of the reservoir. Usually, small lily-covered ponds can be seen beyond the dams. Unfortunately, these ponds are a breeding ground for mosquitoes, although deer and other wildlife can be observed here, too. When you decide to explore the area on foot, be sure to cover yourself appropriately, even during the middle of the day.

If camping on an island does not appeal to you, there are other options. One area that has many good features, namely, being far enough away from the noisy scout camp and the main body of other paddlers, is located at the mid-point of the right (northeastern) finger-like channel fed by an intermittent stream *(See sections 21 and 22 of the Carson-Iceberg Wilderness Map).* Paddle past the cluster of small islands, past the second entrance into Boy Scout Cove, enter the narrow channel, and the site is on your left, above a granite lip near a small pine grove.

Another option is to take a hike up the granite streambed for some outstanding views of the reservoir.

If you are planning to include Union Reservoir as part of the paddling experience, make the portage between Utica and Union rather than driving and putting in at one of the shoreline sites. In the summer, most sites along Union Reservoir are crowded with campers; consequently, the narrow parking area has few, if any, areas for easy unloading and loading of boats. Compounding this, you have to carry your boat and gear through the trees onto a shoreline that provides no easy access to your boat.

Portage Route from Utica to Union Reservoir

As I mentioned earlier, there are two access points from Utica into Boy Scout Cove where the portage route is located. If you access the cove directly from the put-in beach at Utica, paddle down the main channel until you spot the sandy beach of Bare Butt Island. Look to your right for a narrow entrance. Paddle past the entrance into Boy Scout Cove. Looking due east, you will spot a flag pole and a line of beached boats. This is the general area of the camp, and the location of the portage site.

As you paddle across the cove, look to your left and you will spot the mouth of the second entrance used by paddlers entering from upper Utica.

Approach the eastern end of the cove and look for a bare granite ledge with a flagpole and a lineup of beached paddle craft and sailboats. Continue past the flagpole and take- out at the flat granite ledge that extends into the water. If the ledge is occupied, look for a submerged grassy area to the right of it and around the belt of trees growing at the base of a granite knoll. You will have to take-out in the shallow, grass-choked shore. Hike to the top of the same granite knoll, past the campfire circle and onto the concrete base of the dam (the entire hike is approximately 200 feet).

Near a gate leading to a walkway at the top of the dam, where the scouts' motorboats are beached, is a level, sandy area, large enough for two paddle craft. This beach is part of the cove of Union Reservoir which you will notice leaving the tree line above the granite knoll.

The second access into Boy Scout Cove and the portage site is located east of the first entrance and around the tip of the large island that acts as the left (upper) shoreline of the first entrance. More then likely, however, your approach will be from the northeast, especially if you have been exploring or camping on upper Utica. Because of the many nearby islands, locating the entrance may require judicious route finding along with some downright good guesswork. The trick is to separate the islands' shorelines from the mainland shoreline. Once that is accomplished, use the mainland shoreline to guide you to the entrance located between the mainland and the eastern shore of the large island across from "Bare Butt Beach."

Enter the channel leading into Boy Scout Cove and proceed, using the same directions described earlier, as if you were entering from the first entrance, whose channel mouth you spotted on your right as you entered the main body of the cove. *(See Paddling Area 2: Union Reservoir for a description.)*

Sources and References:

Whitney, Stephen, *The Sierra Nevada A Sierra Club Naturalist's Guide*. San Francisco: Sierra Club Books, 1979.

http://www.funtigo.com/troop5/historyunionArea/uticaWaterHistory.jsp *History of the Union/Utica Water Company.*

REGION III: LAKES WITHIN
THE STANISLAUS RIVER DRAINAGE
PADDLING AREA 2: UNION RESERVOIR

Position: 38°25.50'N, 119°59.50'W

Difficulty: You will find similar paddling conditions on Union as on Utica. The lower half of Union is more open then the upper half. Use caution if paddling against the strong afternoon winds.

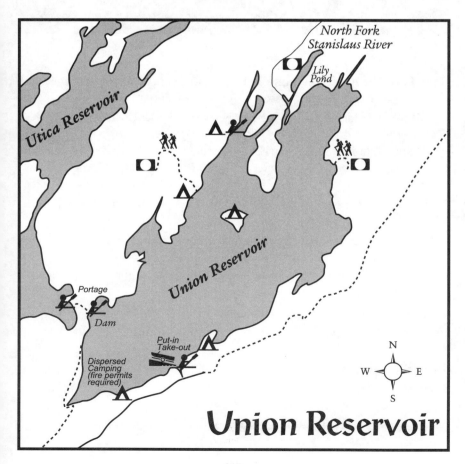

A large bay where the North Fork of the Stanislaus River flows.

Trip Length: About the same as Utica Reservoir. With an early start, you will finish paddling the reservoir by late afternoon.

Portage: If entering Union Reservoir by way of Utica Reservoir, a short (approximately 200 yard) carry over the berm separating the two reservoirs is required. (Hint: Part of the portage is through a Boy Scout camp; challenge any scouts you see to do their good deed by helping you carry the boat.)

Paddling Distance: 1 mile, one-way from the portage site to mouth of North Fork Stanislaus River;

0.5 mile, one-way from portage site to southern tip of center-most island;

0.5 one-way from mouth of stream at entrance to second lily pond to SW shoreline campsite;

0.5 one-way from SW shoreline campsite to boat ramp via dam.

Season: Same as Utica Reservoir: late spring through summer and into fall.

Lake Size: 1.25 by 0.5 mile.

Elevation: 6,850 feet.

County: Alpine County (close to Tuolumne County).

National Forest/Wilderness Area: Stanislaus National Forest, Calaveras Ranger District.

Wilderness Area: The northern end of the reservoir is close to the boundary of the Carson-Iceberg Wilderness.

Maps:

USGS 7.5-Minute Quadrangle Topographical Map Series: Tamarack, CA, and Spicer Meadow Reservoir, CA.

National Forest Service/Wilderness Area: Stanislaus National Forest Carson-Iceberg Wilderness (Stanislaus and Toiyabe National Forests) This map is the best one for the area.

Road Maps:

Compass Maps Inc.: Alpine, Amador and Sacramento Counties, Calaveras and Tuolumne County Communities.

California State Automobile Association (AAA) Maps: Lake Tahoe and Northern Sierra Map and Guide.

Historical Background:

The reservoir was originally called Highland Reservoir. The first dam was constructed in October 1858, by the Union Water Company. Upon completion, it was the largest log crib dam in the state. In 1883, improvements were made to the 1858 reservoir by rebuilding the dam using granitic boulders lined with concrete. Pacific Gas and Electric Co. (PG&E) purchased the entire system of reservoirs, flumes, ditches, and watercourses from the Union/Utica Water Company in 1946. The company still operates the Utica Project

A typical campsite, west shoreline, upper end of Union Reservoir.

today (for additional information on the history of the Union/Utica Water Company, see the Sources and References section).

Access:

Access California State Hwy. 4 East at Angels Camp, CA. Continue on Hwy. 4 for approximately 32 miles. Prior to your turnoff, look for a sign indicating Spicer Reservoir Road Exit. Turn off at Forest Service Road 7N01 (Spicer Reservoir Road).

Follow the Forest Service road for approximately 8.5 miles before turning left onto Forest Service Road 7N75. *This turnoff is easily missed. It is not clearly marked. Look for a wooden sign adjacent to a gravel road exit on your left. The gravel exit and sign will appear in the middle of a series of sharp bends.*

Continue approximately 1 mile up the road to the fork. If you are planning to camp along the shoreline of Union Reservoir, take the right fork and follow it to the end. On a light-use day, you will have a good chance of parking near the area where you hope to camp. Otherwise be prepared to park creatively and hike to your site.

There is a boat ramp, but it is on a steep, unpaved, rock-strewn road. On a crowded day, it would be easier to drive to the put-in/take-out at Utica Reservoir, paddle the distance (approximately 1 mile), and portage your boat the 200 feet onto the shoreline of Union.

Heads Up:

- Last minute "Oops, I forgot" items may be purchased in Tamarack approximately 1 mile past the Spicier Reservoir Road exit off Hwy. 4.
- Located within the Calaveras Ranger District Hwy. 4, PO Box 500, Hathaway Pines, CA (209.795.1381).
- A Fire Permit is required for dispersed camping. You may pick one up at the Calaveras Ranger District Office, or at the U.S. Forest Ranger Station off Hwy. 4 east of Dorrington.
- The three lakes, Utica, Union and Spicer have become a major canoe/kayak destination spot. Be prepared for crowded conditions on summer weekends and summer holidays.
- Although Utica and Union Reservoirs do not require a permit other than the free campfire permit, a *wilderness permit is required* for shoreline camping in the eastern (non-motorized) portion of Spicer Lake. *No-Trace Camping guidelines* are the proper camping procedures for this region.
- Bear country—pack and camp smart!
- No potable sources of water—bring your own or use a filtration system.
- Unlike Utica, the dispersed camping around the lake does not have easy access. This is especially true for launching your boat into the lake.

- Many of the camping sites are on bare granite; bring a foam pad or other *tush cush*. . . it keeps those aches and pains down to a tolerable minimum.

Description:

Unlike Utica Reservoir, Union Reservoir does not show off its secrets until you have paddled some distance into the upper half of the reservoir. You get a taste of the beauty, seeing the large granite islands arranged throughout the lake, but the main course is waiting beyond the islands.

You have two choices for your put-in: at the boat ramp on the southeast shore, or from a combination paddle and portage via Utica Lake. Either way, you want to be on the water early to avoid the wind and have the time to explore the outer islands. Many of these islands are steep and have no easy area to get out of your boat. But the clusters of smaller islands at the upper mid-section of the lake are easily accessible and provide some excellent camping sites. If you are exploring these islands in the late spring, be careful not to disturb the nesting sites of the Canada geese, which have established semi-residency at both reservoirs.

Upper Reservoir

In studying either the Spicer Meadows topographical sheet or the Carson-Iceberg map, you may mistakenly believe that there is no access between the two upper fingers of the lake. In reality, there is a well-defined channel draining from the mouth of the North Fork Stanislaus River to the tip of the hook-shaped finger channel lying west of the river mouth. Because of this access way, you can leisurely enjoy messing about the many coves, drainages, and miniature islands, too numerous or too small to appear on the maps.

One other important feature about paddling here is that all these islands provide a natural windbreak, allowing you to experience the area without fighting the wind.

If you paddle along the south shore past the main group of islands, there is a take-out with a short hike to a fantastic view of the entire lake. Take-out at the short cove on the upper end of the southeast shore before the lake bends northward. Walk through the thin belt of trees bordering the beach, and you find a lightly impacted trail. Follow it upward, boulder hopping if you have to, until you reach the upper terrace of the ridge. The view from here is, indeed, panoramic. Not only do you have a clear view of the lake, but by turning northward you can also follow the gorge of the North Fork of the Stanislaus until it recedes in a misty haze. Continue to turn, and you get a clear view of a volcanic plug called Elephant Rock (7,425 feet). With a pair of binoculars, you can spot the trail crossing the dome of the plug.

Back in your boat, continue along the shoreline and paddle into the enchanting cove containing fern-covered joints and lichen-encrusted sidewalls of light-colored granite. Pines and cedars of various heights jut from the fissures in the rock walls and along the rim of the granite. In the mid-morning light, the entire scene takes on the soft texture found in some Chinese prints.

This part of the lake is where the magic begins. Small granite outcrops topped with trees and flowers are everywhere. The light-green coloration of the sedges softens the harsh contrast of the granite. Mallards, mergansers, an occasional great blue heron and the ubiquitous Canada geese, are seen in almost every pool and cove. Gliding by some of the smaller, more protected pools, you hear a grunt followed by a splash—a sure sign of a frog beating a hasty exit to a safe underwater haven until you have passed.

Lily Pond and Mouth of the North Fork of the Stanislaus River

Eventually, you paddle around the upper end of the lake, and just as you begin the downward leg, you see a small entrance to your right, immediately past a lengthy wall of granite that extends into the lake. The two smaller granite boulders sitting at the mouth of the entrance serve as a resting spot for the Canada geese. But they also mark your entry point into the sedge-filled mouth of a classic lily pond. Just before you enter into this gem, look for another mouth hidden among the willows to your left. This is the entrance to the North Fork of the Stanislaus River.

Entering the pond, particularly if you played your hunch and followed that inner voice telling you to "check out that partially hidden clearing, just beyond the willows," is indeed satisfying!

The pond is oval-shaped and surrounded by a shoreline rimmed with pines and juniper. At the lower right or south edge of the pond is an extension of a granite outcrop. Its stone wall marks the nearby mouth of the pond, and it dominates the shoreline. The tea-colored, glassy calm creates a mirror image of the belt of conifers bordering the upper beach.

At the entrance itself, lily pads, belonging to the Indian Pond Lily, float on the surface. Bobbing alongside are the bright yellow cup-like flowers of the plant. Some Native American tribes collected the seeds from the plant, and roasted them like popcorn. In addition, when oxygen from the mud holding the lily's stem gives out, small amounts of alcohol are formed instead of carbon dioxide. . . no, sucking on the stalk does not work!

Once you are past the lilies, you may either paddle to the end of the pond and back, or beach your boat under the impressive juniper growing on the left bank, mid-way into the pond. A short hike up the bank puts you on a low ridge overlooking the riverbed to the North Fork of the Stanislaus. Following the river as it makes a sharp bend to the left, you can just make out the mouth where it enters the lake. The entire area around the mouth is heavily overgrown with willows. This habitat makes an ideal spot for water birds of every kind. They gather and feed among the willows and use the dense undergrowth for shelter and nesting. Attracted by the numbers of ducks, geese, and other smaller birds, raptors of every type may be spotted cruising the river mouth and nearby coves. On one trip, I was fortunate to observe two American bald eagles for several days as they cruised the lake and river mouth. I was hoping to locate a nest but had no such luck. When I reported the sightings at the ranger station, I was told that the bald and golden eagles were not uncommon to the region, but nest sites were rare.

If you see any eagles, or have the good fortune to locate their nest, be sure to report the sighting to the nearest ranger station *(See Heads Up Section)*.

This same dense growth around the river bend also confuses paddlers seeking the mouth of the river. Instead of paddling through the willows to reach the mouth on the opposite side, paddlers pass by and continue into the next finger cove.

Second Lily Pond and Hike

Upon leaving the pond and adjacent river mouth, follow the willows around the opening that is not indicated on your maps, into a cove whose northern end is overgrown with willows. Many paddlers, who are not familiar with the lake, or do not have a map at their disposal, mistake this overgrown delta for the main mouth to the Stanislaus River, This mistake is not unreasonable, considering that the site has all the characteristics of being a mouth to a flowing river: a silted bank and broad cobble bar bordered by a dense grove of willows. This deceptive locale, however, is the mouth to a shallow stream that feeds from a series of ponds located beyond the overgrowth.

Both are well worth the side trip to explore and use as a hiking base.

The entrance to the shallow stream is located next to the granite wall that is part of the far left (west) shore. This entrance is not visible from your approach; consequently, you have to paddle around the finger of granite extending from the willow-covered mouth. As you make your way around the point, watch for families of mergansers who use the wind-protected point as shelter for their young. If you startle a resting mother and her chicks, back off to allow the brood to paddle off as a group. If any of the chicks become separated, they may not re-join the family group, and hence may fall victim to the elements or any meat-eaters in the area.

As you meander with the stream up to the ponds, watch for trout swimming beneath your boat. They dart in zigzag patterns as the shadow of the boat approaches them. Frogs and turtles are easily spotted all along the banks. As you paddle, you can hear the liquid melodies of black birds being carried on the wind.

A short distance upstream you come to a fork; to the left is a small pond and on your right the stream continues past a deep-water pool. Continue on the stream to your right.

Tracks of the different birds and animals that have passed through the area are imprinted in the wet mud at the fork. Although deer hooves and geese pads predominate, raccoon and skunk tracks are also present. Don't be surprised to find the distinct pad of a bear, coyote, or even a mountain lion. This area is a natural throughway between the high country and the lower lakes.

A short paddle later, you spot the entrance, located just beyond a shallow sand bar, to the granite-encased pond. Magnificent pines and cedars stand as sentinels around the pond. Paddling past the lilies, you encounter a massive slab of stained granite criss-crossed by countless fracture lines, called joints. In addition to the fracture lines, the entire ridge of granite shows characteristic rounding as a result of a weathering process known as exfoliation. *(Exfoliation is the leafing away of rounded shells of rock.)* With some imagination, this tortured hunk of rock bears a keen resemblance to the weathered face of an old, old person – complete with wrinkles and warts.

Opposite the weathered face is a small sandy beach where you may take-out and camp or use as a base for further exploration. If you are planning to camp overnight, several level spots with a commanding view of the pond are located above the manzanita. Hiking higher, additional sites are to be found, again with exceptional views.

Whether you are here for the day or are spending the night, do not miss the opportunity to hike above the granite to the top of the ridge. A brief meander through the hodgepodge pile of erratics brings you to the edge of the ridge. From here, you have a stunning view of Utica Reservoir with its myriad islands. Looking south across the ridge separating the two reservoirs, you spot the shimmer of blue, marking the location of lower Union Reservoir.

Sweeping your eyes northward, follow the gorge of the North Fork of the Stanislaus River, before it fades out of sight among the bare granite domes. These ridges profiling the horizon are part of the Carson-Iceberg Wilderness, a gateway into the high country flanking the west side of the Central Sierra Nevada Mountain Range.

Hiking among the boulders that make up the ridge top allows you to study the effects of glaciation on the granite. Shiny, slick surface areas called glacial polish are visible wherever the sunlight reflects off the rock. Deep grooves mark the path of the former ice sheet as it worked its way down the valley. The telltale debris of boulders, whose composition bears no similarity to the present bedrock, litters the surface as far as the eye can see. Many of the larger erratics contain pines or junipers whose roots have exploited the joints within the body of the boulder. As the trees grow, their roots continue to expand the fracture until the boulder is cleaved into two or more pieces.

Where soil has a chance to build, vegetation in the form of pine mat manzanita and huckleberry oak covers the surface.

Continue on your hike, following the slope of the ridge to the northeast and you come upon a shallow depression filled with melt-water. This tank acts as a source of water for the birds and mammals living in the area. Find a spot well away from the water source, then sit and observe the varieties of birds, chipmunks, and ground squirrels that slowly make their way for a quick drink before darting back into the brush. Butterflies and an occasional dragonfly flit above and around the tank.

On your return hike, follow the ridge bordering the southeast side to obtain a good view of Elephant Rock (7,425 feet).

Lower Reservoir (The Islands)

When you leave the wind-protected area of the upper reservoir and paddle down the lake, you are suddenly pummeled by wind and waves. Here, you have a choice: either paddle into the belt of islands on your left, or stay along the western shoreline. If you are anxious to locate a camp, steer for the islands where there are several sheltered sites. These provide a grand view, particularly of the sunrises and sunsets upon the lake and surrounding ridges.

Look for huge boulders facing the windward side. Take-out on the leeward side and walk your island of choice; former campfire rings mark sheltered camp spots.

Remember to tie down your beached boat in case the wind shifts!

If you are keen for a campfire, look for driftwood on the windward side, or piled under the duff near any standing pine.

When you've finished your food preparation, immediately seal and store your remaining provisions. It's not the bears foraging in the late night that you need worry about as much as it is the rodents.

One of the main benefits of camping on the islands is evident in the late afternoon or early morning, when the surface of the lake appears glass-like. Ospreys and bald eagles hunt fish from the limbs of the tall pines growing on the islands. If you are fortunate, and an early riser, you will witness the incredible display of flight demonstrated by an osprey as it captures its meal. If your luck really holds, the aerial dance takes on a new tempo when a bald eagle attempts to bluff the osprey into dropping its fresh fish.

The Southwest Shoreline

For those of you wishing to continue, paddle along the shoreline and enjoy the changing scenery before you. From the fairy-tale islands of granite and pine, a tall forest of second-growth pines, cedars, and an occasional juniper suddenly confronts you. The body of the lake opens, revealing its personality.

Great blue herons, feeding in the secluded shallows, let out a guttural *squawk*, then take wing as you approach. Families of mergansers and Canada geese scurry along the surface, eventually settling down to watch you paddle by.

In those same sheltered coves, the water surface reflects the racing clouds and blue sky from overhead.

As the belt of islands recedes behind you, new vistas emerge with every paddle stroke. The shining domes of rounded peaks that mark the presence of granitic rock suddenly give way to the brooding angular heights of dark colored basalt. Sheer, vertical walls rise up, looking like a battleship emerging over the clear horizon. At first, the morning sun hides any details that shape these darkened walls. By late afternoon, however, the setting sun highlights the red and orange hues, along with the many shades of black. These magnificent remnants of former volcanic activity are The Dardanelles, named for their resemblance to the original rock formations at Dardanelles Strait, the entrance from the Aegean Sea to Marmara and Black Seas.

If you seek a camp on this side of the lake, be sure to stop as you paddle by and hike to any site that might appeal to you. Many places are not standouts from the water, but if you go ashore to look at them, they have all the right ingredients for a good campsite.

Eventually, you reach the main dam and the beach where you portage to the lower Utica Reservoir. If you put-in at Union Reservoir boat ramp, the dam is a good reference point from which you can spot the boat ramp located on the opposite shore.

Sources and References:

Hill, Mary, *Geology of the Sierra Nevada*. Berkeley: University of California Press, 1975, 9th Ed.

Webster's New Geographical Dictionary. Springfield: G. & C. Merriam Company, 1972.

Whitney, Stephen, *The Sierra Nevada: A Sierra Club Naturalist's Guide*. San Francisco: Sierra Club Books, 1979.

http://www.funtigo.com/troop5/historyunionArea/uticaWaterHistory.jsp

REGION III: LAKES WITHIN THE STANISLAUS RIVER DRAINAGE
PADDLING AREAS 3 and 4: SUMMIT LAKE / ELEPHANT ROCK LAKE

Paddling Area 3, Summit Lake

Position: 38°25.57'N, 119°58.23'W

Difficulty: A little afternoon wind; otherwise, a great place to launch a boat for a lazy day on the water.

Trip Length: Put the coffee pot on to boil, launch your boat for an early morning paddle; upon your return, the coffee will be ready to pour.

Portages: A short walk from the parking area to each lake is necessary.

Paddling Distances: The lakes are too small for any meaningful paddling distances

Lake Size: 0.75 mile long by 0.40 mile wide.

Elevation: 7,068 feet.

Paddling Area 4: Elephant Rock Lake

Position: 38°26.30'N, 119°58.34'W

Difficulty: Same conditions as Summit Lake.

Trip Length: Put the coffee pot to boil . . .

Portage: Short carry from the parking area to the lake.

Paddling Distances: The lakes are too small for any meaningful paddling distances.

Season: Late spring through early fall, or until the road closes.

Lake Size: 0.40 mile long by 0.20 mile wide.

Elevation: 6,922 feet.

County: Alpine County.

National Forest Service: Both lakes are within the Stanislaus National Forest, Calaveras Ranger District.

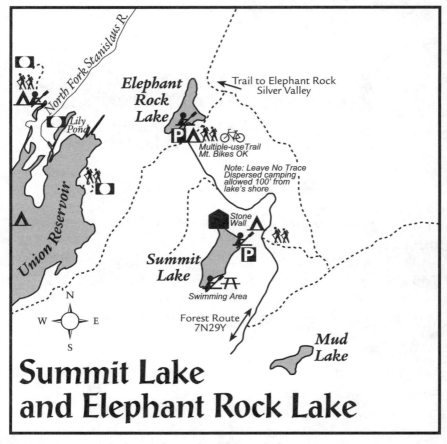

Summit Lake and Elephant Rock Lake

Wilderness Area: Elephant Rock Lake is within the Carson-Iceberg Wilderness boundary; Summit Lake is situated near the edge of the boundary.

Maps:

USGS 7.5-Minute Quadrangle Topographical Map: Spicer Meadow Reservoir, CA.

National Forest Service/Wilderness Area: Stanislaus National Forest, Carson-Iceberg Wilderness.

Road Maps:

Compass Maps Inc.: Calaveras and Tuolumne Counties, Alpine, Tuolumne, and Sacramento County Communities.

California State Automobile Association (AAA) Maps: Lake Tahoe and Northern Sierra Map and Guide.

Summit Lake in the morning calm.

Historical Background:

Both reservoirs were constructed in the summer of 1858 by the Union Water Company to provide additional water to the newly completed Union Reservoir.

> *"More than one hundred years later, remnants of a small earthen dam,*
> *A square wooden culvert for delivering water and pieces of a wooden sluice*
> *gate were found at Elephant Rock Lake. At Duck Lake parts of the ditch built*
> *to drain the lake are still visible."**

Access:

(See Paddling Areas 1 and 2 for detailed description on reaching the main Region).

A gravel road (Forest Route: 7N29Y) located on your left immediately past the exit for Utica-Union Reservoirs. The parking area for Summit Lake is 3 miles up the road. Look for a wooden marker set away from the road and on your left. The parking area will be on your right. The access trail to the lake is across the road facing southwest.

To reach Elephant Rock Lake, continue for another mile, staying to the right, until the road ends at the parking area to the lake and trail head. The access trail to the lake faces north just beyond the clearing for a campsite.

Heads Up:

- Two small secluded natural lakes; ideal for a family canoe paddle.
- Sheltered from strong winds by surrounding forest.

- Both lakes have a wind-protected, shallow area ideal for swimming.
- Elephant Rock Lake has an outstanding view of Elephant Rock.
- Dispersed (*No-Trace Camping* allowed) 100 feet above the lakeshores—look for the wooden boundary marker.
- A fire permit is required.
- No potable sources of water—bring your own or use a filtration system.
- Bear country—pack and camp smart!
- Because the boundary line between the Stanislaus National Forest and Carson-Iceberg Wilderness Area is blurred here, call the Calaveras Ranger District Office (209.795.1381) for verification of a wilderness permit.
- A mountain-bike trail may be accessed at the Elephant Rock Lake parking area. The trail to Elephant Rock is approximately 1 mile, one-way.
- Trailheads accessing other wilderness trails are near the parking areas of both lakes.
- Although the road is gravel, watch for potholes and high rocks if driving a low clearance vehicle.
- Range cattle abound—keep an eye out!

Description:

If the thought of listening to a Boy Scout bugle at different times of the day does not appeal to you, then it is worth the drive to these natural lakes to partake of their stillness.

Each time I have made the trek into these lakes, I have met only a handful of people, and of all those only one was a fisherman in a fishing tube; he was my only companion on Summit Lake. The short driving distances between the two lakes allow you to paddle both in a given day. Each lake has its own charm and personality.

Summit Lake

The short hike into the lake creates anticipation, which is pleasantly fulfilled upon viewing the lake for the first time. Small and oval-shaped, the lake is bordered by tall pines and defines serenity. Depending on the time of day you arrive, the lake is either a glassy surface reflecting the pines and sky, or it shimmers brightly with each passage of a breeze. Across the lake to the west, an outcrop of granite breaks the monotony of the pines. Northward, a group of dead pines in the lake creates a small ghost forest. Their dull silver sheen contrasts against the greens of the living trees.

Breaking the surface shape of the lake is a lone, Zen-like granite slab at the southern end.

Across the surface, hundreds of brown damselflies, along with blue-colored bluets dart and weave near the sedges that grow along the shoreline.

Whenever a breeze picks up, the pines begin to sway, and you hear the needles swish with the rising tempo of the wind. Somewhere nearby a raven croaks, and is answered by another hiding in the trees.

In the early morning and late afternoon, fish jump high to swallow insects skimming the surface. Taking the next step in the food chain, an osprey flying overhead suddenly swoops down to snatch a small trout, then flaps away to consume its catch.

If a swim is in order, paddle to the southern end, to the granite slab where the water is shallow and warms quickly. Beach your boat on the sedges and swim to the slab, then lie on its surface basking in the sun before going back.

Hidden among the trees at the extreme northern end of the lake is a rock wall; you may think it's a dam, because it retains some water, but it actually acts as a bridge for a trail bordering the lake.

The portage from vehicle to lakeside is short and sweet. Put your boat in the water, paddle away and explore, or just let 'er drift for a truly a fine day in God's country.

Elephant Rock Lake

Don't let the gloom of the trees dissuade you from taking the short hike to view the lake. Once you break free of the forest, the lake appears as a bright light of shimmering reflections. Standing as a sentry over the entire scene is the dark-hued mass of Elephant Rock, a former volcano. Yellow, Indian water lilies float over the southeast finger of the lake, forming a carpet of green. The entire lake sparkles with an airiness that brings the excitement of a sense of being to anyone viewing the lake for the first time.

After a short portage, you arrive at a large open space where launching your boat is easy. Once upon the water, slowly paddle into the lily pond. Keep an eye out for frogs that seem to be everywhere. In the very late afternoon or in the early mornings, if you are very quiet approaching this part of the lake, you may observe a great blue heron stalking the frogs. The bird will stand absolutely still, its long slender beak poised in wait. Suddenly, with a blur of motion, the bird's head stabs downward and almost always comes up with its prey.

The countless blur of gossamer wings marks the presence of Green-Darners (*Anax junius*), one of the largest and most common dragonflies in the state. Their flying skills are impressive and extraordinary. From your boat, take the time to observe these highly territorial insects as they perform their aerial maneuvers, either with each other or with other insects of similar size. Among the lily pads and the sedges growing along the shore are many American Bluets, possibly the Boreal Bluet (*Enallagama boreale*), a blue-colored damselfly, common in all kinds of aquatic habitats.

Eventually, you reach the end of the lake where a clearing allows you to alight easily from your boat. Just beyond the shoreline you intersect the trail that leads north to Silver Valley and Duck Lake. If you hike along the northern shoreline, you come to the first of two streams that drain into the lake. This stream forks from the parent approximately 0.5 mile above. The main stream drains into Union Reservoir where its drowned channel may be entered by canoe or kayak *(See Paddling Area 2, Union Reservoir, Upper Reservoir section)*. The second stream is visible where it flows adjacent to the access trail leading to the lake from the parking area. If you hike the trail to Elephant Rock, you intersect it on the way.

Although there is a fire ring near the lake, you must be at least 50 paces away from the shoreline if you're going to camp. I prepare my meals above the lake then paddle across to spend the night without using a fire.

With these restrictions, day use of the area makes more sense; however, by following the 50 paces, (100 foot) rule, you insure the lake stays pristine for the future.

Sources and References:

History of the Union/Utica Water Company. (The quotation is attributed in the main text of the article), San Andreas Independent Newspaper, February 24, September 11, and November 20, 1858; June 24, 25, and October 29, 1859). http://www.funtigo.com/troop5/history/unionArea/uticaWaterHistory.jsp Page 5 of 11, (accessed January 25, 2003).

Powell, Jerry A. and Charles L. Hogue, *California Insects.* Berkeley: University of California Press, 1979.

http://www.fs.fed.us/r5/stanislaus/calaveras/index.shtml
The Calaveras Ranger District of the Stanislaus National Forest Website.

REGION III: LAKES WITHIN THE STANISLAUS RIVER DRAINAGE
PADDLING AREA 5: SPICER MEADOW RESERVOIR (NEW SPICER RECREATION AREA)

Position: 38°23.35'N, 119°59.45'W

Difficulty: The calm appearance of the reservoir in the early morning and late afternoon is very misleading. Spicer Reservoir is notorious for its fierce winds. Because of this, paddling here is recommended for intermediate to advanced boaters who possess solid paddling skills.

The combination of the wind, the wind-generated waves, plus waves rebounding off cliff walls makes for some hair-raising crossings.

If you're caught on the reservoir when the wind comes up, there are a few sheltered coves that may be reached in a relatively short time.

Once you have reached the narrow upper reservoir, the strength of the wind diminishes, but does not die down. In addition, you still have wind-caused fetch to deal with.

A clear view up Spicer, toward the Narrows. This photograph was taken at the Reference Point across the main body of the reservoir, located on the map.

233

Trip Length: If you are seeking a day paddle, there are several large coves good for that purpose once you round the point beyond the boat ramp. However, be prepared to fight a head wind upon your return.

For overnight paddles, you may either explore the shoreline leisurely or locate a campsite within the main body of the reservoir. If you wish to enter the non-motorized area of the upper reservoir, plan on 2 hours of steady paddling from the boat ramp. For a non-hurried crossing give yourself a half-day.

Portage: None.

Paddling Distances:

0.60 mile one-way from the boat ramp to 1st point;

2.1 mile one-way from boat ramp to 5th point (entrance into upper reservoir);

0.80 mile one-way from 1st point to 2nd point;

0.30 mile one-way from 1st point to opposite shore (marked on map as reference point);

0.5 mile one-way from 2nd point to 3rd point;

0.37 mile one-way from 3rd point to 4th point;

0.37 mile one-way from 4th point to 5th point;

1.5 mile (approximately) one-way from 5th point to buoy line;

4.3 mile one-way from 5th point to junction of Highland and Bull Run Creeks.

Season to Paddle: Late spring through fall.

Lake size: 227 acres; 6.5 miles from the dam to the high-water line at junction of Highland and Bull Run Creeks.

Elevation: 6,619 feet.

County: Lower reservoir located in Tuolumne County. Upper reservoir located in Alpine County.

National Forest / Wilderness Area: Located in the Stanislaus National Forest, administered by the Calaveras Ranger District. Upper Reservoir above the Buoy line is part of the Carson-Iceberg Wilderness Area and part of their jurisdiction.

Maps:

USGS 7.5-Minute Quadrangle Topographical Map Series: Tamarack, CA and Spicer Meadow Reservoir, CA.

Note: the USGS maps do not reflect the current shoreline of the reservoir. Use the 6,600-foot contour line for any trip plans.

National Forest Service/Wilderness Area: Stanislaus National Forest (shows the correct elevation level of Spicer Reservoir) and Carson-Iceberg Wilderness Maps. (*The most accurate. It shows the current shoreline along*

One of the dead trees that makes up the "dead forests" located in the bays of the reservoir.

with the relief of the area). The small scale (1:63360), however, precludes using it for any serious trip planning.

Road Maps:

Compass Maps Inc.: Calaveras and Tuolumne County Communities, Alpine, Amador, and Sacramento Counties.

California State Automobile Association (AAA) Maps: Lake Tahoe and Northern Sierra Map and Guide.

Historical Background:

Built originally in 1927, the reservoir was completed in 1929 by the Utica Company as part of their improvement projects to their water systems. The original reservoir had a capacity of only 9,000 acre-feet of water. This is the reservoir shown on many of the maps prior to the completion in 1990 of the New Spicer Meadow Reservoir, which has a capacity of 62,000 acre-feet of water.

Access:

Access California State Hwy. 4 East at Angels Camp, Calif. Continue on Hwy. 4 for approximately 32 miles. Prior to your turnoff, look for a sign indicating Spicer Reservoir Road Exit. Turn off at this exit. You are now on Forest Road 7N01 (Spicer Reservoir Road).

Follow the forest road for approximately 9 miles, and then make a left turn at the sign for the family campground and boat ramp. Follow the road to the lake.

Heads Up:

- *Note:* That the USGS 7.5-Minute Quadrangle Topographical Map of Spicer Meadow Reservoir does not reflect the present levels of the reservoir. The water level on the map is the height of the old reservoir. Use the 6,600 feet contour line for a more current configuration of the reservoir. The U.S. Forest Service map: Carson-Iceberg Wilderness (1987 edition shows the correct shoreline of New Spicer Meadow Reservoir.

- A fire permit must be obtained prior to any overnight dispersed camping at the lower reservoir up to the non-motorized zone. A wilderness permit and a campfire permit are necessary for camping above the non-motorized zone. For information about the permits, contact Calaveras Ranger District Office (209.795.1381).

- Bear country—pack and camp smart!

- A family campground is located on the same road exit that leads to the boat ramp. Take the first left after exiting from Forest Road 7N01. The campground is run by Sierra Recreation Managers. The mailing address is: Sierra Recreation Managers, c/o Bill Cramer, Box 278, Pioneer, CA 95666.

- A paved road leads to the boat ramp. The ramp itself is fully paved and a parking area is located above the ramp. For vehicles with no trailers, park at the day-use area lot located near the restroom and fish cleaning location.

- A pay phone is available on the right, off the same road leading to the boat ramp.

The inlet into 3rd Point.

- The boat ramp gets a lot of use; to prevent conflict with other boaters, use the sandy beach to the left (northeast) of the ramp for loading or unloading your boat.
- The reservoir is noted for its strong afternoon winds, so a late afternoon departure and an early morning time frame for your return are recommended. This also allows you to paddle with the sun on your back and not in your eyes, and these times are also the best viewing/photography hours.
- If you plan to paddle to the Upper Reservoir, upon launching, paddle directly for the far point (*listed as point #1 on the map*) visible to the south of the boat ramp. From here, use the points of land, numbered 1-5 on the map, that jut out from cove entrances as your headings.
- Don't hesitate to get out of your boat and explore when seeking a choice campsite. Many good sites are located above the waterline where the conifers grow. These sites are not always visible from a cockpit or canoe seat.

Description:

To appreciate the grandeur of Spicer Reservoir for the first time, depart from the boat ramp in the late afternoon. Not only will the paddling be less strenuous, but also the setting sun will highlight the exposed granite domes, deepen the greens of the forests, and provide a detailed view of the imposing heights of The Dardanelles.

Back your vehicle down the ramp and park it close to the granite, if the boat ramp is not too busy. Unload in the turnaround area before parking in the day-use area above.

Fill any water bottles at the nifty brass pump adjacent to the bathrooms and fish cleaning area. Take the time to view the many varieties of wildflowers that grow in the stream flowing between the day-use area and the boat parking lot before you leave.

Walk down the concrete ramp to the shoreline. The creek that flows on your left is Hobart Creek and originates from Summit Lake (*See Paddling Area 3*).

Because the reservoir covers such a large area with many interesting coves, I have separated the description into two sections: Lower or Main Body and Upper Reservoir.

Lower Reservoir

To facilitate the location and descriptions of the larger coves within the main body of the reservoir, there is a handy set of numbered reference points on the map. The land points that jut outward from the larger coves are located along the northeast shoreline, and are numbered 1 through 5 on the chapter map.

Located directly across the lake from Point 1 on the map, is a knuckle of land to which I gave the term *Reference Point*. It provides a handy location for a mileage check for paddlers wishing to know the distance from the boat ramp to the opposite shore.

The point of land that extends outward from the shore to the south, and at first appears to be an island, is *1st Point*. This is the first reference point to paddle toward. From there you have an unobstructed view and can decide whether you want to explore the coves to the south and east, paddle across the lake, or visit the lower islands near the dam.

Once you round the tip of 1st Point and enter the cove, follow the shoreline to *2nd Point*. These finger coves are the remnants of stream drainages that emptied into the main channel of Highland Creek, now located beneath the waters of Spicer Reservoir. All of these drainages are worth paddling into, because they provide easy access into the backcountry. Beach your boat, and use the streambeds for short or long hikes to explore the surrounding terrain. The presence of water in these beds insures the existence of wild

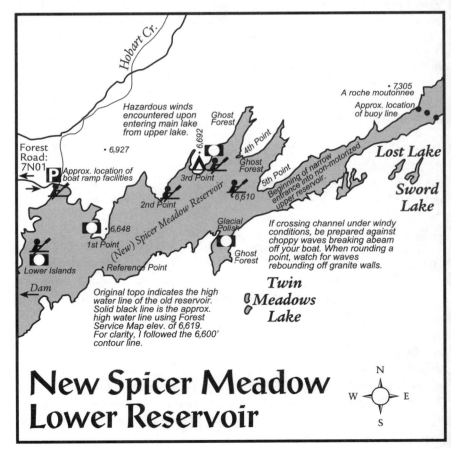

Hobart Cr.

• 7,305
A roche moutonnée

Hazardous winds encountered upon entering main lake from upper lake.

Ghost Forest

Approx. location of buoy line

6,692

4th Point

Forest Road: 7N01

• 6,927

Lost Lake

Approx. location of boat ramp facilities

Ghost Forest

3rd Point

5th Point

Beginning of narrow entrance into non-motorized upper reservoir.

Sword Lake

2nd Point

(New) Spicer Meadow Reservoir

• 6,610

Glacial Polish

• 6,648

1st Point

If crossing channel under windy conditions, be prepared against choppy waves breaking abeam off your boat. When rounding a point, watch for waves rebounding off granite walls.

Ghost Forest

Lower Islands

Reference Point

Dam

Original topo indicates the high water line of the old reservoir. Solid black line is the approx. high water line using Forest Service Map elev. of 6,619. For clarity, I followed the 6,600' contour line.

Twin Meadows Lake

New Spicer Meadow Lower Reservoir

N
W ← → E
S

flowers, birds, and animals. Deer like to bed in the thick, shaded brush that grows nearby, and hawks cruise the ridgelines in search of ground squirrels and chipmunks.

If you are seeking a campsite, then, upon reaching *3rd Point*, beach your boat on the south-facing leeward shoreline. Hike up the south-facing ledge, where a large, level area contains a stone fire ring, with a homemade wooden bench. A spectacular view of the reservoir, the Dardanelles (8,875 feet), and Dardanelles Cone (9,524 feet) stretches before you. Dardanelles Cone is a plug or neck of leftover Andesite lava that erupted over 20 million years ago. The neighboring Dardanelles is part of the volcanic debris that flowed out of this volcano. Elephant Rock, visible from Elephant Rock Lake, Utica and Union Reservoirs, is a similar volcanic feature; however, it is on a much smaller scale.

From the same height as the campsite, walk to the edge fronting the small finger cove that extends northward. If the water level is low, peer down onto the barren boulder-strewn granite shoreline. There, you will spot a long and deep rectangular trench bisecting the granite landscape. This perfectly straight-gauged track is mute testimony to the power of former glacial ice. The trench was excavated by debris-laden ice sliding over the bedrock.

Moreover, the large Volkswagen-sized boulders, resting on the granite floor of the point to the right of the campfire, were also left behind by retreating glaciers. Because the extraction of many of these boulders originated many miles from where they now rest, their mineral composition does not always match up with the existing terrain.

From this vantage point, you may view the other coves to plan your next day's paddle. As you head up into the Upper Reservoir, the narrow entrance is clearly visible just behind and to the left of the barren island standing alone in the main body of the reservoir.

The silver sheen of standing dead wood marks where the ghost forest is located within the drowned drainage of Wilderness Creek. The entrance is shown on the map as the cove located between 4th and 5th points. Upon paddling into this area, look for the exposed granite outcrop with its lone erratic resting on the barren rock. Nearby, is the bizarre sight of a dead forest with hundreds of skeletal trees standing eerily in the water. Paddling through these trees is rather spooky, especially since many of the branches are twisted into strange and weird shapes.

Once through the trees, you spot the mouth of Wilderness Creek where you can hike along its streambed or relax by the flowing creek.

The small island featured with the take-out symbol plays an important role if you are caught by strong winds while crossing the reservoir. The prevailing winds blow out of the southwest, strike the south-facing wall of the island, and create a wind shadow on the lower eastern end. The graduated slope of this end of the island allows you to take out, even on the windiest days, without too much trouble. Here, take a break before deciding on your next move, or wait for a lull in the wind. The only alternative requires paddling abeam to the wind for the nearest cove.

Another interesting feature about this island is its shape. The steep, rough and exposed granite face slopes gently downward with smooth sides. It is characteristic of a glacial feature known as a *roche moutonnee (row-sh-moot-o-nay)*, a French term meaning sheep rock which, refers to the fact that the rock shape resembles the profile of a woolly sheep.

Bill Guyton, in his book *Glaciers of California*, describes how they were formed:

> *"Each has a gentle streamlined slope where it faces up-valley, against the flow of the ice, but steep and rough sides facing down-valley where ice flowing away from the hill pulled, or plucked, blocks of rock loose from the mountain and carried them away."* (P. 22)

Roche moutonnees come in all sizes, but it is their unique shape that allows one to identify them. For example, the huge mass of granite guarding the north side of the channel leading into the non-motorized area is also a roche moutonnee. Paddle past it and look for the characteristic rough, plucked, steep end that slopes downward with its smooth-tapered back.

Upper Reservoir

Upon entering the narrow channel, stay on the right or south shoreline. You will enter a bay that provides excellent protection from the wind and contains many choice campsites. If you have time and energy, take-out at the far southern end. Locate the streambed that flows from the south, and follow it for approximately .30 miles to the Lost Lake outlet. Hike to Sword Lake, the second lake, over the tree-covered ledge on the opposite shore.

Both of these are natural lakes formed after the last glacial period.

Smaller lakes, almost ponds, are nearby. In the late afternoon and on into evening, their shoreline reverberates with the sound of frogs. Sometimes you spot a great blue heron, stalking or standing still in its characteristic hunting stance, its neck and bill aimed downward, ready to strike at the slightest movement.

The camping symbol on the map indicates an area containing at least three sites spread out over the level ground high above the shoreline.

A short distance beyond the cove and inside the narrow channel, you cross the buoy line that separates the motorized, lower reservoir from the upper, eastern reach that allows paddle craft only and requires a wilderness permit for any camping. A short distance from the buoys is a ghost forest. Upon paddling through this forest, you reach the start of your trip into the upper end of the reservoir. This entire section contains many stands of bleached trees. The unique character of so many dead trees, standing within the body of the reservoir, also invites different species of birds to perch and hunt from their limbs. One of the more interesting is the osprey. You hear it's distinct but loud *kyew kyew kyew* just before it abandons a limb and soars off to another section of the forest.

Scolding you with its chattering cry, the belted kingfisher seems to lead you forward as it flies from limb to limb, staying just ahead of your boat.

All around you are ravens watching over the entire scene, missing nothing, ready to take advantage of any opportunity that provides them with a meal.

If you are really fortunate and attentive, you will spot an American bald eagle perched on one of the limbs and hiding beside the trunk. Although they are capable of catching their own fish, they often bluff an osprey into releasing the one it caught. That is why, when you spot ospreys fishing the lake, they are keeping an eye out for a bald eagle. It is quite a show watching this earnest duel between the two birds.

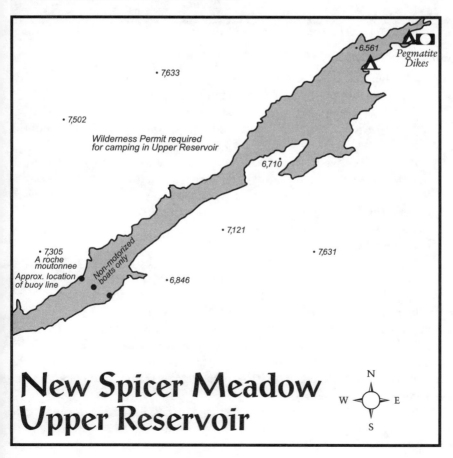

New Spicer Meadow Upper Reservoir

The author, surrounded by a dead forest with the Dardanelles looming in the background.

Families of mergansers, varieties of ducks, and the ever-present Canada goose paddle around the base of the standing deadwood also.

Eventually, you reach the far end where the two streams, the smaller Bull Run Creek and the larger Highland Creek, converge into the tail of the reservoir.

Besides the obvious shoreline camping readily visible on the left or north side of the reservoir, don't hesitate to seek out other sites above the boulders on your right or on the southeast shore. If you take the time to search for them, they often prove to be far superior to those on the more exposed beach. Two campsites that are on the higher ground above the rocky shelf are marked. But others are also prevalent.

If you follow the reservoir to its termination at the mouth of Highland Creek, you will pass a large vertical wall of granite off your right side just as you round the short bend and begin to enter into the stream channel. High on the slab's slick wall and running the length of it in a crisscross pattern, are two well-defined *aplite* dikes. Aplite is a fine- to medium-grained igneous rock that occurs as thin veins (dikes) within the coarser plutonic parent rock. To non-geologists, these veins may be mistaken for quartz. Unlike the glassy look and slick feel of quartz, aplite appears creamier in color and has a sugary texture.

When you are ready to start the return journey, if there is any wind, hug the northern shore. It provides the best protection and you can use any of several small coves and landings. Remember, however, to be prepared for strong gusts and choppy fetch as the wind and water funnel into the narrow channel near the dead forest.

Sources and References:

Guyton, Bill, *Glaciers of California: California Natural History Guides.* Berkeley: University of California Press, 1998.

National Geographic Society, *Field Guide to the Birds of North America.* Washington D. C.: National Geographic Society, 1987.

Whitney, Stephen, *The Sierra Nevada: A Sierra Club Naturalist's Guide.* San Francisco: Sierra Club Books, 1979.

APPENDICES

APPENDIX I
MAPS & MAP SOURCES

Note: The higher the map scale ratio, the smaller the detail available. One inch on a map scale of 1:24,000 represents 2,000 feet; one inch on a scale of 1: 250,000 represents about 4 miles.

A small-scale map = greater detail. This terminology is often misunderstood.

The most common map for the paddler and backpacker is the topographic (also known as a contour map) map series put out by the United States Geological Survey (USGS). The type that shows the most detail and is the easiest to use, be it on the water or on the trail, has a scale of 1: 24,000. This map series is also known as the **7.5-Minute Topographical Quadrangle,** often called a quad.

The scale: **1: 24,000** is to be interpreted as a scale of reference meaning one inch on the map represents 2,000 feet on the ground.

The **7.5-Minute** refers to the corresponding number of minutes of longitude and latitude this map quadrangle covers at a scale of 1: 24,000.

The symbol ' refers to a minute of either longitude or latitude; the term **minute** pertains to a placement in space that is divided into 60 minutes, rather than time. For a more precise location, the minutes are subdivided further into 60 seconds.

For example, the Carson Pass Quadrangle lies between:

119°52.30' and 120°00.00' Longitude and 38°37.30' and 38°45.00' Latitude. Each one of the 7.5-Minute Quadrangle Topographical Map Series covers an area of 49 to 70 square miles.

Within this area, symbols are used to designate all features natural and manmade. For example, land and water features are shown as a series of lines called contours. The shape, distance between these contours, their width and color (brown for areas above sea level and blue for features below sea level) all describe how a specific three-dimensional terrain feature will look on a flat piece of paper, the 7.5-Minute Quadrangle Topographical Map Series.

Unfortunately, topographic maps required by many of the places paddlers, hikers and other backcountry users are out of date. (USGS is updating their map series based on budgetary availability and area priorities).

Besides the government agencies, private map companies also put out maps that cover many of the popular lakes and reservoirs of California. Almost all of these maps use the USGS topographical quads as their base map and then overlay their information onto the existing data. As a result, although you may obtain a map with current roads, structures and even some terrain changes, the primary data is as current as the original topographical quadrangle. In addition, these maps are aimed at the sportsperson. Hence, the majority of overlaid data pertains primarily to choice fishing and hunting areas.

Private company maps provide not only places to fish, but also current roads and buildings, and a smaller scale map of the lake or reservoir itself, without any extraneous details.

Unfortunately, no known private company maps exist for retail sales that cover the majority of lakes described in this volume. If a current map is required, the best available type is made by remote sensing techniques: either from aerial photography or from satellite imagery.

However, for the places described in this book, the cost for satellite imagery maps does not seem warranted.

7.5-Minute Quadrangle Topographical Map Series Used in Text:
Region I:

Caples Lake, CA
Carson Pass, CA
Freel Peak, CA
Markleeville, CA
Pacific Valley, CA
Woodfords, CA

Region II:

Bear River Reservoir, CA
Caples Lake, CA
Calaveras Dome, CA
Mokelumne Hill, CA
Peddler Hill, CA

Region III:

Spicer Meadow Reservoir, CA
Tamarack, CA

APPENDIX II

PADDLING CLUBS, ORGANIZATIONS, OUTFITTERS, & RETAILERS

American Canoe Association (ACA)
Phone: 703.451.0141
www.acanet.org

American Red Cross
www.redcross.org

Becoming an Outdoors Woman
Sponsored by: California Department of Fish & Game
& University of Wisconsin-Stevens Point,
College of Natural Resources
Phone: 916.657.4333
www.dfg.ca.gov/bow/owoman.html

CSUS Aquatic & Boat Safety Center.
Phone: 916.985.7239
www.csusaquaticcenter.com

California Floaters Society
Phone: 916.482.8548
www.cfsonline.org

Central California Canoe Club
Phone: 916.482.5592
www.carlwoodard.com/c4/

Chico Paddle Heads
Phone: 530.345.2453
http://groups.yahoo.com/group/chicopaddleheads
www.chicopaddleheads.com

Friends of Hope Valley
www.greatbasin.net/~fohv

Marin Canoe Club
Email: marincanoe@aol.com

Sierra Nevada Alliance
Phone: 530.542.4546
www.sierranevadaalliance.org

Sierra Nevada Canoe & Kayak Club
www.4myclub.com/snckc

Sierra Sea Kayaking
Email: Rwelch4060@sbcglobal.net

Western Waters Canoe Club
Phone: 408.243.6115
www.westernwaterscanoeclub.org

Retail Stores:

Adventure Sports
Phone: 916.971.1850
www.sierrgear.com

California Canoe & Kayak, Sacramento
Phone: 916.353.1880
www.calkayak.com

California Canoe & Kayak, Oakland
Phone: 510.893.7833
www.calkayak.com

Current Adventures
Kayak School & Trips
Phone: 530.642.9755 or 888-4-kayaking
www.kayaking.com

Kayak Tahoe
Phone: 530.544.2011
www.kayaktahoe.com

Klepper West
Western Folding Kayak Center
Phone: 888.692.8092 or 530.626.8647
www.klepperwest.com

Mountain Hardware
Phone: 530.587.4844
www.tahoeadventuresports.com

Mr. Canoe's Paddlesports
Phone: 707.887.7416
www.MrCanoesPaddlesports.com

North Rim Adventure Sports
Phone: 530.345.2453
www.northrimadventure.com

RackNRoad Truck and Vehicle Outfitters
Phone: 800.722.5872
www.racknroad.com

The Raft Store
Inflatable Boats, Etc.
Phone: 916.638.0808
www.theraftstore.com

Recreational Equipment Incorporated (REI)
www.rei.com

Tahoe City Kayak Shop
Phone: 530.581.4336

Tahoe Paddle & Oar
Phone: 530.581.3029
www.tahoeadventuresports.com

The River Store
Phone: 530.626.3435
www.theriverstore.com

Sierra Nevada Adventure Company (SNAC)
Phone: 888.900.SNAC or 209.795.9310 or 209.532.5621
www.snacattack.com/ContactSNAC/contactinfo.htm

Sierra Outdoor Center (SOC)
Phone: 530.888.7066
www.sierraoutdoorcenter.com

Sierra South Mountain & Paddlesports
Phone: 800.376.7303
www.sierrasouth.com

Sports Fever Ski ' N ' Sport
Phone: 530.477.8006

Wolf Creek Wilderness
Phone: 530.477.2722
www.wolfcreekwilderness.com

Resorts, Cabins to Rent, Restaurants and Other Amenities
Region I: Hope Valley and Highway 88

Caples Lake Resort

Phone: 209.258.8888

www.capleslakeresort.com

A finer place to stay, either at the resort itself or in one of the cabins, is hard to match. On top of that, throw in the stupendous view of Caples Lake and the Carson Range, and you have a glimmer of what your stay will be like at this well-kept resort. As a guest, be sure to take in their sauna overlooking the lake. At the end of a day of paddling, this amenity is well worth it. The resort also rents canoes and kayaks by the hour.

Carson River Resort

Phone: 530.694.2229

www.carsonriverresort.com

The resort rents cabins, RV spaces and has a campground and a general store with gas or propane pumps.

Kay's Silver Lake Resort

Phone: 209.258.8598

Another historical site along the former Pioneer Road. The present day store, marina and cabins, are owned and operated, since the 1930s, by the Kay Family. The easy access from Highway 88 insures a quick stop for groceries, fuel or other services. The marina and boat launch are available for a fee.

Kirkwood Mountain Village Resort

Resort: 209.258.6000

Kirkwood Sports and Adventure Center: 209.258.7240

Kirkwood Vacations: 800.967.7500

www.kirkwood.com

An assortment of stores and other amenities in the world-renowned ski resort.

Kit Carson Lodge

Summer Phone: 209.258.8500

Winter Phone: 530.676.1370

www.KitCarsonLodge.com

No address line as the lodge has its own post office. This is a rustic lodge with incredible and elegant charm. One of the friendliest resorts I have visited. In addition to the delightful cabins, the lodge is known for its local art gallery displaying the works of talented local artists, mini-concerts, and a first-class European chef, whose morning brunches are simply scrumptious.

Plasse's Resort
Phone: 209.258.8814
www.plassesresort.com
A young Frenchman named Ramon Pierre Plasse founded the resort in 1853. The resort has continued to be run by the same family for five generations! The facilities include a campground for tents as well as RVs, in addition to cabins and rooms at the lodge. In the summer, the resort puts on a first-class barbecue that brings visitors from all over California and Nevada.

Markleeville General Store
Phone: 530.694.2448
The wooden structure that houses the store is over one hundred years old, Bob and Dee Rudden the proprietors, are much younger. The store carries groceries, ice, fishing supplies, hardware and the best wine selection in this part of the county.

Mountain Creek Cabin
Phone: 530.694.2454
www.mountaincreekcabin.com
A modern cabin with loads of amenities to spoil you, including 3 bedrooms with queen beds, plus additional sleeping spaces for up to 10 people, 2.5 baths, a full kitchen and dining room, private hot tub, etc.

Mountain Family Shuttle Service
Phone: 530.694.1833
The only shuttle service in the area of Hope Valley; call the number for details.

Sorensen's Resort
Phone: 800.423.9949 or 530.694.2203
www.sorensenresort.com
Sorensen's Resort embodies the spirit of the region with its understated charm and friendly, knowledgeable staff. If an overnight stay is not part of your plan, then at least stay for a meal; you won't be disappointed.

Hope Valley Resort (Sorensen's sister resort)
Phone: 800.423.9949
www.hopevalleyresort.com
More camping oriented with river front campsites and RV capability.

Sierra Pines Country Store
Phone: 530.694.2949
Quoted as, "Serving the best honest hamburger this side of the Sierra." In addition to the restaurant, they also sell gas, groceries, propane, and have a laundry and RV Park.

The Woodford's Inn, UC

Phone: 530.694.2410
www.woodfordsinn.net
A charming AAA approved 20-unit motel, with a spa.

Woodfords Auto Service

Phone: 530.694.2916
The ONLY local towing and limited repair facility in the Markleeville, Hope Valley areas.

Region II: High Country Lakes of the Mokelumne River

Bear River Lake Resort

Phone: 209.295.4868
Fax: 209.295.4585
www.bearriverlake.com
A resort lodge with all the amenities for an enjoyable time on the lake.
If camping is not your style, then reserve a unit, complete with a kitchen, for your stay. There is a marina with boat launching and rentals, coin operated showers, Laundromat and grocery store.

Annotated Bibliography of Technical References

Acorn, John and Ian Sheldon, *Bugs of Northern California*. Renton: Lone Pine Publishing, 2002.

The best paperback book on the creepy-crawlers that abound in our part of the state. The text is informative, witty and geared for us, the interested amateur. Older kids will appreciate the author's approach and irreverent humor. The illustrations are oversized, easy to compare against the real bug, and very detailed.

Aiken, Zora and David Aiken, *Simple Tent Camping: Basics of Camping from Car or Canoe*. Camden: Ragged Mountain Press, 1996.

A simple introductory guide to camping. Contains excellent tips for beginners insuring that the first trip will not be the last.

Alt, David D. and Donald W. Hyndman, *Roadside Geology of Northern California*. Missoula: Mountain Press Publishing Company, 1994.

The entire Roadside series of books are an excellent introduction to the geology of California and the United States. All the books provide maps with geologic features superimposed over the roads and highways of the state. The text is clearly written and easy to comprehend.

Butruille, Susan G., *Women's Voices from the Motherlode: Tales from the California Gold Rush*. Boise: Tamarack Books, Inc., 1998.

A wonderful book that covers the lives of pioneer and Native Californian women.

Daniel, Linda, *Kayak Cookery: A Handbook of Provisions and Recipes*. Chester: The Globe Pequot Press, 1988.

Current edition printed by Menasha Ridge Press, Birmingham, AL, 2nd ed. 1st printing. 208 pp. Not only do the recipes work, and the outcome deliciously satisfying, the book has some excellent tips on packaging and stowing the foodstuff prior to touring.

Dennis, Jerry, *From a Wooden Canoe: Reflections on Canoeing, Camping, and Classic Equipment*. New York: Thomas Dunne Books/St. Martin's Press, 1999.

Personal commentary on all aspects of canoeing and camping. A book to take with you and read on your own trip.

Diaz, Ralph, *Complete Folding Kayaker.* Camden: Ragged Mountain Press, 1994.

The only book available devoted exclusively to the folding boat kayaker. Although the author covers many different folding kayak designs, his emphasis is toward the Klepper style of kayak.

Dowd, John, *Sea Kayaking: A Manual for Long-Distance Touring.* Vancouver: Douglas & McIntyre; Seattle: University of Washington Press, 1988.

This book is a very readable primer written by an individual who has kayaked for 35 years all over the world. He has the ability to communicate his knowledge clearly without the use of jargon. The chapter on Sea Kayaking for People with Disabilities is worth the price of the book.

Gardner, Lee and Will Hart, "The Uniqueness of Sierra Saprophytes." *Sierra Heritage Magazine,* Vol. 18, No. 5, May/June 1999, p. 24.

About beautiful plants that live on organic matter and do not require chlorophyll to sustain life.

Getchell, Annie, *The Essential Outdoor Gear Manual: Equipment Care & Repair for Outdoorspeople.* Camden: Ragged Mountain Press, 1995.

This is the best reference book on the repair, maintenance and care of outdoor gear being sold today. I rely heavily on this book before I attempt any boat repair or description of how to repair any damaged gear. Every serious outdoors person should have a copy of this book in his or her library.

Harrison, David and Judy Harrison, *Canoe Tripping with Children: Unique Advice for Keeping Children Comfortable.* Merrillville: ICS Books, 1990.

This book has great common sense ideas on how to entertain the kids without losing your own enjoyment of the trip.

Hoover, Mildred Brooke et al, *Historic Spots in California.* Stanford: Stanford University Press, 1990.

The emphasis is on the historical background of the many communities that sprung up at the time of the Gold Rush and after. Many of these places no longer remain except as "names on the side of the road." I find this book to be extremely valuable when researching the names of the sites destroyed by the reservoirs.

Hubbell, Sue, *Broadsides from the Other Orders: A Book of Bugs.* New York: Random House, 1993.

Did you know that if you lost a cow, the best way of finding her is to locate a Daddy longlegs spider and see which way his 2nd legs are pointing, that is the direction the cow went; Furthermore, the ancient name for the daddy longlegs is Shepherd spider. This bit of trivia and others like it makes the book a pleasure to read.

Jacobson, Cliff, *Canoeing and Camping: Beyond the Basics.* Merrillville: ICS Books Inc., 1992.

You will never be wrong purchasing a book written by this author. He is opinionated, but those opinions carry the weight of "been there, done that." This handy little booklet contains the same practical information, as does his primer.

Jacobson, Cliff, *The Basic Essentials of Map and Compass,* Merrillville: ICS Books Inc., 1997.

This short but easy to comprehend guide will give you the confidence to plan and read a route using a map and compass.

Johnston, Verna, R., *Sierra Nevada: The Naturalist's Companion.* Berkeley: University of California Press, 1998.

A thoroughly enjoyable natural history of the Sierra Nevada, written with an eye for detail that covers the work of early naturalists and explains updated material.

Johnston, Verna, R., *California Forests and Woodlands: A Natural History.* Berkeley: University of California Press, 1994.

An excellent companion to the Naturalist's Companion to the Sierra Nevada; both books provide the reader with a comprehensive natural history guide to California's forests and woodlands.

Mason, Bill, *Song of the Paddle: An Illustrated Guide to Wilderness Camping.* Toronto: Key Porter Books, 1988.

This is a follow-up to the author's first volume. Stunning photography followed by clear advice and information on wilderness canoe camping.

McKown, Doug, *Canoeing Safety and Rescue: A Handbook of Safety and Rescue Procedures for Lake and River Canoeists.* Calgary: Rocky Mountain Books, 1996.

Written for both flat water and river runner canoeists. Contains solid information with good illustrations and photos.

McPhee, John A., *The Survival of the Bark Canoe.* New York: Farrar, Straus and Giroux, 1975.

The author builds a history of the birch bark canoe around the biography of Henri Vaillancourt, a modern day canoe builder, who follows the traditional methods and uses the same tools that the Indians used in the construction of his birch bark canoes.

Mills, Sheila, *The Outdoors Dutch Oven Cookbook.* Camden: Ragged Mountain Press, 1997.

If you have ever tasted a meal properly prepared in a Dutch oven, then you know this book will be a favorite resource guide. I was given this book as a gift and am preparing and eating my way through it.

Montgomery, M. R., *Many Rivers to Cross: Of Good Running Water, Native Trout, and the Remains of Wilderness.* New York: Simon & Schuster, 1995.

More than just a book on trout fishing . . . there is a contemplative wisdom on the meaning of wilderness and what we stand to lose, eloquently written.

Nilsson, Karen B., *A Wild Flower by Any Other Name: Sketches of Pioneer Naturalists Who Named Our Western Plants.* Yosemite National Park: Yosemite Association, 1994.

A book of biographical sketches on pioneer naturalists.

Ornduff, Robert, *Introduction to California Plant Life.* Revised by Phyllis M. Faber and Todd Keeler-Wolf. Berkeley: University of California Press, 2003.

Its one thing to be able to identify a particular plant, tree or shrub, it is a lot more complicated to know and understand why that particular species grow where it does. This revised version of the late Prof. Robert Ornduff's 1974 classic introduces the student to the natural history of California's rich and varied landscapes in a clear, concise and above all, very interesting style.
    The pocket-size guidebook format allows one to easily slip it into a pocket or backpack.

Pickett, Edwin R., "Birds of Central California." *Sacramento Bee Newspaper,* Reprint, Sacramento, 1972.

If you come across this out of print gem, snag it immediately. The book is a compilation of articles that were written in the Sacramento Bee under the heading: The Bird Watcher. I have yet to find a source book that covers the subject in such depth. 160 birds are described.

Powell, Jerry A. and Charles L. Hogue, *California Insects.* Berkeley: University of California Press, 1979.

This is a technical, but thorough, source book on bugs of California.

Ray, Slim, *Canoe Handbook: Techniques for Mastering the Sport of Canoeing.* Harrisburg: Stackpole Books, 1992.

Still one of the best introductory guides for novice and "mossback" canoeists on the market.

Roberts, Harry, *The Basic Essentials of Canoe Paddling.* Edited by Steve Salins. Guilford: The Globe Pequot Press, 2000.

This volume is part of the Basic Essentials Series of books and is a fast-paced introduction to canoe paddling. No philosophy on paddle grips or scientific treatise on wood versus synthetics . . . just how to paddle a canoe properly.

Rowlands, John J., *Cache Lake Country: Life in the North Woods.* Woodstock: Countryman Press, 1998.

Amongst the thoughtful homespun observations on living in the woods, is some practical woodcraft that any aspiring woods person should know.

Ruark, Robert, *The Old Man and the Boy and The Old Man's Boy Grows Older.* Harrisburg: Stackpole Books, 1989.

These two classics on growing up are a must read for any outdoors person. A real "hoot" to carry and read on a paddle trip.

Seagraves, Anne, *Women of the Sierra.* Lakeport: Wesanne Enterprises, 1990.

The book is a great companion book to the one written by S. Butruille; it includes modern day women, as well as the women of the 19th Century.

Seidman, David, *The Essential Sea Kayaker: A Complete Course for the Open-Water Paddler.* Camden: International Marine Publications, 1992.

For a while, this book was the only descent introductory instruction book on the American market. The updated version is still an excellent source of information on getting started on all aspects of the sport.

Spielman, Andrew and Michael D'Antonio, *Mosquito: A Natural History of Our Most Persistent and Deadly Foe.* New York: Hyperion Books, 2001.

Everything . . . and some things you wish you didn't know . . . about that #%* little denizen of nature.

Stratton, George, *Camping California's National Forests* (formerly: *The Recreation Guide to California's National Forests).* Helena: Falcon Press, 1991.

A basic guide to what's available at our National Forests; including information on camping, sports, and some historical background.

Tekiela, Stan, *Birds of California: Our Nature Field Guide.* Cambridge: Adventure Publications, Inc., 2003.

Finally... an updated, pocket-sized field guide that is devoted specifically on the birds residing in California! The guide contains excellent photographs taken by the author and uses a key, based on the coloration of the birds.

Van Dyke, Elizabeth, "The Silent Sea: Paddling with Deaf and Hard-of-Hearing Kayakers." *SeaKayaking,* Issue 61, December 1997, page 52.

Upon reading this informative and personal article, you come to realize that the term "handicapped" is, in part, only a state-of-mind.

Walbridge, Charlie, *Nuts 'n' Bolts Guide: The Nuts 'N' Bolts Guide to the American Canoe Association's Knots for Paddlers.* Birmingham: Menasha Ridge Press, 1995.

A knot-tying guide specifically for boaters that is written by a well-known ACA instructor and paddler.

Wyatt, J. Michael, *The Basic Essentials of Sea Kayaking.* Revised by Jan Shriner and Roger Schumann. Old Saybrook: Globe Pequot Press, 1991.

This book is an excellent introduction to the sport of sea kayaking, as this material is well researched without the techno jargon. Lots of helpful sketches and photos.

Glossary

This Glossary provides a quick and handy reference to the Reader upon encountering a scientific, nautical or other bit of jargon from the variety of fields of study that were utilized in the text. To provide the Reader with the source from which I used a word or phrase in question, the field of study is provided in parenthesis following the word. Some of these words may have similar definitions but are used in a different context depending on the discipline they derive from. Whenever possible, I include a website that covers the subject in more detail.

Alpine Glacier/Mountain Glacier (glaciology, geology): A glacier that forms in and is confined to: mountains.
http://nsidc.org/glaciers
http://www.uwsp.edu/geo/faculty/lemke/alpine_glacial_glossary

Andesite (geology): A fine-grained extrusive igneous rock of volcanic origin, light gray to dark colored fine with a mineral composition similar to diorite.
http://seis.natsci.csulb.edu/basicgeo/ANDESITE/ANDESITE.html
http://volcanoes.usgs.gov/Products/Pglossary/andesite.html

Angle of Repose (geology): The steepest slope on which the talus material will rest without rolling further. This slope angle, although varied by the shape and size of the rock fragments, is usually about 30°.
http://www.icsi.berkeley.edu/~dbailey/gallery/image/angleofrepose.html
http://phoenix.liunet.edu/~divenere/notes/angle_of_repose.htm
http://www.brookes.ac.uk/geology/sedstruc/repose/landslid.htm

Area (geography): Any particular extent of surface; geographical region or tract: Grouse Ridge Area, the area near the Yuba River Drainage Region.

Bar (geology/hydrology/geography/mining): A mixture of unconsolidated materials such as mud, sand, gravel, cobbles and other sediments that form mounds, ridges or banks and are partially or fully submerged in stream channels, river mouths, estuaries and along the coast.

Basalt (geology): Extrusive igneous rock formed on the surface from volcanic activity such as lava flows, dikes, shield volcanoes and cinder cones.
www.geo.mtu.edu/volcanoes/

Batholith (geology): A large mass of plutonic rock at least 40 square miles in extent, composed of coarse-grained rock that originally crystallized below the surface. The **Sierra Nevada Batholith** is made up of many smaller *plutons*, intrusive masses composed largely of granitic rock.
http://www.colorado.edu/GeolSci/Resources/WUSTectonics/Tectintro.html

Bedrock (geology): The solid rock underlying the top layer of soil or other unconsolidated material. Sometimes incorrectly called country rock.

Bedrock Mortars (archaeology): Holes formed into bedrock by early Gatherers for the purpose of pounding nuts and seeds into flour. The holes themselves are called mortars, and the elongated tool used to pound the foodstuff is called a pestle.
http://www.geocities.com/cvas.geo/potter.html

Bench (geology): A flat or gentle slope of land usually narrow in width bounded by steeper slopes below it and above it.

Berm; Berme (geology/geography): A narrow ledge or shelf along a slope.

Broach (nautical): Causing your boat to turn broadside (sideways) to the wind and waves. The effect to this movement may cause the boat to capsize.

Bulbous (geology, archaeology): In archaeology, the term refers to where a platform of rock was intentionally struck by Man during tool making. The detached chip is called a flake. The bulbous head of the struck flake is called the bulb of percussion. In geology, this same pattern of flaking occurs naturally when two or more rocks collide or come in contact with each other.
http://www.wku.edu/~darlene.applegate/introtoarch/lab3/lab3.html

Canal (mining/engineering): In the northern mines, the terms canal, ditch and flume were used to describe a specific type of man-made water conveyance system that carried water for the purpose of hydraulic mining operations.
www.cwo.com/~ditches/index.htm

Cap Rock (geology): A hard layer of rock overlying softer more erosion prone layers.

Chinking (construction/engineering): Filling the empty spaces of a structure such as a log cabin, or a rock wall with a substance like mud, mortar, small rocks or even paper.

Cinder Cone (geology): A steep conical hill formed over a volcanic vent. They are built as a result of eruptions of small lava fragments called cinders, and more recently, under the collective term of: "tephra." The tephra fragments are ejected from the vent and accumulate around the base of the vent as they fall back down to earth.
http://www.educ.uvic.ca/faculty/mroth/438/VOLCANO/cinder.html

Cirque, Glacial (geology, glaciology): A rounded amphitheater-like basin with steep sidewalls and backwall. Formed as a result of glacial erosion on a mountainside. The basin of a cirque often contains a glacial lake called a tarn.
http://www.uwsp.edu/geo/faculty/lemke/alpine_glossary/landforms/cirque.html

Cobble (geology): A stone with a diameter between 2.5 and 10 inches (64 and 256 mm). Cobbles are larger then pebbles, but smaller then boulders.

Columnar Jointing (geology, volcanology): Formed in lava flows during cooling. The joints or fractures form perpendicular to the direction of the flow, hence the term columnar.
http://volcanoe.und.nodak.edu/vwdocs/vw_hyperexchange/col_joint.html

Contour (cartography): An imaginary series of lines used on a topographic map that run along the ground points having the same elevation. The color of these lines indicates above or below sea level, with brown for ground points and blue for features below sea level.
http://www-sci.lib.uci.edu/SEP/CTS98/topographic.html

Country Rock (geology): Rock that surrounds or is penetrated by various mineral veins; rock surrounded by an igneous intrusion such as magma.

Cove (geography): A small sheltered bay in the shoreline of a sea, river or lake.

Deciduous (botany/biology): Trees or other plants that lose their leaves annually at a particular season.

Dike (geology): Cracks or fissures in the earth that are filled with molten matter. As the molten material cools and hardens, it forms into various minerals. In Sierran granite, dikes composed of pegmatite or aplite are common.
http://www.angelfire.com/extreme4/lkrwork/x170.htm

Dome (geology): 1. A circular or elliptical, almost symmetrical uplifted deformation. 2. A large igneous (volcanic) intrusion or extrusion whose upward surface is concave.

The Sierra Nevada Range contains many such igneous intrusions that have the characteristic dome shape.
http://www.tec.army.mil/research/products/desert_guide/lsmsheet/lsdomea.htm

Diorite (geology): A medium- to coarse-grained intrusive rock. If the presence of quartz is found in the rock, then it becomes granodiorite (quartz diorite).
http://www.geocities.com/RainForest/Canopy/1080/diorite.htm

Duck (backpacking): A stack of rocks, one on top the other, to be used as a trail marker. Sometimes called a cairn.

Eddy (hydrology): An area where the current is flowing contrary to the main current. Usually found on the downstream side of obstructions in the water.

Fetch (geography): 1. An area where ocean waves are being generated by the wind. 2. The uninterrupted distance traveled by a wind or an ocean wave. The longer the fetch, the larger the waves that may be formed by wind action.

Flank (geography): A side or lateral part: the flank of a mountain.

Flume (mining/engineering): A wooden or metal structure with a center channel for carrying water. In the area covered by this volume, flumes were constructed where ditches could not be dug, along the side of steep ravines at a prescribed gradient.
See: www.cwo.com/~ditches/index.htm

Friable (geology): Describes material that can be broken down into grains by slight pressure, such as one's fingertips.

Fungus, pl. fungi (botany): Any group of organisms that include moulds, yeasts, rusts, smuts, mildews, mushrooms and toadstools. They are not considered true plants because they have no leaves or roots. They contain no chlorophyll, therefore are not able to make their own food (photosynthesis); they also reproduce by spores rather than pollination.
Fungi are either parasites, or saprotrophs (living on dead matter).
www.herb.lsa.umich.edu.kidpage/factindx.htm
Specific to California and the Sierra Nevada fungi:
www.mykoweb.com

Gorge (geology, geography): A narrow passage.

Gradient (geology/hydrology): The rate of descent or ascent of any topographic feature; the steepness of slope. In hydrology, the term applies to the grade or fall of a stream. Gradient is expressed in feet per mile.

Granite (geology): A plutonic igneous rock consisting primarily of the minerals quartz, feldspar and biotite.

Granitic: Of or like granite but containing fewer or additional minerals than associated with true granite.
The Sierra Nevada Mountains are a former batholith; when it cooled, the rock became a granitic intrusion.
http://www.sierra.cc.ca.us/museum/Rxrockln.htm

Gruss; Grus (geology): Loose fragments of coarse rock associated with the weathering of granite.

Gunnel; Gunwale (nautical): Structural supports that run end to end along the top of the hull. Can be made out of wood, vinyl, or aluminum. Inside strips of the gunnels are called *inwales* and the outside strips are *outwales.* Derived from an old English word pertaining to the area on a warship that braced the guns.

Hornblende (geology): Green or black rock-forming mineral. It is a silicate composed mainly of calcium, iron, magnesium, and aluminum. Hornblende is found in both igneous and metamorphic rocks.
http://mineral.galleries.com/minerals/silicate/hornblen/hornblen.htm
http://hyperphysics.phy-astr.gsu.edu/hbase/minerals/hornblende.html

Hydraulic Mining (mining): An extraction process whereby high-pressure hoses wash enormous amounts of earth and other overburden. This form of mining required huge amounts of water to wash the soil into sluice boxes for extraction of the ore. To meet the demand for a continuous flow of water, rivers gorges and existing small Sierra lakes were dammed; deep reservoirs were constructed and vast tracts of land were criss-crossed with ditches, canals and flumes.
See: www.calgoldrush.com/graphics/evolution.html

ice age (geology, glaciology): A major interval of geologic time during which extensive ice sheets (continental glaciers) formed over many parts of the world.
http://www.museum.state.il.us/exhibits/ice_ages

Ice Age (Pleistocene): A time period that spanned from 1.8 million years ago to 11,000 years ago. It was during this time period that episodes of global cooling or Ice Ages took place. In North America, the northern portion of the continent was buried under massive

glaciers. The locking of so much water as ice lowered the sea levels by many hundreds of feet.
http://www.ucmp.berkeley,edu/quaternary/ple.html

Igneous Rock (geology): Rock formed by the cooling and solidification of magma or lava. ***Intrusive* or plutonic igneous rock** forms and crystallizes beneath the earth's surface, such as the intrusive igneous rock that makes up the Sierra Nevada Batholith.

Extrusive igneous rock occurs as a result of volcanic action on the earth's surface. Examples of this type of rock are varieties of lava, volcanic ash, cinders and the glass-like obsidian.
See: www.geo.mtu.edu/volcanoes/

Inlet (geography): A bay or recess in a shore.

Intermittent Stream (geography/hydrology: A body of water that flows on a seasonal or irregular basis.

Joint (geology): Fractures (cracks) in a mass of rocks that do not show displacement on one side or the other, such as in a fault.
http://www.naturalfractures.com/1.1.1.htm

Knob (geology): A prominent, usually isolated, rounded hill.

Knoll (geology): A small rounded hill; hillock.

Krummholz (botany): From German meaning "crooked wood." The term itself describes environmentally dwarfed plant species surviving at timberline in high altitudes. In a friendlier environment, these species would grow into trees.
http://www.ltrr.arizona.edu/sngc/studies/treeline.htm

Lahar (volcanology/geology): An Indonesian term that describes a hot or cold mixture of water, rock and rock fragments flowing down the slope of a volcano or adjacent drainages. When moving, a lahar looks like a mass of moving wet concrete carrying rocks of various size from minute pebbles to boulders over six feet in diameter (see: pyroclastic flow).
http://volcanoes.usgs.gov/Hazards/What/Lahars/lahars.html

Leeward (nautical): Also called *windward*. It is the side toward which the wind is blowing. A sheltered or protected place out of the wind.

Lichen (botany): Organisms that consist of both a specific fungus and a specific alga living together in a mutually beneficial relationship *(symbiotic relationship)*. The alga provides the food and the fungus provides water and protection. Lichens are a sponge-like mass, somewhat resembling moss. They grow in patches on trees, rocks, and other surfaces.
http://mgd.orst.edu/hyperSQL/lichenland/index.html

Life Cycle (Biology): The successive stages of development that members of a given species pass, such as birth, juvenile growth, adulthood, old age and death.

Life Zone (geography): The affects of climatic variables such as altitude, temperature, and precipitation on the distribution of plant and animal life. The term, life zone was introduced by C. Hart Merriam in his classic study on the relationship between temperature and elevation on the distribution of plants and animals in the western U. S. http://www.runet.edu/~swoodwar/CLASSES/GEOG235/lifezone/lifezone.html

Massif (geology): 1. A compact portion of a mountain range, containing one or more summits. 2. A massive block of rock, generally more rigid than the surrounding rocks, and commonly composed of crystalline basement or younger plutons. http://www.slackpacker.com/geology101.html

Matrix (geology): The rock in which minerals, gems or fossils are embedded.

Mélange (geology): A mixture of assorted rock fragments having a variety of shape, size and composition.

Metamorphic Rock (geology): Rock formed by the transformation of preexisting rock in response to increased heat, pressure or chemical change. The Scottish geologist Charles Lyell coined the term in 1833. The process that creates this form of rock is termed metamorphism. http://www.geocities.com/RainForest/Canopy/1080/metamorphic.htm http://seis.natsci.csulb.edu/bperry/ROCKS.htm

Military Crest (Army engineers): Opposite from *topographical crest*. An area on the forward slope of a hill or ridge, below the topographical crest which is the highest point, from which maximum observation covering the slope down to the base of the hill or ridge can be obtained. http://roundtop.arthes.com/pipermail/gettysburg/2004-February/018991.html

Moraine, Glacial (glaciology/geology): A ridge of unsorted, primarily rock debris called till, in or on a glacier, or deposited by an older glacier. Moraine piles are given a variety of names dependent on where the moraine was deposited. As an example, a lateral moraine lies on the side of a glacier, and an end moraine forms around the frontal edge of the glacier's snout and sometimes connects to the lateral moraine. www.ship.edu/~cjwolt/geology/slides/gl23.htm www.ship.edu/~cjwolt/geology/slides/gl25.htm

Moss (botany): Any class of very small, soft, green or brown non flowering (bryophytic) plants that grow close together in clumps or like a carpet on the ground, on rocks, or on trees. Mosses have small stems and numerous, narrow leaves.
http://www.perspective.com/nature/plantae/bryophytes.html

Nectar (botany): A sweet liquid found in many flowers, which attracts many insects and birds that feed off the sugar and insure survival of the plant through pollination. Bees gather nectar and make it into honey.
http://koning.ecsu.ctstateeu.edu/Plant_Biology/pollination.html

Node (geography/geology): A protuberance or *knob*.

Ore (mining): The naturally occurring material from which economically valuable minerals can be extracted at a profit.

Oxidation (chemistry): The act of or process of oxidizing; combination with oxygen. When a substance burns or rusts, it oxidizes. The rusting of iron is a common example of the original meaning of oxidation. Iron combines with oxygen in the presence of moisture to form rust. In geology, this process occurs when rocks are broken down into soil through the agents of weathering, specifically, chemical weathering.
www.chipr.sunysb.edu/eserc/longis/chemicalweathering.html

Patina (geology): A surface appearance of something grown beautiful with age or use.

Pegmatite (geology): An exceptionally coarse-grained igneous rock or vein that consists largely of quartz, alkali, feldspar and mica. Pegmatite and pegmatite dikes are relatively small and light (white to pink) in color and most are of granitic composition.
http://www.sp.uconn.edu/~geo253vc/granite.html

Phenocrysts (geology): Any of the large or conspicuous crystals usually found in certain types of (porphyritic) igneous rocks.
http://www.google.com/search?q=define:Phenocrysts

Pitch (mountaineering): A stretch of rock or snow, usually of some technical difficulty. In mountaineering, a pitch has a measurement not longer than a rope's length. The term has been broadened to include any section of difficult ground to be covered.

Plagioclase (geology/mineralogy): One of two major types of feldspar, containing sodium and calcium and having its two prominent cleavage directions oblique to one another. Plagioclase is a common rock-forming mineral, also known as sodium-calcium feldspar.
http://volcano.und.nodak.edu/vwlessons/lessons/Slideshow/Show1/Show1-13.html

Pollen (botany): A fine yellowish powder consisting of grains, or microspores, all of which contain a mature or immature male gametophyte. In flowering plants, pollen is released from the anthers of the flower and fertilizes the pistils.

Pollination (botany): For flowering plants, pollination involves the transfer of pollen from the flower's anthers to its stigmas for fertilization, either by insects or by wind. During springtime in the Sierras, the pollen in the air is so thick that it causes a yellow haze. The surface of many lakes and ponds are coated with a thin yellow layer that under certain lighting conditions appears to give off a neon glow.

Pond (hydrology): A permanent small body of water with no discernable wind-swept beach; plants whose roots have attached to the silty bottom of the pond dominate the surface area of the pond. http://www.twingroves.district96.k12.il.us/Wetlands/LakesPonds/LakesPonds,html

Pleistocene (geology): 1.8 million to 11,000 years ago. An epoch of geologic time of the Quaternary period, following the Tertiary and before the Holocene. Also known as Ice Age. http://www.ucmp.berkeley.edu/quaternary/ple.html

Pluton (geology): A single massive body of plutonic rock (rock formed at considerable depth and usually medium to coarse-grained such as granite) consisting of intrusive igneous rock of a size that may be mapped. An assemblage of plutons is a *batholith.* The Sierra Nevada Mountain Range is an example of a granitic batholith. http://www.colorado.edu/GeolSci/Resources/WUSTectonics/Tectintro.html

Porphyritc (geology): Pertaining to or resembling **porphyry**: any igneous rock containing large phenocrysts that are enclosed in a very fine-grained matrix. www.dc.peachnet.edu/~pgore/geology/geo101/igneous.htm

Portage (Old French): Synonymous with carry. To carry a canoe and gear overland to a distant river, lake or around an obstacle in the water.

Put-In (paddling): The location on a body of water where a canoe or kayak is placed prior to a paddle. (See: *Take-out.*)

Pyroclastic Flow (volcanology/geology): Sometimes called, Nuees ardentes, French for *glowing clouds.* An avalanche of hot ash, rocks, and gas, produced by an erupting volcano. These avalanches reach temperatures of 1500 degrees F. and travel at speeds up to 100–150 miles per hour (See: *lahars*). http://volcanoes.usgs.gov/Products/Pglossary/PyroFlow.html

Quadrangle (cartography): The rectangular area represented by U. S. Geological Survey topographical and geological maps. The two common sizes depict tracts about 13 miles wide by 17 miles north to south and 6.5 miles wide by 8.5 miles north to south. http://mac.usgs.gov/mac/isb/pubs/booklets/topo/topo.html

Quartzite (geology): A granular rock composed mainly of quartz and formed by the metamorphism of sandstone. http://seis.natsci.csulb.edu/bperry/metarock/QUARTZITE.htm

Rain Shadow (geography): A condition whereby little rainfall occurs on the downwind side of mountainous areas. Rain shadows are due to the warming of air as it moves down slope, preventing the occurrence of rain. http://www.weatherpages.com/rainshadow/ http:/www.sp.uconn.edu/~geo101vc/Lecture19/sld020.htm

Reef (geology, oceanography): An offshore chain or range of rock or sand at or near the surface of the water.

Ridge (geology/geography): An elongated, narrow and steep sided elevated feature on the earth's surface.

Riparian (biology): pertaining to the life along a natural watercourse such as a river, stream or surrounding a lakeshore. http://www.rivers.gov.au/acrobat/riprap11.pdf

Rip-Rap (engineering): A foundation of loose rock or stone thrown together without order onto a shore or embankment to prevent erosion.

Saddle (geography/geology): 1. A gap that is broad and gently sloping on both sides. 2. A relatively flat ridge that connects the peaks of two higher elevations.

Scree (geology): A steep mass of loose rock lying at the base of a cliff or on the side of a mountain. A.k.a. talus.

Seep (geology): A small area where water or another liquid percolates slowly to the surface.

Spring (geology): A small stream of water flowing naturally from the earth.

Stratum, pl. strata (geology): Latin *stratum*: something spread out, from *sternere* to spread. A bed or formation of sedimentary rock consisting of approximately the same kind of material throughout.

Striations (glaciology/geology): Scratches cut into the surface area of the bedrock a glacier moves over. www.ship.edu/~cjwolt/geology/slides/gl10.jpg

Swale (geology/geography): 1. A slight depression, sometimes swampy, in the midst of generally level ground. 2. A shallow depression in an undulating ground moraine due to uneven glacial deposition.

Take-out (paddling): Opposite of a put-in. The place where a canoe or kayak is removed from the water.

Talus (geology): A.k.a. rubble; scree. Coarse and angular rock fragments derived from and accumulated at the base of a cliff or on a steep slope.

Terrace (geology/geography): A flat raised level of land bordered by vertical or sloping sides, especially one of a series of such features placed one on top of the other.

Terrain (geology): Any tract of land in respect to its breadth and natural features.

Topography (geography/cartography): The surface features of a place or region, including hills, mountains, valleys, streams, lakes, bridges, tunnels, roads, etc. In cartography, the term applies to the detailed description or drawing of the surface features of a place or region.

Topographic Map (cartography/geography/geology): A map showing the elevations as well as the positions of the physical and cultural features of a given area, often in color and with contour lines. http://mac.usgs.gov/lsb/pubs/booklets/symbols

Volcanic Plug (geology, volcanology): A crater filling of lava, the surrounding material of which has been removed by erosion. http://library.thinkquest.org/17457/volcanoes/features.plugs.php

Volcanic Vent (geology, volcanology): The opening of a volcano in the earth's crust, similar to fumarole. http://library.thinkquest.org/17457/volcanoes/structure.php

Western Gall Rust (forestry): A disease produced by certain types of fungus that infects several hard pine species, such as lodgepole pine in the Sierras and causes round to pear-shaped outgrowths or galls to form on branches, stems and trunks of the host tree. http://plantbio.berkeley.edu/~bruns/papers/vogler1991a.html

The following texts were used as sourcebooks for the definitions:

Barnhart, Robert K., *The Hammond Barnhart Dictionary of Science*, Hammond Incorporated, Maplewood, NJ, 1986.

G. & C. Merriam Company, *Webster's Seventh New Collegiate Dictionary*. G. & C. Merriam Company, Publishers, Springfield, MA, 1972 Ed.

McGraw-Hill, *Dictionary of Geology and Mineralogy*, Sybil P. Parker, Editor-in-Chief. McGraw-Hill, New York, NY, 1997.

Quality Paperback Book Club, *QPB Science Encyclopedia*, Quality Paperback Book Club, New York, NY, 1998.

About The Author

The author was born in Pau, France. He was raised in both San Francisco and Santa Cruz, California. Bill has enjoyed surfing, snorkeling, backpacking and museum viewing since he was a teenager. Having completed his Air Force commitment with a tour in Vietnam as an Aerial Reconnaissance Photographer, he graduated from San Francisco State University with a Bachelor of Arts Degree in Anthropology (Archaeology) followed by a Teaching Credential.

Bill worked as a caretaker at the Calico Early Man Site under the tutelage of Ruth DeEtte Simpson. He also participated in several projects and field surveys conducted by the Paleontology and Geology Department of the Museum of Northern Arizona with William J. Breed as curator. In the early 1980s, Bill volunteered as a docent, then became a paid staff member at the Año Nuevo State Reserve, in San Mateo County, California.

Bill's love of nature, archaeology and geology, plus his skill as a photographer, brought excitement to the classroom where he taught social studies, science and history classes for over ten years.

In 1984, he moved to Sacramento where he worked for California Canoe and Kayak.

Currently, he is a naturalist/guide for **Current Adventures**, a kayak school and trip outfitter located in Lotus, California.

Bill is married to Louise Anne Cherry, the father of one 18-year-old son Peter Karl, and a stepfather to Eric, a returned veteran from the second Iraqi War.

Other Publications by the Author

"These books are a gift . . . for this and future generations."
—JOHN SEALS, DAGGER CANOE AND KAYAK

Up the Lake with a Paddle, *Volumes 1, 2 and 3 are the first guidebooks to address the growing needs of canoeists and kayakers. User-friendly, with photographs and detailed diagrams, of the great places to paddle in the foothills and mountains of California's Sierra Nevada, these guides provide information on how to get there and what to expect. Well-researched routes detail classic trips for families or solo paddlers.*

Up the Lake with a Paddle, Volume 1:
Sierra Foothills and Sacramento Region
0-938665-54-5, 18.95

Up the Lake with a Paddle, Volume 2:
Tahoe Region, Crystal Basin, and Foothill Reservoirs
0-938665-70-7, 21.95

Up the Lake with a Paddle, Volume 3:
Tahoe National Forest-West and the Lakes within the Yuba River Drainage
0-938665-82-0, 19.95

Up the Lake with a Paddle, Volume 4:
The High Country Lakes of the Central Sierra Nevada
1-932310-30-4, 19.95